THE CIVILIZATION OF THE AMERICAN INDIAN SERIES

The Indian

AMERICA'S UNFINISHED BUSINESS

The Indian

AMERICA'S UNFINISHED BUSINESS

𝕏𝕏

Report of the Commission on the Rights,
Liberties, and Responsibilities
of the American Indian

COMPILED BY

William A. Brophy and Sophie D. Aberle

W. W. KEELER · KARL N. LLEWELLYN · SOIA MENTSCHIKOFF

ARTHUR MEIER SCHLESINGER · CHARLES ARTHUR SPRAGUE

O. MEREDITH WILSON

UNIVERSITY OF OKLAHOMA PRESS
NORMAN

LIBRARY OF CONGRESS CATALOG CARD NUMBER: 66–16528

Copyright 1966 by the University of Oklahoma Press, Publishing Division of the University. Composed and printed at Norman, Oklahoma, U.S.A., by the University of Oklahoma Press. First edition.

Preface

IN 1953 the Eighty-third Congress of the United States adopted House Concurrent Resolution 108 setting forth the policy of terminating "as fast as possible" the special relationship existing between American Indians and the federal government. This reversal of the policy which had been followed for well over a century made highly desirable a fresh, up-to-date appraisal of the status of the Indians. Thus the Commission on the Rights, Liberties, and Responsibilities of the American Indian was established for this purpose by The Fund for the Republic, Inc., in March, 1957.

The final report of the investigation is published in the pages which follow. The Commission hopes that it will help to promote a better understanding of the historical relationship between the federal government and the Indians and that it will provide guidelines as the Indians move forward to enjoy the rights, exercise the liberties, and assume the full responsibilities of American citizenship. It should be pointed out that the report concerns primarily Indians who through their tribal membership have a constitutional relationship to the federal government. Other Indians, numbering perhaps 75,000 to 100,000, who dwell mostly east of the Mississippi River and in Alaska, are beyond the scope of this inquiry.

The Commission published an abbreviated preliminary report in January, 1961, which contained seven sets of recommendations, each preceded by an introduction. The recommendations appear at the end of each chapter in this final report.

At the time of its inception, the Commission included the following members: O. Meredith Wilson, chairman; William A. Brophy, executive director; W. W. Keeler, Karl N. Llewellyn, Arthur Meier Schlesinger, and Charles Arthur Sprague. Upon the resignation of Mr. Brophy, Sophie D. Aberle, M. D., became executive director; and after the death of Professor Llewellyn, Soia Mentschikoff was appointed to the Commission. Each of these persons brought unique talents and resources to the investigation and to the preparation of this report.

W. W. KEELER of Bartlesville, Oklahoma, a trained engineer, is now chairman of the executive committee of Phillips Petroleum Company. He is also principal chief of the Cherokee Nation, and, following the publication of the Commission's preliminary recommendations, he served on the late President Kennedy's Task Force on Indian Affairs. Since he belongs to both cultures, he has been able to interpret the Indians and the whites to each other.

ARTHUR MEIER SCHLESINGER was Francis Lee Higginson Professor of History at Harvard University from 1931 to 1954 and professor emeritus until his death in October, 1965. In addition to producing an impressive list of books and papers in American history, he served as a member of the Commission on the Freedom of the Press from 1943 to 1946. Few men have had as clear a grasp of the American scene or have been as wise in searching for new points of view that might explain our history and resolve our national problems. The Commission was fortunate that he would set aside his own heavy writing schedule to help with its work.

CHARLES ARTHUR SPRAGUE is currently editor and publisher of the *Oregon Statesman*. Governor of Oregon from 1939 to 1943, he has repeatedly served on national commissions where justice and public interest were at stake. He brought experience, judgment, and searching inquiry to bear upon the Commission's problems.

KARL N. LLEWELLYN's research into the nature of law and the origins of legal systems resulted in fundamental contributions

in the field of legal methods. These inquiries, as well as his natural sympathies, brought him into intimate association with
American Indians. To his special competence he added a rare
instinct for justice and a deep appreciation of the problems of
minority groups. He was a valuable member of the Commission
on the Rights, Liberties, and Responsibilities of the American
Indian, and with his death on February 13, 1962, the Commission sustained a severe loss. Fortunately, SOIA MENTSCHIKOFF
(Mrs. Llewellyn), who is professor of law in the University of
Chicago and who had participated in the work of the Commission
from the first meeting, accepted membership in order to complete the work in which her husband had so keen an interest.
Her own great legal talents and her sympathies thus remained
available.

O. MEREDITH WILSON, chairman of the Commission, has had
a long and distinguished career in the academic world and in
the area of human rights, a career characterized by devotion
to a search for the truth and by unusual courage in support of
his deep convictions. He was president of the University of Oregon when our work began and is currently president of the University of Minnesota. In addition, he has served in many other
academic capacities and has been a member of many commissions and committees dedicated to the advancement of learning,
to the achievement of true academic freedom, and to the dignity
of the individual. This Commission has been fortunate indeed
to have him as its chairman.

WILLIAM A. BROPHY was the first executive director of the
Commission. From the beginning the Commission profited from
his work and wisdom. In addition to serving as director of research he also did research of striking insight and power himself, writing the chapter on tribal governments (Chapter Two)
and the section on water rights in Chapter Seven. Notwithstanding his retirement from active directorship, he provided counsel
as skillful as it was generous to further each portion of the work.
Both our debt and our gratitude require expression.

Mr. Brophy had been closely connected with Indian affairs

since 1933. From 1945 to 1948 he served as United States commissioner of Indian affairs and accumulated a wealth of knowledge from his experience. Through his efforts many policies important to Indians were established—aboriginal rights (Walpai Supreme Court opinion, December 8, 1941); the Indians' right to vote in Arizona; religious freedom in the *Toledo* v. *Pueblo de Jemez* case, 1954; and the Indian Claims Commission Act of August 13, 1946. He resigned from the Commission on the Rights, Liberties, and Responsibilities of the American Indian in September, 1957, to become the Indians' special legal consultant on Indian policy. He died on March 24, 1962, after the facts for this account had been collected and policies laid down; thus the report reflects his thinking.

Mr. Brophy's successor, DR. SOPHIE D. ABERLE (Mrs. Brophy), is a graduate of Stanford University and the Yale University School of Medicine. From 1935 to 1944 she served as general superintendent of the United Pueblos Agency, with supervision of federal activities for nineteen Pueblo tribes as well as for three off-reservation Navaho groups in New Mexico. From 1944 to 1948 she was a member of the Division of Medical Sciences, National Research Council, and from 1950 to 1958 was a member of the board of the National Science Foundation. Her scientific training combined with her experience in Indian affairs made her a logical choice to direct the Commission's research, organization, and compilation of facts for this report.

The report rests on investigations made by the Commission, its research staff in Albuquerque, New Mexico, and its consultants in many parts of the country. The Commission itself visited reservations in all sections (except Florida and Alaska) and discussed polities, needs, and problems with Indians, Bureau of Indian Affairs officials on the ground, and other representatives of the Department of the Interior.

Various studies were made by the Commission staff, including termination of government responsibility for the Paiutes and the Menominees, discrimination against Indians, relocation, assimilation, and an analysis of current legislation. Other, special studies directed by the Commission include the following:

"American Indian Arts and Crafts at Mid-Century" (June, 1959), by Réné d'Harnoncourt, director of the Museum of Modern Art and vice-president of the Museum of Primitive Art in New York City and long-time chairman of the Indian Arts and Crafts Board of the Department of the Interior.

"The Economic Position of the American Indians" (February, 1959), by Peter Dorner, associate professor of agricultural economics, University of Wisconsin.

"Indian Arts and Crafts" (September, 1958), by Dorothy Dunn, founder in 1933 of the Studio of Indian Painting, United States Indian School, Santa Fe, New Mexico.

"Constraints on Economic Progress on the Rosebud Sioux Indian Reservation," by Carl K. Eicher; Ph.D. dissertation, Department of Economics, Harvard University, 1960.

"Interim Report on Indian Health to the Commission on the Rights, Liberties, and Responsibilities of the American Indian" (June 30, 1959), by Walsh McDermott, M. D., Livingston Farrand Professor and chairman of the Department of Public Health and Preventive Medicine, The New York Hospital–Cornell University Medical Center, New York City; Kurt Dueschle, assistant professor of public health and preventive medicine, and Edwin Kilbourne, associate professor of public health and preventive medicine, The New York Hospital–Cornell University Medical Center; David Rogers, formerly associate professor of medicine in The New York Hospital–Cornell University Medical Center and professor and chairman of the Department of Internal Medicine, Vanderbilt University Medical College, Nashville, Tennessee.

"A Case Study of the Termination of Federal Responsibilities over the Klamath Reservation" (October, 1959), by Vincent Ostrum, associate professor of political science, University of California at Los Angeles, and Theodore Stern, associate professor of anthropology, University of Oregon, Eugene.

"A Study of the Changes in Policy of the United States Toward Indians" (February, 1959), by S. Lyman Tyler, director of libraries, Brigham Young University, Provo, Utah.

"Indian Education" (June, 1959), by Virgil Whitaker, dean of the Graduate School, Stanford University, and former superintendent of schools of the United Pueblos Agency, Bureau of Indian Affairs, Albuquerque, New Mexico (1942–45).

Professor Peter Dorner not only supplied the study on the economy of the American Indians, but also assisted with Chapter Three in determining policy and in bringing some of the material up to date.

Mr. Lawrence Stevens, associate director of the Bureau of Outdoor Recreation in the Department of the Interior, supplied the section on the acreage, use, and potential for recreation on Indian lands from the "Study Report," Outdoor Recreation Resources Review Commission, published in June, 1962.

Professor E. J. Workman, former president of the Institute of Mining and Technology, Socorro, New Mexico, kindly lent the Commission a member of his staff to assist with the footnotes.

In addition, there are the many employees of the Bureau of Indian Affairs who have discussed policy matters either for or against the final recommendations made; and there are many, many Indians who have assisted in supplying the Commission with a deeper understanding of their problems.

Chapter One and parts of Chapter Seven were edited by Arthur Schlesinger. Chapter Two was written and edited by William A. Brophy and was read and approved by Karl N. Llewellyn and Soia Mentschikoff.

In conclusion, it should be restated that the Commission on the Rights, Liberties, and Responsibilities of the American Indian is an independent commission operating under a grant from The Fund for the Republic, Inc., which has also generously supplied a grant-in-aid toward the publication of this report.

COMMISSION ON THE RIGHTS, LIBERTIES, AND
RESPONSIBILITIES OF THE AMERICAN INDIAN

July 1, 1966

Contents

Contents

Contents

Chapter Seven: Policies Which Impede Indian Assimilation

Illustrations

xix

The Indian

AMERICA'S UNFINISHED BUSINESS

1

Introduction

I. FACTS ABOUT INDIANS

Indian Values and Attitudes

THE INDIAN HIMSELF should be the focus of all public policy affecting him. Money, land, education, and technical assistance should be considered as only means to an end—making the Indian a self-respecting and useful American citizen. This policy involves restoring his pride of origin and faith in himself after years of crippling dependence on the federal government and arousing his desire to share in the advantages of modern civilization. These are deeply human considerations. If disregarded, they will defeat the best-intended government plans.

To encourage pride in Indianness is not to turn back the clock. On the contrary, it is to recognize that the United States policy has hitherto neglected this vital factor as a force for assimilation, with a corresponding loss to our national culture. As a result, Indians who have already entered the greater society have tended to disdain their historical background, drawing away from it as though ashamed. Instead of seeing it as a bridge to enable others to follow in their footsteps, they have too often misinterpreted their heritage to the dominant race and misrepresented their adopted culture to their own people. Yet men who have a foot in each world with an appreciation of both can effectively lessen the gap that divides the two and thus cross-fertilize both.

No program imposed from outside can serve as a substitute for one willed by Indians themselves. Nor should their ostensible

3

consent to a plan be deemed sufficient. Such "consent" may be wholly passive, indicating only a surrender to what seems unavoidable; or their consent may be obtained without their full understanding or before they are either able or desire to shoulder additional obligations. What is essential is to elicit their own initiative and intelligent co-operation.

While emphasis should be put, as it has hitherto been, on fitting Indian youth for its new opportunities and responsibilities, yet it would be unwise to dismiss all that is in the traditional Indian culture as being necessarily a barrier to change. In their society and in their religion Indians believe that they have values well worth preserving. These are sometimes stated in mystical terms and, if related to the Supreme Being, are sometimes a close secret. Nonetheless, these values exist and should be reckoned with. Two examples out of many involve their idea of unity or mutual assistance and their reverence for Mother Earth.

Unity is evidenced by each individual voluntarily working with the community. He gives his unstinted devotion to perpetuate ancestral usages. Status as well as personal security often rests on such service. In many tribes this selflessness derives vitality from a veneration for elders and their wisdom. By the same token, the merging of self in the group tends to deter competitiveness or a pride in material possessions for their monetary worth. Indian values have not customarily included the amassing of valuables for private benefit because of the ingrained tradition of sharing. These attitudes perhaps account in part for the improvidence often attributed to Indians. These conceptions, however, are not consistently achieved. Modifications and exceptions to the norm exist in every group.

The spiritual attachment to nature, an essential aspect of many pre-Columbian cultures, has brought the Indian into an intimate accord with the elements. That harmony appears strikingly in his feeling for the earth. Indians have traditionally regarded land as part of a benevolent Mother and, like her, indispensable to life. It was not considered a merchantable property but one that the users had an innate right to enjoy. This sentiment still tends to persist.

These and related ideas, if given due weight as part of the Indian's heritage, will prevent the confusion brought about by the assumption of persons in both races that assimilation can be achieved merely through the Indians' adopting certain attitudes common to their white neighbors. For example, is is said that all that is necessary is for the Indian *to be thrifty, to acquire habits of diligence,* and *to learn the importance of punctuality.*

Yet by the standards and needs of their own culture, the Indians historically have been economical, hard-working and appreciative of time. Thrift caused them to utilize every part of animals killed in the chase, as well as to gather and dry berries and roots for later consumption. Hunting or tilling the soil with wooden sticks to grow the family food demanded unflagging industry. The element of time for the agriculturist was determined, not by the white man's clock, but by the coming of the planting and harvesting seasons, and for the hunter by the habits of the animals he stalked.

Nor should it be overlooked that Indian attitudes are not theirs alone. "Honor thy father and thy mother," for instance, is a sacred commandment to many peoples. The importance of any set of values does not arise from its origin, existence, uniqueness, or validity. What is of paramount concern is that the mores of the Indian should be recognized in helping plan his future.

Besides tribal values vital in framing policy, neighbors and local officials must make it a point to help the Indian participate on a basis of equality in their political and economic life. Let them not expect him to conform to their image of how he ought to be, but accept him as the fellow human creature he is, with freedom to shape his own life as they do.

At the time time the Indian, too, has obligations to assume. He must devote his energy, ability, and perseverance wholeheartedly to the effort to improve his education, political participation, health practices, and standard of living.

The matter of government aid also requires a new look. Since

1933 the dominant society has been meeting its human needs by means not unlike those traditional to Indian tribes, inasmuch as sharing their possessions with others was also their way of helping the helpless. The United States has in similar fashion supplied relief through Social Security, through aid to the old, the blind, and the dependent, to crippled children, and to the unemployed, and also through the free distribution of surplus commodities. More strikingly, it has been extending to the entire population the kind of help it formerly gave only to Indians. Such benefits as federal financial aid to public schools, vocational education, scholarships, housing, construction of highways and hospitals, and medical assistance to the elderly are now available to other Americans. These services have arisen from acts of Congress. The Indians through the years have received their services as the result of bargains set forth in treaties, agreements, statutes, and administrative policies.

As the ways of the two civilizations converge and the government services to the mass of the people—financed partially or largely by the United States—actually outstrip those once granted only to Indians, the passage of the tribesmen into the broader society will be facilitated. What the members of this underprivileged race require for self-reliant participation is more and better education, improved economic assistance, better health, and a more carefully designed preparation for the responsibilities of the white man's way of life. Provided that they can fully share in the social services enjoyed by the non-Indian population and also that they find material opportunities appropriate to their abilities, Indians can profit from the merging of the two cultures.

Indian Background

Indians through their history have repeatedly had to adapt themselves to changing circumstances. Before Columbus discovered America, bands unable to preserve internal harmony divided and separated; vanishing water supplies forced others to abandon long-established locations; and adjustments to constant intertribal wars determined in part the form of their governments.

Then came the white man. Into the Southwest the Spaniards brought horses, sheep, silverwork, and new methods of weaving. Along the Atlantic seaboard the French and English introduced medicine, tools, rum, firearms, and new food products. Both groups brought the Christian religion to the Indians. These innovations brought a major revolution in native ways of life.

Then with the establishment of American independence factors of a different kind entered the situation. In the century or more of reservation existence Indians have of necessity developed a complex of legal ties with the United States government—with "Washington," as they call that distant authority, which operates so powerfully and often so incomprehensibly on their lives. Agents of the Bureau of Indian Affairs reside in or near the reservations. The Indian people know them, sometimes as friends, sometimes as critics and antagonists; but, paradoxically, in spite of loud complaints against "Washington" and its ways, few Indians want to relinquish the relationship, recognizing as they do their need for Bureau help.

Over the last century, government policy has more than once swung with disconcerting swiftness from one extreme to the other—from recognizing tribes as independent nations to dealing with the members as virtual prisoners; from ignoring or suppressing Indian culture to extolling it; from requiring that all decisions, even the most trivial, originate in Washington, to permitting a high degree of self-rule.

This instability has arisen both from actions of the Washington government and from those of the reservation superintendents, where the confusion is compounded by the fact that attitudes change so frequently. As a consequence, Indian groups have within a short span been alternately advised to utilize their land and to lease it to outsiders, to strengthen their tribal governments and social institutions and to relinquish them through the process of the termination of federal supervision. Even in the matter of school attendance the policy has swung from one extreme to another. These shifts of direction frequently, as in matters governing the child's education, were made without adequate preparations on the part of the persons involved.

Why has the Bureau of Indian Affairs (the B. I. A.), charged with the responsibility, not followed a uniform course? Why has it swung from pole to pole? The answer lies in the fact that no commissioner today can be sure of more than four years' tenure or eight years at the most. He must act quickly if at all. In addition, he must work with a staff, many of whom fail to understand the complexities of a culture which has not developed a level of achievement which predisposes a society to vigorous economic activity.[1]

The Indian, for his part, moreover, cannot say, "I am going to adopt all the white ways immediately." In view of his heritage, he must proceed step by step. Consider his inner struggle, for instance, over deciding whether to give up the medicine man for an M.D. Such an act could mean renouncing deep-rooted ideas of his tribe regarding the relationship of health to the spiritual forces of his world.

A Zuñi or a Rosebud Indian in Chicago or California faces a further series of exacting experiences. For the first time in his life, he must pay rent, wear different clothes, mingle with strange people, speak a language imperfectly mastered, and eat new foods.

But these various reasons account only in part for what by white standards is considered the Indian's backwardness. More important is the fact that the mass of Americans know little of the red man's history and hence lack interest in his condition. They are better informed about underdeveloped peoples in Asia and Africa than about those in their own country. They have read self-serving white versions of Indian wars, have seen the painting of "Custer's Last Stand," perhaps have bargained with basket-sellers, or watched painted dancers at railway stations. But beyond such superficial contacts, they see Indians as they

[1] David McClelland, *The Achieving Society* (Princeton, N. J., Van Nostrand, 1961), 63–70.

learned to see Indians in schoolbook days—contradictory creatures who on the one hand are ruthless savages with scalping knives, and on the other are heroic woodsmen and hunters, faithful until death to their friends.

Another widely held myth is that all Indians receive regular payments from the government *because* they are Indians. In fact, the federal policy of issuing regular food rations to tribesmen ceased long ago. Like other citizens, they receive general assistance and surplus farm products only when they are in need. An Indian on or off the reservation may, however, get a government check remitting land rent or royalities from mineral production paid to the local Indian agency for him as owner, but such payments are not due to his Indian heredity.

Overlooking the obstacles in the way, an articulate group of whites has advocated that all Indians be thrust without delay into the mainstream of American life. The group has succeeded from time to time in securing federal legislation and regulations for opening Indian resources more freely to non-Indians, for banning tribal customs and ceremonials, and for transporting the children to be "civilized" in distant boarding schools where the very use of their language was denied them.

Nothing that has happened to the Indians in recent generations, whether good or bad, has reflected views consciously and thoughtfully held by any substantial number of Americans. The public has had insufficient interest or knowledge to develop an adequate policy. Ideally, a major requirement, then, is for a program commanding the support of an informed citizenry, stable in aim, and yet flexible in application to differing situations.

Assimilation

Assimilation has often been variously defined. The B. I. A. at one time considered an Indian assimilated if he wore "civilian dress."[2] More recently, William Zimmerman, Jr., when he was

[2] *Report of the Superintendent of Indian Schools to the Commissioner of Indian Affairs* (Washington, G.P.O., 1905), 10.

assistant commissioner of Indian Affairs in 1947, construed the attainment in terms of admixture of white blood, literacy, business ability, acceptance of non-Indian institutions, and acceptance of the tribesmen by whites.[3] But even this wide-ranging definition falls short of the mark.

Ostensible familiarity with the English language and the adoption of white manners and customs by no means demonstrates that the Indian also adopts the white man's ethics. He may only be aping the ways of a society alien to him. Below the surface he may still form judgments based on tribal usages. As a case in point, he may lack the necessary urge for individual initiative and reject a competitive life despite his verbal acceptance of the white man's ways. The absence of adequate words in his language to convey the meaning of many concepts, values, and institutions further complicates the difficulty of communication between the two races.

No tests yet devised show whether an individual Indian has changed his basic emotions. Regardless of the degree of acculturation, studies show that a persistent core of aboriginal goals and expectations is still discernible in some Indians.[4] For a tribe, a rough index of the extent of the adoption of white ways could be had from the vital statistics of the group.[5] Infant death rates, particularly, have been shown to be directly related to the socioeconomic level.[6] The Committee on Indian Affairs to the Commission on Organization of the Executive Branch of the Gov-

---

[3] *Report with Respect to the House Resolution Authorizing the Committee on Interior and Insular Affairs to Conduct an Investigation of the Bureau of Indian Affairs,* 82 Cong., 2 sess., *House Report 2503* (Calendar No. 790), 163.

[4] Irving A. Hallowell, "Ojibwa Personality and Acculturation," *Acculturation in the Americas, Proceedings and Selected Papers of the XXIXth International Congress of Americanists* (ed. by Sol Tax; Chicago, University of Chicago Press, 1952), XXIX, Part 2; Irving A. Hallowell, *Culture and Experience* (Philadelphia, University of Pennsylvania Press, 1955); Ernestine Friedl, "Persistence in Chippewa Culture and Personality," *American Anthropologist,* Vol. LVIII, No. 5 (1956), 814–23.

[5] Clark Wissler, "The Effect of Civilization upon the Length of Life of the American Indian," *The Scientific Monthly,* Vol. XLIII (July, 1936), 13.

[6] Marion E. Altenderfer and Beatrice Crowther, "Relationship Between Infant Mortality and Socioeconomic Factors in Urban Areas," U. S. Public Health Service, *Public Health Reports,* Vol. LXIV, No. 11 (March 18, 1949), 331–39.

ernment recognized that assimilation has failed if shedding the old culture takes the joy out of life, produces a feeling of inferiority, and destroys the drive and purpose of the Indian.[7]

How Many Indians Are There?

The answer depends on how the question of what constitutes an Indian is defined. The census of 1960 records 508,675 on and off reservations. It uses the term to embrace all persons in whom Indian characteristics predominate and those who are considered to be tribesmen by the community (see Appendix, Table 1). Professor Sol Tax, of the University of Chicago, arrived in 1956 at a larger over-all figure for the Indian population, based on the 1950 census. He put the number of 571,824.

The Indians of primary concern in this report are members of tribes, bands, and communities so recognized by the United States. They number, according to the recent federal census, approximately 308,103, most of them residing on reservations or on individual allotments and said to be "under the jurisdiction" of the B. I. A. (see Appendix, Table 1). Some who dwell elsewhere may maintain their ties with the tribe and still consider the reservation their home; others, although also members, retain only tenuous connections and do nothing to advance the tribal community.

Excluded from any special relationship to the federal government are approximately 96,000 Indians of mixed blood in the eastern seaboard states, who zealously keep their Indian and tribal identity and some of the ceremonies (see Appendix, Table 1).

Behind such contrasting estimates of the Indian population as those of the 1960 census and of Sol Tax lies a host of difficulties. Splinter groups often completely escape classification as Indians. Migratory workers may cause the reservation population to shrink or expand according to the season. In the large communities of the Southwest, moreover, it is easy to overlook individuals who were born outside a hospital or who live in isolation

7 "Report of the Committee on Indian Affairs to the Commission on Organization of the Executive Branch of the Government," Oct., 1948 (mimeographed), 56.

and who speak no English. The Bureau of Indian Affairs in 1960 reckoned 74,000 as the probable number on the Navaho Reservation; but, if the findings of the Cornell Field Health Research Project as to a single area were extended to the entire region, the figure may well be 100,000. After reviewing all available sources of information about present-day tribal population, irrespective of whether they lived on the reservation, on allotted lands, or on adjoining areas, it is estimated that there are 80,364 Navahoes.[8]

For purposes of determining land titles and receiving the B. I. A.'s services, the degree of Indian blood is very important. For example, some statutes and regulations define the minimum amount of "Indian blood" necessary for an applicant to obtain educational assistance. In other respects, however, the ratio of the admixture may be meaningless. A person with only a single Indian grandparent—that is, a quarter-blood Indian—can still dwell on the reservation and be accepted by the tribesmen as of their race. On the other hand, a full-blood may reside in an eastern city and for all practical purposes be accepted and think of himself as a white man. An undetermined but considerable number of Indians have over the years merged with the general population, acquiring the white man's culture and competing successfully in industry and the professions. All these considerations complicate the problem of determining how many Americans should be called Indians.

Where Are the Indians Concentrated?

The 1960 census reports Indians present in every state in the Union, but the B. I. A. in that year acknowledged those under its jurisdiction in only twenty-five states (excluding Alaska). Of this number, 15,000 and upwards are in each of the following states: Arizona, Oklahoma, New Mexico, South Dakota, and Montana. Arizona leads all the rest with over 83,000 and Oklahoma and New Mexico follow with more than 64,000 and 56,000

[8] *The Navajo Yearbook, 1951–1961: A Decade of Progress*, Report No. VIII (1961), 311.

each. Except in Oklahoma, the Indians as a rule live on reservations (see Appendix, Table 1).[9]

What Is a Reservation?

A reservation is land owned by a tribe, where the members have their homes. The tracts vary in size from the one acre of Strawberry Valley Rancheria in Yuba County, California, to the Navaho Reservation, straddling New Mexico, Arizona, and Utah, with an area about the size of West Virginia. However, the definition of a reservation varies. The B. I. A., for purposes of census enumeration, designates as "units" the land on which Indians live (see Appendix, Table 1). A federal statute (except for purposes of liquor prohibition) defines a reservation as "land within the limits of any Indian reservation under the United States jurisdiction." Reservations may also include land covered by exclusive titles—including right of ways—dependent Indian communities, and Indian allotments where the title has not been extinguished (18 United States Code 1151, 1154, 1156). More than 300 separate stretches of land are so occupied by Indian groups and held in federal trusteeship for their use and benefit.[10]

An Indian on a reservation enjoys absolute freedom as to his person and earnings. He may go and come as he chooses, rear his children as he sees fit, and spend his own money wisely or foolishly, just as other American citizens do. Restrictions pertain to the control of tribal or trust funds and property. Most of the reservation land cannot be sold without an express act of Congress, while the sale of other land needs only the consent of the secretary of the interior. The land, however, can be leased for all purposes with government approval, the income going to the tribe or the owners of allotments.

Most reservations date prior to 1871, having resulted from

9 Although the state of Texas took over federal supervision of the Alabama and Coushatta Indians by the act of August 23, 1954, they are still eligible for admission to federal schools and hospitals on the same terms as other Indians. They were omitted from the list prepared by the B. I. A. from which Table 1 was compiled.

10 *Answers to Your Questions on American Indians* (U. S. Dept. of Interior, B. I. A., Haskell Institute, Lawrence, Kansas, 1959), 10.

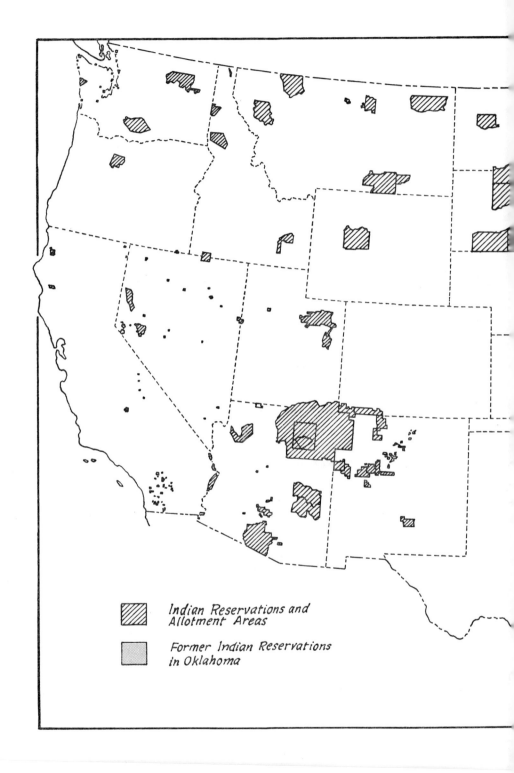

Indian Reservations and Allotment Areas

Former Indian Reservations in Oklahoma

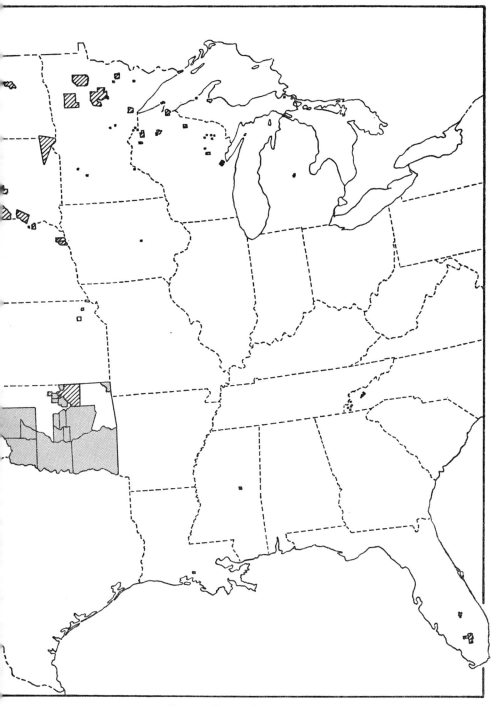

INDIAN LAND AREAS, 1965
Based on a map issued by the Bureau of Indian Affairs, U.S. Department of the Interior

treaties between the United States and the Indians. Those established after 1871 originated in agreements with tribes approved by Congress, in executive orders of the President, or in federal statutes.

The reservations are not gifts to the tribes concerned. They are either the part of their homeland which they kept when they ceded the rest to the United States or land which they got in exchange for their holdings when they were forced to move West.

Are Indians Citizens?

On June 2, 1924, Congress conferred citizenship on all Indians born in the United States who were not already in that category. Since then, therefore, they have possessed the same rights, privileges, and obligations as other citizens.

To imply, as is sometimes done, that Indians have not assumed their full civic duties does them injustice. They have borne their fair share of the most onerous responsibility of all—military service. They possess the suffrage and are exercising it in increasing numbers. Indians, moreover, are subject to jury duty, although some localities seldom call them.

Similarly, Indians pay federal income, excise, and other taxes, and all state levies on their salaries, off-reservation earnings, purchases, and property. Only their reservations and allotted lands are immune. They enjoy an exemption from land taxes because—among other reasons—Indians provide their own local governments. Outside of reservations, taxes from land are used to administer the affairs of a county.

What Is the Bureau of Indian Affairs?

The Bureau of Indian Affairs is the government agency which handles many of the common services which are administered for non-Indians by states, counties, and municipalities. When the B. I. A. was established in 1834, settlements near Indian country were mostly army outposts, so the Bureau was established in the War Department. It was transferred to the Department of the Interior in 1849, where it is today. The Snyder Act of 1921 (42

Stat. 208; 25 U.S.C. 13) provided the substantive law for appropriations covering B. I. A. activities. This was broadened by the Indian Reorganization Act of 1934 (48 Stat. 984; 25 U.S.C. 461, *et seq.*). The commissioner of Indian Affairs is appointed by the President and confirmed by the Senate, and his authority is delegated to him by the secretary of the interior.

The Bureau has three distinct functions. One is to carry out federal programs authorized by Congress according to government rules and regulations. The second is to act as trustee for Indian lands and resources. The third and increasingly important one is to create a climate in which Indian groups can operate by and for themselves.

II. LANDMARKS IN INDIAN LAW

United States policy toward the Indians is embodied in countless treaties, statutes, judicial decisions, administrative regulations, and opinions of law officers in different federal departments. Six enactments, however, constitute the landmarks: the Northwest Ordinance of 1787, the Constitution of the United States, the Trade and Intercourse Act of 1834, the General Allotment Act of 1887, the Indian Reorganization Act of 1934, and House Concurrent Resolution 108 of 1953.

The Northwest Ordinance

This law, passed in 1787 prior to the Constitution, expresses the following attitude toward the Indian, which should have been basic and continuing toward the race:

> The utmost good faith shall always be observed towards the Indians; their land and property shall never be taken from them without their consent; and in the property, rights, and liberty, they never shall be invaded or disturbed, unless in just and lawful wars authorized by Congress; but laws founded in justice and humanity shall from time to time be made, for preventing wrongs being done to them, and for preserving peace and friendship with them.[11]

This action of the Confederation Congress was reaffirmed in

[11] Felix S. Cohen, *Handbook of Federal Indian Law* (Washington, G.P.O., 1942), 69.

1789, with minor changes by the first Congress under the Constitution.

The Constitution of the United States

The basic authority for the conduct of Indian affairs is the Constitution of the United States. That document, adopted in 1789, conferred on the federal government the power to regulate commerce with the Indian tribes and to make treaties with them, to control the public land Indians occupied, and to prescribe the terms of admission for new states.[12]

Arizona, Montana, New Mexico, North Dakota, Oklahoma, South Dakota, Utah, and Washington were required by Congress to disclaim jurisdiction over Indian land before they were admitted to statehood. All reservations are, nevertheless, politically and legally parts of the states.[13]

The Trade and Intercourse Act

This measure of 1834, incorporating provisions of earlier laws with amendments, broadly expresses the power the Constitution bestowed on Congress over the tribes. It defined Indian country, prescribed the method of making contracts with the natives, and empowered the commissioner of Indian affairs to appoint traders as well as to regulate the kind, quantity, and prices of goods they sold to tribesmen. It further provided that interests in their land, whether by lease or by purchase, could be acquired only by treaty or other agreement pursuant to the Constitution. To this end it penalized trespassers on Indian holdings.

The relationship between tribesmen and the federal government still rests in large degree on these provisions of more than a century ago.

The General Allotment Act (Dawes Act)

This enactment of 1887 (24 Stat. 388) and amendments in 1891 (26 Stat. 794), 1910 (36 Stat. 855), and 1906 (34 Stat. 182)

12 *Ibid.*, 89.
13 *Langford* v. *Monteith,* 102 U.S. 145 (1880), *ibid.,* 119.

authorized the President to parcel tribal land to individual members in tracts of 40, 80, or 160 acres, called allotments. The secretary of the interior was to negotiate for the purchase of the surplus land remaining after all eligible Indians had received their shares, and the proceeds were to be devoted to the education and civilization of the tribe. The General Allotment Act did not apply to the Five Civilized Tribes, certain other tribes in Indian Territory, or the New York Senecas.

Each allotment was to be held in trust by the United States for twenty-five years or longer, at the President's discretion, after which the government would issue a fee patent, free of all liens and debts, to the allotee or his heirs. Inheritance was to be determined by state law.

Individual members of a tribe upon receiving patents were to become citizens (including the right to vote), subject to the civil and criminal laws of the state or territory where they resided. This provision was changed in 1906 in order to postpone citizenship and the application of state law (except for determining heirship) until a fee simple patent was issued. A further amendment permitted a fee patent to be granted, with the secretary of the interior's approval, to a "competent" Indian before the twenty-five-year trust terminated (or the land was leased). Even this, however, caused complexity in view of other legislation and the Indian's refusal to abandon his tribe. According to the solicitor of interior, the provision became practically a dead letter (61 I. D. 298; 1954).

The General Allotment Act was based on the theory that an Indian who possessed his own plot would automatically thereby become a farmer or livestock operator. Contact with whites and ownership of land were expected to teach him to become educated, civilized, and self-supporting—like his neighbors—thus relieving the government of further supervision and also throwing open large quantities of surplus land to non-Indians. Some allotments had been made earlier under treaties or laws, but the Act of 1887 subdivided land on a wholesale basis.

The framers sadly misjudged the nature of the Indian. He

was not familiar with private ownership or farming. Unfortunately, there was no provision for training him in agriculture or for granting him credit for livestock, feed, and implements. However, the "surplus" land and many of the allotments passed into the hands of whites.

In 1934, when the process of allotting stopped, 246,569 assignments totaling nearly forty-one million acres had been made.[14] The Meriam Survey *Report* in 1928, however, caused a slowdown of the parceling; and in 1934 the Indian Reorganization Act prohibited it altogether. This measure prolonged the trust period of allotments on reservations whose members accepted the Act, while an executive order extended the periods of other allotments.

Under the operation of the law of 1887, tribal landholdings were cut from approximately 138,000,000 acres to roughly 48,000,000 in 1934.[15] This reduction provides one reason for the Indian's present impoverishment and shattered morale.

Indian Reorganization Act

The Wheeler-Howard Act of 1934, also known as the Indian Reorganization Act, endeavored to repair the damage of the allotment era. By it the United States recognized the importance of Indian communal life as an agency for preserving and encouraging social controls and values on which the people could base innovations made by themselves. To this end it sought to transfer the initiative from the B. I. A. to the tribesmen concerned.[16]

Besides stopping the alienation and allotment of tribal land, this act authorized appropriations to purchase new holdings, established a system of federal loans, confirmed Indian self-gov-

[14] *Indian Heirship Land Survey,* Memorandum of the chairman to the Committee on Interior and Insular Affairs, 86 Cong., 2 sess., Senate, *Committee Print,* Part I, p. 2.

[15] Cohen, *Handbook of Federal Indian Law,* 216.

[16] Clyde Kluckhohn and Robert Hackenberg, "Social Science Principles and the Indian Reorganization Act," *Indian Affairs and the Indian Reorganization Act. the Twenty Year Record* (ed. by William H. Kelly; Tucson, University of Arizona, 1954 [mimeographed]), 29–30.

ernment, and provided for the setting up of tribal business organizations to be chartered as federal corporations. It required the groups accepting the act further to conserve their soil, water, vegetation, and timber resources; and it directed the secretary of the interior to inform them of all estimates of the cost of federal projects for their benefit before submitting the figures to the Bureau of the Budget. The act also made Indians eligible for B. I. A. posts without regard to Civil Service laws. Throughout, the intent was to assist Indians to assume greater responsibility for their own affairs which was not always realized. Some persons criticized the act as a scheme to push the Indians back to the blanket. Actually, the direct opposite was the aim, as is evidenced in the provisions for encouraging native arts and crafts as business careers.

The Act had been operating for only seven years when America entered World War II. Many superintendents and other local officials, as well as younger Indians competent to assume tribal leadership, left for military service. There was a reduction in B. I. A. appropriations. Physical plants, schools, roads, hospitals, vehicles, telephone systems, and other facilities deteriorated. During these years of national peril very little advancement—if not, indeed, retrogression—took place on the reservations.

For this and related reasons doubts arose concerning the wisdom of self-directed community life; and in 1944 a penetrating investigation by the O'Connor-Mundt House Committee on Indian Affairs reported that, although the Wheeler-Howard Act (I.R.A.) had in some instances aided the Indians, progress toward assimilation had lagged because of inadequate land, education, health guidance, and the government's failure to settle claims and to consolidate scattered holdings owned by several heirs.[17]

In 1953, at an American Anthropological Association symposium, it was pointed out that more than three-fourths of all tribes were then operating under the Indian Reorganization Act, evidence that the race wanted community responsibility and self-determination; also, in the twenty years since the passage of the

17 *Aspects of Indian Policy, 79 Cong.,* 1 sess., Senate Committee Print., 17.

measure, only one tribe had revoked its constitution or surrendered its charter. Those tribes not under the Indian Reorganization Act, such as the Navaho, had nevertheless adopted and benefited from some of its provisions. Indeed, Congress in 1950 expressly authorized the Navaho to adopt their own frame of government (64 Stat. 46).

The shortcomings of the Indian Reorganization Act in action have stemmed in part from the failure of administrators to understand how to motivate the Indians to take full advantage of its benefits, in part from the skepticism of superintendents about the Indians' ability to look after themselves, and in part from the inadequacy of appropriations for credit facilities, land purchase, and administration.[18] However, in agencies with sympathetic superintendents, able tribal governments, and emphasis on local decision, the Indian Reorganization Act has amply proved its worth.[19]

House Concurrent Resolution 108

House Concurrent Resolution 108, passed by Congress in 1953, did not take the form of a statute, but administrative action has given it almost the effect of one. This declaration of official policy reversed most of the principles of the Indian Reorganization Act. Its stated purpose was to free Indians from federal control and supervision, end their wardship, and make them subject to the same laws and entitled to the same privileges as other citizens.

Indians, however, were already citizens by federal law, with all the rights possessed by their white neighbors. The term "wards" applied to them was, and had for a long time been, misleading. Except for the federal prohibitions against selling alcoholic liquor to Indians—repealed in 1953—they were subject to no greater federal control of their persons than any other citizens; they paid state and federal taxes the same as non-Indians,

18 Theodore H. Haas, *Ten Years of Tribal Government Under I. R. A.* (Washington, Indian Service, 1947), 6–7.

19 *United Pueblos Quarterly Bulletin, 1939–43,* issued by the United Pueblos Agency, Albuquerque, N. M. (mimeographed).

unless specifically exempted by treaty agreement or statute. Most of the exemptions applied only to real estate or income from trust property. The property the government held in trust for them was supervised like any other trust, although some Indians claimed that the government's management was not effective. The restrictions and the trusts, moreover, had not been imposed by the government but by and large had resulted from covenants made by the Indians with the United States in the form of treaties, agreements, statutes, and policies designed to protect them from losing their land and to assure the right of self-government, the inalienability and immunity from taxes on their land, and the services which the United States provided.

III. RECOMMENDATIONS

An objective which should undergird all Indian policy is that the Indian individual, the Indian family, and the Indian community be motivated to participate in solving their own problems. The Indian must be given responsibility, must be afforded an opportunity he can utilize, and must develop faith in himself.

2

Tribal Governments

I. Legislative and Executive Powers

Self-Government by Tribes

A TRIBE is not only a social group; it is also a body politic whose right of self-rule in local matters the white man has recognized since the country began. Except as limited by federal law, a tribe has governing powers similar to those of a state or municipality. Following the practice of other European nations, the English colonial governments and later the United States recognized the tribes—in Chief Justice Marshall's words—as "distinct, independent, political communities" and "domestic dependent nations"[1] and entered into nearly 400 treaties with them. These agreements under the Constitution possess the same validity as those with foreign powers.

Although the documents varied in content, a rough pattern appears in the long succession. The tribe agreed to keep the peace with the dominant race and with other Indian bands and acknowledged dependence on the white man's government. It further ceded all its territory except for a part retained for its own use. Reservations, as these withheld portions were called, arose also in other ways. Sometimes they were created in lieu of land the tribes surrendered elsewhere, or, if the Indians had failed to keep back enough for subsistence, Congress or the

[1] *Worcester* v. *Georgia,* 5 Peters 515 (1832); *Cherokee Nation* v. *Georgia,* 5 Peters 1, 12 (1831).

Executive might later add to their holdings. It was by such means that the West was opened to white settlement.

In return for a tribe's cessions the United States pledged its protection and typically agreed to pay the concerned groups cash and annuities; to erect schools, hospitals, churches, gristmills, sawmills, and the like; to provide teachers, physicians, millers, and blacksmiths; to furnish food, tobacco, and domestic animals; and to supply the fruits of modern progress such as vaccines, farm implements, guns, steel, and blankets. The Ute treaty of 1868 (15 Stat. 619), for example, promised an annual sum sufficient in the discretion of Congress for the absolute wants of the tribesmen (but not to exceed $30,000) for clothing and articles of utility and another $30,000 for food "until such time as said Indians shall be found capable of sustaining themselves."

Over the years the complex of contractual agreements, the dependent-nation status of the Indians, the constitutional authority of Congress over Indian affairs, and the thousands of statutes, judicial decisions, and administrative regulations defining the mutual rights and responsibilities of the Washington government, the tribes, and the states—all these gave the Indians every warrant to believe that they could retain their lands, their governments, and their way of life as long as they wished. Added to these legal sanctions were the special circumstances of their situation: their isolation, their ignorance, and even disdain, of the white man's language and institutions and his of theirs; their inability to cope with competitive, acquisitive whites seeking their land; the mutual fear and animosity between Indians and their neighbors; the impossibility of state governments' controlling warlike tribes or giving them any public services; and the acknowledged duty of the United States to "civilize" them. Out of these many circumstances arose the immunity of their land from taxation, their freedom from state control, the duty of the federal government to supply educational, medical, and other "civilizing" services, and their right to local self-government. Their emotional attachment to the land and their conception of the reservation as a final refuge created additional complications.[2]

In 1871, Congress ended further treaty-making by a law, which, however, recognized the validity of all existing compacts.[3] But the principle of securing tribal consent thereafter was not wholly abandoned. In fact, the Indian Reorganization Act of 1934 went so far as to encourage community, tribal, and corporate action as the best way for the race to learn modern practices. The Act, moreover, was applicable only to tribes that voluntarily accepted it.[4] Indeed, when the government has acted without Indian acquiescence, particularly in matters involving property, it has frequently had to pay the tribesmen at a later date if they failed to benefit as had been anticipated. Thus when the United States built certain irrigation projects and laid the cost on the Indians without their consent, the Leavitt Act of 1932 authorized cancellation of the charges.[5]

[2] Williams v. Lee, 358, U.S. 217 (1959); Native American Church v. Navajo Tribal Council, 272 F. 2d 131, C.A. 10 (1960); Your Food Stores v. Village of Española, 68 N.M. 327, 361 P.2d 950 (1961); Cohen, Handbook of Federal Indian Law, 33–34; Constitution, Article II, sec 2, clause 2 (make treaties); Article I, sec. 8, clause 3. (regulate commerce, general welfare); Article VI, sec. 2 (supremacy section).

A number of recent court decisions refer to the "sovereignty" of the tribe, as: Native American Church v. Navajo Tribal Council, above; Iron Crow v. Oglala Sioux Tribe, 231 F. 2d 89, C.A. 8 (1956).

Whatever the meaning of "nation" or "sovereignty" may be, Indian tribes and nations "are in no sense sovereign States," Stephens v. Cherokee Nation, 174 U.S. 445 (1899). Failure to recognize this ruling has misled Indians to deny that citizenship could be conferred on them by the 1924 act, to discuss submitting their grievances to the United Nations, and to talk as though their tribe were not an integral part of the United States.

[3] " . . . hereafter no Indian nation or tribe within . . . the United States shall be acknowledged or recognized as an independent nation, tribe or power with whom the United States may contract by treaty; but no obligation of any treaty lawfully made and ratified with any such Indian nation or tribe prior to March 3, 1871 shall be hereby invalidated or impaired . . . " (act of March 3, 1871, 16 Stat. 544, 25 U.S.C.A. 71). For many years thereafter formal agreements with tribes were embodied in acts of Congress. These compacts, sometimes inconsistently called treaties by Congress and the courts, had practically the same effect as treaties. See Laurence F. Schmeckebier, The Office of Indian Affairs (Baltimore, Md., 1927), 57–58, 64, 85.

[4] Act of June 18, 1934, 48 Stat. 984, 988, 25 U.S.C.A. 461.

[5] 47 Stat. 564, 25 U.S.C.A. 386(a).

Treaties and Agreements

Although treaty-making ceased almost a century ago, the treaties and the later agreements remain important bases of Indian law.[6] The courts interpret ambiguities in treaties and agreements favorably to the Indians on the ground that they did not understand the white man's language and ways, that their bargaining position was weak, and that they had trusted the good faith of the government.[7]

Indians sometimes say that Congress lacks the power to supersede a treaty and that, therefore, they have merely to trace their rights to such a document to stop Congress in its tracks. True, some property rights vested in Indians by treaty, such as exemption of an allotment from taxation, are constitutionally protected from Congressional infringement; and when an agreement has pledged certain services, then morally the government should observe its plighted word. From a strictly legal standpoint, however, if a later act of Congress should alter a treaty, generally speaking it is the will of Congress which governs.[8]

All the government's treaty engagements to expend money and construct schools, hospitals, and other community buildings have been met. A few perpetual annuities are still being paid and some treaty goods are being delivered.[9] Certain things promised, such as a "plough maker," have not been needed for gen-

6 Cohen, *Handbook of Federal Indian Law;* see also Cohen's *Federal Indian Law* (Washington, G.P.O., 1958). 139.

7 Cohen, *Handbook of Federal Indian Law;* 37; *Federal Indian Law*, 145; *Worcester* v. *Georgia,* 6 Peters 515–82 (1832). Indian treaty language "should never be construed to their prejudice...." Agreements with Indians are interpreted according to the same principles as foreign treaties: *Marlin* v. *LeWallen,* 276 U.S. 58 (1928); *Carpenter* v. *Shaw,* 280 U.S. 363 (1930).

8 *Choate* v. *Trapp,* 224 U.S. 665 (1912): "Of course, an Act of Congress may repeal a prior treaty as well as it may repeal a prior Act," declared the court with reference to both foreign governments and Indian tribes; *Ex parte Webb,* 225 U.S. 663 (1912): "Great nations, like great men, should keep their word"; Justices Black, Douglas, and Chief Justice Warren's dissenting opinion in *Federal Power Commission* v. *Tuscarora Indian Nation,* 362 U.S. 99 (1960).

9 Felix S. Cohen, "Original Indian Title," *Minnesota Law Review,* Vol. XXXII, No. 1 (Dec., 1947), 28; Letter from Assistant Commissioner Fred H. Massey to the Commission on the Rights, Liberties, and Responsibilities of the American Indian, Feb. 2, 1962.

erations. On the other hand, small outlays promised for education, medical doctors, and medicines and for "civilization" have been merged in the general educational, medical, and other services to the tribesmen.

The United States authorities overreached some tribes in negotiating treaties and intimidated others into compliance; and undeniably Congress at times has violated solemn compacts—both treaties and agreements—by enacting later conflicting laws or by arbitrarily moving one band onto the land of another. In some cases, too, either deliberately or unwittingly, Congress has reduced the treaty land. Still, President Truman assessed the historical record fairly enough when he signed the Indian Claims Commission Act in 1946:

> This bill makes perfectly clear what men and women, here and abroad, have failed to recognize, that in our transactions with the Indian tribes we have at least since the Northwest Ordinance of 1787 set for ourselves the standard of fair and honorable dealings .... Instead of confiscating Indian lands, we have purchased from the tribes that once owned this continent more than 90 percent of our public domain, paying them approximately 800 million dollars in the process. It would be a miracle if in the course of these dealings—the largest real estate transaction in history—we had not made some mistakes and occasionally failed to live up to the precise terms of our treaties and agreements with some 200 tribes. But we stand ready ... to correct any mistakes we have made.

In recognition of these injustices the government paid large damages to injured tribes. Thus in 1950 it gave the Utes over $31,750,000 for taking their land, and in 1938 it paid the Shoshones of Wyoming $4,408,444.23 because a commissioner of Indian affairs had moved Arapahoes to the Shoshone Reservation. Likewise in 1942, it compensated the California Indians with $5,000,000 as an offset for part of the goods and the land they had expected to get under treaties signed but never ratified by the Senate. Similarly in 1938, the Klamaths won a judgment for $5,313,347.32 for a tract the tribe had reserved for its own use but which the government had wrongly conveyed to Oregon.[10]

The establishment of the Indian Claims Commission in 1946 provided a regular means of adjudicating any claims arising out of the Constitution or laws or treaties, or involving negligence by the United States, or the taking of Indian land. If fraud, duress, or mistake exists in connection with any treaty or agreement or an insufficient consideration has been paid Indians for any land, the Commission awards damages to the tribe. Even "claims based upon fair and honorable dealings that are not recognized by any existing rule of law of equity" are allowed. As a result, the Otoe and Missouri Indians in 1955 received a gross award of $1,681,892 for the loss of land they occupied but to which they did not own recognized title.[11] As of January 1, 1964, Indian tribes had filed 588 claims; 108 were dismissed and 50 awards totaling $94,915,000 have been made.[12]

Contrary to widespread popular belief, the government has not always cheated the Indians. In some instances at least, the government has itself been the loser. Some of the land bought at $1.25 an acre the government still has on its hands; in other cases, tribes sold the United States tracts to which they had no claim and which, therefore, had to be purchased a second time from a different tribe. Anticipating President Truman, Felix Cohen concluded:

> There is no nation on the face of the earth which has set for itself so high a standard of dealing with a native aboriginal people as the United States and no nation on earth has been more self-critical in seeking to rectify its deviations from those high standards.[13]

[10] Act of August 13, 1946, 60 Stat. 1049, 25 U.S.C.A. 70 and 70(a); Schmeckebier *The Office of Indian Affairs*, 61; Cohen, "Original Indian Title," *Minnesota Law Review*, Vol. XXXII, No. 1 (Dec. 1947), 28, 34–43.

[11] *Otoe and Missouri Tribe v. United States*, 131 F. Supp. 265, 131 Ct. Cl. 593 (1955), cert. den. 350 U.S. 848.

[12] *Department of the Interior and Related Agencies Appropriations for 1965*, Hearings before a Subcommittee of the Committee on Appropriations, U.S. Senate, 88 Cong., 2 sess., on *House Report 10433*, 1110.

[13] Cohen, "Original Indian Title," *Minnesota Law Review*, Vol. XXXII, No. 1 (Dec., 1947), 43.

Today the Indian people look to treaty provisions for perpetual possession of their reservations—for the right to make their own laws and be ruled by them, as Justice Black held in *Williams* v. *Lee* in 1959 (358 U.S.C. 217), and for their exemption from state taxation and state laws. The very water used for agriculture as well as for domestic, municipal, and related purposes depends upon these compacts; and without this natural resource Indians could not grow crops on their arable land. Hunting and fishing rights similarly rest on treaty provisions.[14] Congress and the courts take these guarantees into account in framing legislation and rendering decisions; and administrators and policy makers must likewise respect such assurances, for a treaty cannot be abrogated by purely executive action.[15]

Public Law 280, in 1953, although widely attacked by Indians for extending state law to certain tribes without their consent,

14 *Harrison* v. *Laveen*, 67 Arizona 337, 196 P. 2d 456 (1948). The treaty with the "Shoshone (eastern band) and Bannock" tribes (July 3, 1868, 15 Stat. 673) reserved land "for the absolute and undisturbed use and occupation" of the Shoshones and such other friendly Indians as they might be willing, with the consent of the United States, to admit amongst them. The Indians further agreed to make the reservation their "permanent home," and the United States in turn agreed to permit no persons except those specifically designated to enter, pass over, settle upon, or reside in the area. Similar provisions appear in numerous other treaties, as: Navajo treaty, June 1, 1868, 15 Stat. 667; *Williams* v. *Lee*, above; *Winters* v. *United States*, 207 U.S. 564 (1908) ; *United States* v. *Ahtanum Irrigation District*, 236 F. 2d 321 (1956) cert. den. 352 U.S. 988; *Arizona* v. *California, et al.*, No. 13 original, in Supreme Court. The report of Special Master Judge Samuel Rifkind recognized the right of various tribes to large quantities of Colorado River water, based on their treaties and agreements. See Cohen, *Handbook of Federal Indian Law*, 285, 316–19, and *Federal Indian Law*, 662–71.

15 Strangely, the Commissioner of Indian Affairs wrote, on Nov. 12, 1957, each of the Bureau's area directors as follows:

> The uncertainty of our position and the generally adamant, but in the main equally-uncertain knowledge on the part of Indian people concerning their "treaty rights" make it necessary that such "rights" be clarified without further delay to facilitate program planning with individual groups.
> Accordingly, I am requesting each Area Director to carefully examine all treaties and statutory obligations pertaining to each tribe of Indians within his jurisdiction for the purpose of defining with certainty the remaining obligations of the Government.

Why such information was not available in Washington but was thought to be in the hands of field employees is not evident. Nor is it clear how policies of termination, then being aggressively pursued, could have been formulated without knowing what treaty obligations were outstanding.

nevertheless also recognized existing rights and prohibited the states from regulating Indian property in a manner inconsistent with those rights and from depriving Indians of hunting, trapping, or fishing privileges derived from treaties or agreements.[16]

Powers of the Federal Government

By the Constitution, Indian affairs fall exclusively under the federal government, unless it has delegated some function to the states. Accordingly, the United States and the respective tribes exercise exclusive jurisdiction over Indian affairs and the Indian country,[17] except that the states concerned retain the same authority over non-Indians on reservations as they have anywhere else so long as Indian interests are not involved. Historically, this arrangement has permitted reservation people to maintain their own governments.

The United States currently deals with roughly 250 self-governing tribal societies.[18] Excluded are those in Oklahoma, who at the most have shadow governments, and the groups in Alaska, whose background differs from that in other states. Ninety-five of the 250 framed their constitutions in compliance with the Indian Reorganization Act statute; four had prior ones;[19] others, like most of the New Mexico Pueblos, govern themselves according to ancient customs, which they have more or less adapted to modern conditions without recourse to written codes or laws. "If we had a written constitution and laws, we'd always have to look up what we could do and then maybe ask a lawyer half the time," explained one of the older Pueblo leaders.[20]

In addition, approximately 74 tribes have charters from the United States for conducting their business affairs.[21] The cor-

16 Act of Aug. 15, 1953, 67 Stat. 588, as amended, 18 U.S.C.A. 1162, 28 U.S.C.A. 1360.

17 The Constitutional Convention intended "to give the whole power of managing those affairs to the government about to be instituted, the Convention conferred it explicitly." C. J. Marshall, *The Cherokee* v. *Georgia*, 5 Peters 1 (1831).

18 *Answers to Your Questions on American Indians* (1959), 3.

19 *Answers to Your Questions on American Indians* (1949), 57.

20 Personal communication to William A. Brophy.

21 *Answers to Your Questions on American Indians* (1949), 57.

porate organization and management are sufficiently flexible to be fitted to the needs and capacity of each group, but in most instances the members of the elected council are the directors. Consequently, the anticipated separation of economic from governmental affairs has not generally resulted.

Indian governments vary widely in function, effectiveness, and the extent of review over their actions exercised by the secretary of the interior. The Navaho tribe, with a population of about 80,364 in 1960, budgeted expenditures of $20,149,531 in 1959[22] and employed 3,800 people[23] in legislative, judicial, and executive work, including extensive logging and sawmill operations. By contrast, the Pueblo of Pojoaque in New Mexico, with but thirty-four members in seven families, had no tribal budget at all and no paid employees.

The governments currently functioning are democratic or representative in form, with popularly elected councils and officers who, like public officials in non-Indian communities, are subject to replacement by election. Some constitutions even provide for the recall of officials and allow the voters to initiate laws and refer those already enacted back to the electorate. In general, the codes are patterned after state and local governments, not on the traditional tribal systems. There is nothing exotic or alien about them. They are integral parts of the complex American governing mechanism and, in fact, introduce Indians as nothing else could to the methods of government, administration, public finance, and political activity common to the rest of the United States.

No fully acceptable statistics of tribal voting are available, but approximately 50 per cent of the eligibles in forty-six tribes voted in one or more of the elections in 1958, 1959, and 1960. In October, 1956, the House Committee on Interior and Insular Affairs found that 143,078 Indians over twenty-one years of age

22 *The Navajo Yearbook, 1951–1961*, Report VII (fiscal year 1958), 151. This includes capital investments of $11,267,700 for public needs, such as land purchases, and a sawmill development costing $7,500,000.

23 Communication from Walter Olson, assistant area director, B. I. A., Gallup, N.M., Feb., 1961.

lived on reservations; 57,818 of them had qualified to vote, but only 25,582 had voted in the previous national, state, or local elections.[24] The accompanying table shows the voting record of Indians in tribal elections.

VOTING RECORD OF INDIANS IN TRIBAL ELECTIONS[25]

Year	Eligible to Vote	Voted	Per cent Voted
1958	24,640	9,180	37
1959[26]	50,449	30,437	60
1960	27,400	11,363	41
Total	102,489	50,980	50

So far as the members of the reservations are concerned, tribes exercise powers comparable in breadth to those of a state or of home-rule subdivisions. As recently as 1959, the United States Court of Appeals of the Tenth Circuit held in the Native American Church case that

> Indian tribes are not States. They have a status higher than that of States. They are subordinate and dependent nations possessed of all powers as such only to the extent that they have expressly been required to surrender them to the superior sovereign, the United States . . . .

In short, tribes retain all their original authority except as withheld by Congress. They exercise the right to adopt and operate a government of their own choice, to determine their own memberships, to regulate domestic relations of the members, and to make rules for inheritance of property (except where the inheritance of allotments depends upon federal law). They control the conduct of their members by legislation, tax all persons residing or doing business on the reservation, exclude and evict

24 *Present Relations of the Federal Government to the American Indian,* 85 Cong., 2 sess., *House Committee Print. No. 38,* p. 9.

25 Material obtained in letters from area directors and superintendents. These figures represent one or more elections for officers of 46 tribes, which is 18 per cent of the approximately 250 tribes in the United States (exclusive of Alaska).

26 Voting records for 1959 include Navaho. This explains why the figure is so high. No Navaho voting occurred in 1958 or 1960.

non-members, appropriate money for general purposes, and administer justice through their own courts under codes of civil and criminal justice enacted by the tribal councils or promulgated in the regulations of the secretary of the interior or under customary law.[27]

Unlike the federal and state governments, however, there is rarely a separation of powers. The tribal council in many instances is the legislative as well as the executive branch, both passing and enforcing the laws. Some groups indeed carry the principle of unification to the point of having the council that serves as a legislative body act also as an appellate judicial body for decisions of a tribal court, mingling the functions in much the same way as do many United States administrative agencies.

The members of the council, either in their political capacity or as directors of a tribal corporation, also manage the common resources, determine what use the tribesmen may make of the collective land, lease tracts and minerals, and make other contracts relating to tribal activities. To finance their governments, a few groups tax merchants who do business within the reservation,[28] but most groups depend on income derived from common assets.

The Indian Reorganization Act illustrates how a law intended to strengthen Indian governments and to give the people responsible business experience through making their own decisions has in fact actually increased federal control over them. Prior to the passage of the statute a tribe generally had the inherent power freely to make its own laws and to spend any funds not in the possession of the federal Treasury.[29] Despite the fact that these rights and powers were in words confirmed by the Indian

27 Cohen, *Handbook of Federal Indian Law*, chap. 7; *Iron Crow* v. *Oglala Sioux Tribe*, 231 F. 2d 89, C.A. 8 (1956); *Native American Church* v. *The Navajo Tribal Council; Williams* v. *Lee; Your Food Stores* v. *Village of Española*, 68 N.M. 327, 361 P. 2d 950 (1960), cert. den. 368 U.S. 915; 25 Code of Federal Regulations, chap. 11, cert. den. 358, U.S. 932.

28 *Iron Crow* v. *Oglala Sioux Tribe*, 129 F. Sup.; *Barta* v. *Oglala Sioux Tribe*, 259 F. 2d 553, C.A. 8 (1958), cert. den. 358, U.S. 932.

29 Opinion of the solicitor for the Dept. of the Interior, Oct. 25, 1934, on *Powers of Indian Tribes*, 55 Interior Department Decisions 14; V. Kappler, *Indian Affairs*,

Reorganization Act, in actual practice every constitution adopted under the statute requires the secretary of the interior to review nearly all ordinances in various categories, notably those which define and punish offenses. Similarly, every Indian Reorganization Act corporate charter subjects to such approval almost the entire amount that a tribe can spend or make contracts for. And the same restrictions apply to many other groups not under this law.

This refusal to allow Indians to learn by trial and error may have had warrant in the 1930's at the time the first constitutions were adopted, for most tribes then had little knowledge of how to conduct a modern government and transact business in corporate form. Indeed, the corporate charters provided that the controls could be removed as the tribes gained experience, but in most instances the restraints still remain, continuing to be imposed when new charters are adopted.

This policy probably stems from the widespread belief among the B. I. A. staff that as "guardian" or "trustee," the Bureau itself must make the vital decisions. According to this notion, the United States could be sued for damages if the Indians made mistakes. However groundless this idea may be, it prevails and will continue to hamper tribal self-development until legislation or strong executive direction dispels the doubts of the Bureau employees.[30]

Powers of Tribal Governments

Tribal government is, as has been seen, an integral part of the nation's political system, an evidence both of an unwillingness of the dominant race to exercise its power arbitrarily over these "first Americans"[31] and of a conviction that a people familiar

Laws, and Treaties (76 Cong., 2 sess., *Senate Doc. 194*), 778–808; "Indian Rights and the Federal Courts," *Minnesota Law Review*, Vol. XXIV (1940), 145; Cohen, *Handbook of Federal Indian Law*, chap. 7.

[30] See pages 132–34, Chapter Four below for a discussion of this point.

[31] In 1958, Premier Khrushchev, answering Bertrand Russell's plea that the United States and the Soviets should abandon their efforts to spread their creeds by force of arms, denied, of course, that the Soviets were guilty but charged us with driving "numerous brave Indian tribes, valiant hunters and peaceful farmers" into reservations and amusement parks and of imposing by force of arms

with its own needs can better manage its local concerns than can officials far off in Washington.

President Kennedy's Task Force in 1961 reported that the reservations which had effective governing bodies invariably were the ones most successful in carrying out Bureau programs. In like fashion, the Task Force of the Hoover Commission in 1948 had said regarding the results attained under the I.R.A.: "The dividends from this investment in self-government are just beginning to come in, and there are some real weaknesses in the system as it stands, but Indian self-government is clearly a potent instrument if wisely used."[32]

It is not easy for Indians to conduct their own regimes, but the very difficulty makes it worthwhile for them to try. Many Indians are now obtaining valuable experience in government, which otherwise would seldom be available to them. Although there has been progress, there remains much for Indian tribes to do in this regard. Hence, to put the race willy-nilly under state authority when the members themselves feel as yet unprepared would defeat the national purpose of encouraging all citizens to be politically self-reliant.

The reservation governments are small and flexible enough to allow Indians to use and appraise the effectiveness of modern methods of public administration, including the arrest and treatment of offenders. These regimes need not limit sentences to fines, jail, or public work, for other deterrents such as the kinship, clan, family restraints, or traditional tribal sanctions may prove more effective. The Sioux with their tenacious pattern of freely sharing their personal possessions with others should extend the same concept to the regulation of juvenile conduct. By

the creed of belief in white superiority over the aborigines of America. See letter of March 5, 1958, to Bertrand Russell, *New Statesman*, Vol. LV, No. 1409 (March 15, 1958). The way we have fostered Indian community life and supported the Indians' right to preserve customs and tribal governments at heavy expense to the United States Treasury is a plain answer to Mr. Khrushchev.

[32] *Report* to the Secretary of the Department of Interior by the Task Force on Indian Affairs (July 10, 1961), 70; *Report* of the Committee on Indian Affairs to the Commission on Organization of the Executive Branch of the Government (Oct., 1948), 16, 18, 54–55, 60, 69, 73–74, 96–98.

so doing, the disorganization of youth resulting from conflict with the white man's culture might be greatly reduced. The Indians and the commissioner of Indian affairs, with technical assistance from the Departments of Justice and of Health, Education, and Welfare, should set up machinery for dealing with juvenile offenders among Indians, which takes cognizance of conflicts in values that lie behind social disorganization.

By and large, the defects of the tribal organizations are the same as those which plague many other American political subdivisions: lack of leadership, lack of interest of the members, administrative incompetence, nepotism, too short terms for elective officials, insecure tenure of employees, factionalism, insufficient funds, inadequate tax resources, and inability to remove the causes of crime and of juvenile delinquency.

A unique shortcoming, discussed later, is that the constitutional provisions which forbid all other communities in the nation to infringe basic civil rights do not extend to the Indian people. In addition, the following criticisms are frequently made: (1) the judges on the reservation are not trained lawyers; and (2) it is not possible to get a review of original decisions of the reservation courts by other tribunals. Still other complaints have arisen from vesting the management of large and valuable tribal property in the same persons who operate the political government. It is also argued that by tolerating special Indian governments, the jurisdictional problems of law and order are needlessly complicated.

It is contended that these Indian governments no longer serve any valid purpose and only handicap the tribesmen. Among the reasons given are that they tend to isolate Indians from their neighbors, to keep them from participating in outside state and local affairs, and so delay the process of assimilation.[33] The sys-

---

[33] Kelly (ed.), *Indian Affairs and the Indian Reorganization Act, ii–iii;* William H. Kelly, "The Economic Basis of Indian Life," *Annals of the American Academy of Political and Social Science* (hereafter *Annals Am. Acad. Pol. and Soc. Science*) Vol. CCCXI (May, 1957), 71–79; Arthur V. Watkins, "Termination of Federal Supervision: The Removal of Restrictions Over Indian Property and Person," *Annals Am. Acad. Pol. and Soc. Science,* Vol. CCCXI, 47–55.

tem perpetuates a form of collective land ownerships, which runs contrary to the individualistic economic practices of the rest of the nation and leads the Indians to eke out a bare living from their holdings and from outside work for wages.[34]

Further, critics say, the reservation people have no important customs which would be thwarted by state law; that the regimes are maintained as a matter of pride and to perpetuate tax exemptions for their land and federal services for themselves; that the few remaining tribal resources would be better managed by some form of trust or corporation under state law; that no white discrimination against the Indians exists; and that the outside local governments stand ready to render all the public services needed.

To a varying degree and in a few places, some of these contentions possess merit. Occasional tribes have found it desirable to give up their political organizations, and others will find it beneficial to do so. On the other hand, some of the alleged defects can be better cured by tribal governments than by outside governments. But the distinctions between the Indian and the outside governments have created thorny problems, which will persist regardless of whether the tribal governments continue or the Indians integrate. This is particularly so with respect to jurisdictional clashes, which cannot be completely avoided in a federal system, especially one like ours where potential conflict exists not only between the federal and state governments but between the local subdivisions, competing with one another and with the state for authority. The difficulties, however, are not insurmountable. In fact, such questions tend to receive undue attention as far as the Indians are concerned. Of the thousands of cases tried annually in reservation courts and the many hundreds of laws enacted by the tribal councils, only a handful involving jurisdictional issues have ever reached state or federal courts.[35] Problems of conflict of jurisdiction sometimes grow out of traffic, juve-

---

34 Kelly, "The Economic Basis of Indian Life," *loc. cit.,* 72–73.

35 For example, the Navaho tribe in 1957 and 1958 handled approximately 15,000 offenses with no jurisdictional tangles resulting (see *The Navajo Yearbook, 1951–61,* Report VII [1958], 351). During the same period only three cases in

nile delinquency, and family questions; but they can be resolved by appropriate legislation.[36]

Education and medical care, the principal services reservation Indians receive from the federal government, and freedom of their land from taxes are current payments that the nation agreed to make to most tribes when they ceded their land. The other services tribes receive from the United States are no longer public services that are unique to Indians. Contrary to common belief, Indians bear their share of the taxes—sales, excise, and income—which pay for the cost of these public services. Reservations and allotted lands are generally tax exempt, but land taxes comprise only a small proportion of the total taxes paid by Americans. The Arizona Tax Commission estimated that state taxes on the entire Navaho Reservation in their state would be less than the taxes on a single bank building in Phoenix.[37]

Furthermore, it is only prudent that Indians should not surrender services and tax exemptions unless it is crystal clear, as it is not, that they will get such services from other sources and be able to pay the land taxes. At this time, when their land earnings are so much below those of white-owned land, it is evident that the standard of living of most Indians would be further depressed and that they would lose the land for nonpayment of taxes.

Among the principal grounds for not terminating tribal governments except with willing Indian consent are the following:

1. The United States gave legal guarantees to many tribes that they could govern themselves. The government has implied obligation to others.

state courts involved jurisdiction of the states over Navahos on the reservation, which is in New Mexico, Arizona, and Utah (estimated by William A. Brophy).

36 *The Navajo Yearbook, 1951–61,* Report VII (1958), 139, 351; *State of New Mexico* v. *Begay,* 63 N.M. 409, 320 P. 2d 1017 (1958); *Application of Denetclaw,* 83 Arizona 299, 320 P. 2d 697. Both cases held that the state had no jurisdiction to try a Navaho Indian for violation of state traffic laws committed on the Navaho Reservation. In *Williams* v. *Lee,* 82 Arizona 241, 319 P. 2d 998 (1958), the state court held that a licensed Indian trader could sue a Navaho for a debt contracted on his reservation. The Supreme Court, in *Williams* v. *Lee,* 358 U.S. 217 (1959), reversed the state decision; the state court had no authority.

37 "Economic Progress Indian's Big Need," *Arizona Republic,* Sept.–Oct. 1960.

2. Tribal governments in some form are older than the nation itself. Although the persistence of an institution is not in itself sufficient to justify its continuance, yet it should not be abandoned without convincing evidence that a replacement would be better.

3. The tribal organizations afford essential means for Indians to collaborate with the federal government in making programs for advancing themselves through their initiative and enterprise. As has already been indicated, the most successful projects have been put into effect where the tribal governments are best.

4. Organized administrations are bridges to outside life rather than dams against it. If their neighbors welcome Indian participation in the social, economic, and political life of the community, nothing in the tribal government fosters isolation. Through home rule, moreover, Indians obtain training in government and are thereby enabled to move more easily into the political life of the surrounding society and at a higher level without white resentment. By the same token, they gain otherwise unavailable experience in the management of business. All this is especially important at a time when the younger men are beginning to take the lead in reservation affairs. It is advantageous also to the adjoining communities and to any place in which Indians may relocate.

5. The governments are institutions by which the Indians preserve their identities and their characteristic community customs. By insuring the continuation of such institutions, the American people will continue to demonstrate to the world that wide diversity in cultures and in forms of government and ways of life are the very essence of true democracy.

6. The dissolution of tribal governments would threaten the social controls which now exist, such as the clan, or of the extended family, and dissolve the social cement which holds the group together.

7. Over the years the United States has urged and persuaded

the tribes to strengthen their regimes as the best means of meeting the problems of the modern world. They should not now be forced to abandon what they built with such effort. Clarence Wesley, a San Carlos Apache leader, did not exaggerate when he said in 1953, "Twenty years under I. R. A. at San Carlos is actually seven years old . . . . "[38] There were, in addition, repeated invasions of the right to self-government between 1949 and 1953.[39] Considering all the circumstances, the results achieved by the Indians have been decidedly promising.

8. The large tribal landholdings complicate the shifting of reservations to state rule. The difficulties are forbidding, if the common estate is not to be divided up—something many Indians would resist to the last ditch. Taxation of their land, moreover, would furnish a field day for inequality and either reduce their inadequate income further or force sale of the land for unpaid taxes. The reluctance of Indians to participate in local elections and the fact that they would be an ineffective minority in most places even if they voted would place their lives, liberty, and resources at the mercy of officials less familiar with their needs than they themselves and would expose them to possible exploitation by persons who had no interest at all in Indian welfare.[40]

9. The evidence does not establish that tribal regimes cause or perpetuate discrimination. Indeed, as Indians advance in self-government and economic status, prejudice against them is almost certain to decline, as it has long since declined in the eastern section of the United States.

10. If by democratic process the tribes have the right to retain their regimes, they should be allowed to determine for themselves whether their governments satisfactorily meet their needs

[38] Clarence Wesley, "Tribal Self-Government Under IRA," *Indian Affairs and the Indian Reorganization Act* (ed. by Kelley), 26–28.

[39] Felix S. Cohen, "The Erosion of Indian Rights," *Yale Law Journal*, Vol. LXII (1953), 348.

[40] Helen L. Peterson, "American Indian Political Participation," *Annals Am. Acad. Pol. and Soc. Science*, Vol. CCCXI (May, 1957), 121–26; 83 Cong., 2 sess., *House Report 2680*, pp. 187–249.

or are inadequate and too costly, provided always that the basic civil rights of the Indians and others are properly safeguarded.

Civil Rights and Constitutional Protection

Neither the federal government nor the states may invade the fundamental civil rights of Indians, for they enjoy the same protection in respect to these governments as do all other American citizens. But the federal judiciary has held that official tribal action is not restricted by the Constitutional guarantees of freedom of worship, speech, and the press, the right to assemble and to petition the government, due process of law, and the right to be indicted for infamous crimes by a grand jury.

These determinations stem principally from the 1896 decision to *Talton* v. *Mayes* (163 U.S. 376). A Cherokee sentenced by his reservation courts to execution for murder petitioned for release on the ground that the grand jury which had indicted him had consisted of only five men and so had violated the Fifth Amendment. The United States Supreme Court, however, held that the amendment applied only to the federal government, not to the Cherokee Nation, which had existed before the adoption of the Constitution.

Accordingly, a United States court has held that the Navahos can enforce tribal legislation prohibiting peyote on the Reservation, notwithstanding that this enforcement infringed on the observance of a religion. Nor can a deprivation of religious liberty be redressed under the federal Civil Rights Act, even when the tribal decree withholds the use of the common property from members of a minority faith. Similarly, a tribe's actions are not controlled by Constitutional amendments that forbid the United States or the states to deprive any person of life, liberty, or property without due process of law. A tribe can also tax its members or others who do business within the reservation, without complying with the due-process requirement. The Utah federal District Court, however, has held that the Code of Offenses of the Ute Indians on the Uintah and Ouray Reservation violates due process by denying an accused person the right to be represented by a professional lawyer in a tribal court.[41]

Only a little more than one-fifth of the tribal constitutions contain bills of rights. These typically guarantee liberty of worship, communication, and association, freedom from unlawful searches, and the right to vote and to share in the resources of the reservations. They further assure accused persons of notice of the offense charged, a public hearing, the rights of reasonable bail and of summoning witnesses, a trial by jury if the offense entails more than thirty days' imprisonment, and exemption from cruel punishments. Some tribes have placed comparable provisions in their statute books; others have not.[42]

Such guarantees do, however, require vigilant enforcement to be effective; but they are apparently not enforcible in outside courts by appeal or otherwise. The Kennedy Task Force heard many complaints from Indians and non-Indians of denials of these safeguards. The Task Force accordingly urged the Secretary of the Interior and the respective tribes to require these protections in the Indian courts.[43]

In view of the hundreds of statutes adopted and the thousands of trials conducted each year, remarkably few cases challenging the constitutionality of a tribal law or of the judicial proceedings have reached the outside courts. There are probably two reasons. First, the necessity of obtaining the secretary of the interior's approval for important tribal laws has tended to reduce the number of enactments that patently violate basic human

41 *Native American Church* v. *Navajo Tribal Council; Toledo* v. *Pueblo de Jemez,* 119 F. Supp. 429, U.S.D.C., N.M. (1954) ; *Talton* v. *Mayes,* 163 U.S. 376 (1896); *Barta* v. *Oglala Sioux Tribe of the Pine Ridge Reservation,* 259 F. 2d. 553, C.A. 8 (1958): cert. den. 358, U.S. 932, U.S.D.C. Utah (1961); *Oglala Sioux Tribe* v. *Barta,* 146 F. Supp. 917; *Oliver, et al.* v. Udall—another effort to invalidate the Navaho anti-peyote law—was argued in the Court of Appeals of the District of Columbia in January, 1962, 306 F. 2d 819, June, 1962.

42 It was reported in 1958 that twenty-two of the one hundred written constitutions contain a bill of rights, but some are in constitutions of Oklahoma tribes, which do not enact laws or try cases; Cohen, *Federal Indian Law,* 399–400.

43 *Report* to the Secretary of the Department of the Interior by the Task Force on Indian Affairs, July 10, 1961, pp. 28, 30, 32, 69, 70.

rights.[44] Second, there is a substantial element of fairness in the tribal process.

No government of whatever kind should possess the authority to infringe fundamental civil liberties; government itself must ever be subject to law. Freedom of religion, utterance, and assembly, the right to be protected in one's life, liberty, and property against arbitrary power, and to be immune from double jeopardy and bills of attainder, and the guarantee of a fair trial are not privileges—they are minimum conditions which all Americans should enjoy. For any tribe to be able to override any of them violates the very assumptions on which our democratic society was established. Moreover, the absence of these safeguards will retard the economic development of reservations, since business concerns are not likely to risk their capital when confronted with the possibility of unjust taxation, regulation, or similar oppressive measures.

Efforts to induce the courts to reconsider the decisions denying basic civil protection will undoubtedly continue, but the surest and quickest way of securing these rights is by federal law. The Subcommittee on Constitutional Rights of the United States Senate Committee on the Judiciary mentioned the possibility of Congress' limiting the sovereignty of an Indian tribe so that tribesmen may not be deprived of property or liberty without due process of law.[45]

Immunity of Tribes From Suit

The tribes cannot as a rule be sued in court without express Congressional authorization. This is nothing unusual because governments normally are immune to prosecution without their consent, and prior to the Act of 1946 Indians themselves could

[44] Yet the Navaho anti-peyote ordinance, unsuccessfully challenged in the Native American Church case, had the Secretary's assent. But, in recognizing that federal participation in executing the act would probably violate the First Amendment guarantee of religious freedom, he prohibited the use of federal money or personnel in its enforcement.

[45] "Constitutional Rights of the American Indian," *Summary Report* of Hearings and Investigations by the Subcommittee on Constitutional Rights of the Committee on the Judiciary, U.S. Senate, 88 Cong., 2 sess., pursuant to *Sen. Res.* 265, p. 4.

Homeward-bound Navaho shepherdess carries her sheep
across the saddle.

Bureau of Indian Affairs

Navaho family on the way home from the trading post, winter, 1957.

Bureau of Indian Affairs

A Navaho man wearing a wealth of silver and turquoise jewelry
stands before a winter hogan.

Typical Indian home, Pine Ridge, South Dakota.

Bureau of Indian Affairs

One of fifteen modernized "chickees" on the Miccosukee Reservation
in southern Florida. This up-to-date version of the traditional
thatched-roof 'Glades dwelling is near the tribal
restaurant on the Tamiami Trail.

Bureau of Indian Affairs

Pueblo mother and children enjoy the sunshine in the dooryard of their home.

Bureau of Indian Affairs

Indian woman at San Ildefonso baking bread in the outdoor oven
which resembles a large beehive. These beehive ovens are
landmarks in the Indian pueblos of New Mexico.

New Mexico Department of Development

Constructing a wall of adobe bricks at the pueblo of Cochiti,
New Mexico.

not proceed against the federal government on tribal claims unless Congress agreed by special act.[46] The seventy-five tribes, however, which obtained I. R. A. corporate charters are subject to suit under the provisions of the charters.

But those which rejected the I. R. A. or put themselves under it without obtaining charters continue to be exempt. This situation has unfortunate results, for when leases or contracts with tribes cannot be enforced in an outside court, a brake is put on much needed investments in the Indian country. Such groups can be prosecuted only if Congress so legislates in each particular instance.

Federal legislation enabling a tribe to consent to suits should contain limitations to prevent tribal land and assets from being dissipated by levy of creditors.

II. Administration of Justice

Laws

A. Interrelation Between Federal, State, and Tribal Laws

A consideration of the interrelationships of federal, state, and tribal authority may elucidate some current problems in the Indian country concerning the administration of justice.

Three legal codes—federal, state, and tribal—apply to Indian offenses. Laws from all three codes may be involved in various phases of the same case. For example, that part of an act making it a federal crime to dispense intoxicating liquor to tribal Indians, either on or off the reservation, was repealed in 1953 (67 Stat. 586). Under the amended act tribal governments were given local option to prohibit or to permit the introduction of liquor on the reservation and to regulate its sale. The state law as to license, taxes, hours of operation, and other controls would apply

---

[46] Cohen, *Handbook of Federal Indian Law*, 283, and *Federal Indian Law*, 491; *United States* v. *U.S.F. & G. Co.*, 106 F. 2d 804, C.C.A. 10 (1939), reversed, 309 U.S. 506 (1940). Indian tribes "like the United States, are sovereigns immune from civil suit except when expressly authorized . . . ," act of August 2, 1946, 60 Stat. 1049, 25 U.S.C. 70. The Federal Tort Claims Act consent to suit against the government for damages caused by certain torts of federal employees. Act of August 2, 1946, 60 Stat. 842 as amended, 28 U.S.C. 1346, 2401, 2402, 2671–80.

to the commercial operator of the bar. In other words, both state and tribal laws would be applicable to the operation, neither code abrogating the other but, if the authorities saw fit, adding additional controls. Also federal law would be involved, not alone because the bar was located on a reservation but because the owner was a dealer in distilled spirits.

B. Laws Making No Distinction Between Indians and Others, Either on or off Reservations

1. Federal Criminal and Civil Law

An Indian inside or outside the reservation is subject to all the federal criminal and civil laws that are generally applicable to the public at large. Statutes which apply to all persons in the country are, among others, counterfeiting, smuggling, interfering with the mails, robbing banks, and transporting stolen cars across state lines.

Federal laws protecting Indians and applying to others in the country are those, for example, which prohibit acquiring interest in trust land and receiving money from tribes or furnishing legal services without government approval, embezzling, stealing, or knowingly receiving stolen assets of Indian tribal organizations.

Similarly, Indians are subject in common with non-Indians to many federal civil laws whether beneficial or burdensome, such as (1) Social Security, (2) income and other taxes (by statute, however, the income from certain allotments held by the United States as trustee for individuals under the General Allotment Act is not taxable), (3) military service, (4) veterans' legislation,[47] and (5) federal regulations under which Federal Housing, Area Redevelopment Administrations and the Federal Power Commission operate, since the latter's rules and regulations apply to private companies with which Indians negotiate.

[47] See Cohen, *Handbook of Federal Indian Law*, 147, 363, and *Federal Indian Law*, 449, 882–85; act of August 1, 1956, 70 Stat. 792, 18 U.S.C. 1163; Laurence Davis, "Criminal Jurisdiction Over Indian Country in Arizona," *Arizona Law Review*, Vol. I (Spring, 1959), 76–77; *Squire* v. *Capoeman*, 351 U.S. 1 (1956); Internal Revenue *Bulletin 1956* (July 23, 1956), 30.

2. *State Criminal and Civil Law*

Off the reservation an Indian is subject to all state and local laws. If he violates the state or municipal speeding or traffic laws, he likewise pays the penalty. He pays sales, excise, and general property taxes. His contracts are mutually enforceable, and he is accountable for his own conduct and may recover damages from other persons when injured by them. In short, off the reservation he has the same rights and duties as a non-Indian.

Although he is entitled to be free from discrimination by officials and public organizations, the Indian is, in some places, treated harshly by law enforcement officials. Only recently have New Mexico and Arizona allowed him to vote and then only when he has enforced his right by court action. Although he may serve on juries in nearly all states, he is never called for jury service in South Dakota.[48] As he becomes more politically active and asserts his rights as a voter, discrimination will vanish; for, unless civil rights are backed by political power of the people involved, the law by itself has little force.

Except where Congress has expressly conferred jurisdiction on states or where tribes have been terminated, state legislation does not generally extend to an Indian on a reservation or to his holdings or to tribal property. As examples of federal transfer of authority, a 1929 statute (25 U.S.C. 231) permits states to enforce sanitary and quarantine regulations under rules fixed by the secretary of the interior. A 1946 statute authorizes the state to execute its compulsory school attendance law on a reservation provided the tribe gives consent.

Indians pay rent on state grazing land. They receive from the states welfare, aid to dependent children, old-age assistance, and some extension services. Indians purchase state automobile and driver's licenses. Most tribes have good relations with the fish and wildlife divisions of state governments. State laws are applied

[48] Statement of the chairman, South Dakota Advisory Committee to the National Commission on Civil Rights; "The Indian and State Government," *Program and Proceedings, Sixth Annual Conference on Indian Affairs* (Institute of Indian Studies; Vermillion S. Dak. State University of South Dakota, June 17–18, 1960), 10, 15.

to non-Indians for hunting and fishing on tribal lands. Before issuing a tribal license, tribal governments require sportsmen to show a state license. There are no federal or state laws that prohibit suffrage on reservations. The Supreme Court of New Mexico said:

> It is our considered judgment that the granting of the right to vote and the location of polling places on the reservation in no way interferes with the reservation self-government, or impairs any right granted or reserved by Federal law.[49]

Public Law 280 of 1953 (18 U.S.C.A. 1162: 28 U.S.C.A. 1360) allows state criminal and civil legislation to supersede tribal and federal enactments in the cases of some reservations. (See Chapter Seven, under "Termination by Assumption of Jurisdiction over Indian Country.")

Inasmuch as most Indian tribal laws are not written (unless they have an Indian Reorganization Act constitution or charter), there exists an unexplored legal area between the state and reservation Indians.

C. OFFENSES IN INDIAN COUNTRY
1. By Indians Against Indians

Today, most Indian self-governing groups have adopted law and order codes or use regulations promulgated by the secretary of the interior (25 C.F.R., part 11). But from the earliest days every tribe sat, according to its own local customs, in judgment over offenses, even murders, by Indians against each other. Some tribes treated offenses as crimes against the group and treated offenders in ways calculated to reassimilate them into the group. Others treated offenses as injuries to individuals or families. Settlements were made with the person injured or aggrieved; or, if a person were killed, ponies or merchandise was paid to his family in order to avoid a blood feud.

It was a blood feud that led Congress to pass federal legislation covering murder, among other things. Crow Dog, an Oglala

---

[49] *Montoya* v. *Bolack,* 70 N.M. 196, 372 P. 2d 387.

Sioux chief, in 1881 shot and killed Spotted Tail, a Brulé Teton Sioux chief in South Dakota. The feud originated because Spotted Tail had seduced the wife of Medicine Bear, a crippled friend of Crow Dog. Settlements were made in the Indian way, but Crow Dog was, nevertheless, tried in the federal court, convicted, and sentenced to be hanged. But in 1883 the Supreme Court ordered Crow Dog discharged from custody, holding that the tribe had exclusive jurisdiction over crimes between Indians, as no federal law had curtailed the tribal authority.[50]

This trial led to great consternation throughout the country. In 1885, Congress passed the Major Crimes Act,[51] which provided for the trial and punishment of Indians committing murder, manslaughter, rape, assault with intent to kill, arson, burglary, or larceny against the person or property of another Indian or of any other person on a reservation. Later the crimes of incest, robbery, and assault with a deadly weapon were added.[52] Together, they are known as the "ten major crimes." These offenses, plus embezzlement of tribal funds (70 Stat. 792, act of August 1, 1956) and the infringement of a few federal laws applying to both Indians and non-Indians, constitute the only acts of Indians against each other that are federal crimes.[53] Crimes committed by an Indian against another Indian in Indian country, excluding those enumerated above, are dealt with by the tribal courts.

Offenses between Indians over which the tribal courts have exclusive jurisdiction include simple assault and battery, adul-

[50] *Ex parte Crow Dog,* 109 U.S. 556 (1883).

[51] Act of March 3, 1885, 23 Stat. 385; constitutionality upheld, *United States* v. *Kagama,* 118 U.S. 375 (1886).

[52] Act of March 4, 1909, 35 Stat. 1088; act of June 28, 1932, 47 Stat. 336; now 18 U.S.C. 1153; Cohen, *Handbook of Federal Indian Law,* 363.

[53] Act of August 1, 1956, 70 Stat. 792, 18 U.S.C. 1163; Cohen, *Handbook of Indian Law,* 147, 363; 18 U.S.C. 1853 (timber depredation on Indian land); 1856 (starting fires on Indian land); 1857 (breaking fences or driving cattle on enclosed land), 25 U.S.C. 202 (inducing conveyances by Indians of trust interests in land), 18 U.S.C. 438 (receipt of money under unapproved contracts, such as attorneys' contracts with tribes). Possessing or introducing intoxicating liquor in a reservation where the tribe has not by ordinance permitted liquor to enter is still a federal offense whether committed by Indian or non-Indian (Cohen, *Federal Indian Law,* 381–82; act of August 15, 1953, 18 U.S.C. 1161).

49

tery, various kinds of thefts, cheats, frauds, trespass, blackmail, disorderly conduct, intoxication, prostitution, and failure to support dependents.

The Indian law-and-order codes are simpler, and are aimed at rehabilitation rather than at deterrants or punishment of crimes. They define approximately fifty transgressions, in comparison with the two thousand frequently defined in state codes. The maximum penalty assessed by Indian courts seldom exceeds six months, with the performance of tribal work often being required instead of imprisonment.[54]

2. By Indians Against Non-Indians

Any major crime an Indian commits on the reservation against a non-Indian or his property is tried in a federal court under either the Major Crimes Act, listing the ten most serious offenses referred to above, or the Assimilative Crimes Act (18 U.S.C. 13), covering all the other serious offenses which, if committed off the reservation, would violate state law. As a matter of fact, the penalties for such on-reservation crimes are those laid down by the state. For example, if an Indian breaks into a non-Indian merchant's warehouse on the reservation, he is tried in a federal court but sentenced in accordance with state statutes.

3. By Non-Indians Against Indians (or Indian Property)

Offenses committed by non-Indians against Indians or Indian property on the reservation also belong to the federal judiciary and are federal cases (18 U.S.C. 1152).

Non-Indian petty offenders—the cheats, the frauds, and the brawlers—often are not prosecuted, because the federal courts are so busy with larger matters that they have no time for petty cases. Needless friction results, much of which could be avoided if federal judges would routinely designate special commissioners to handle such less important cases.[55]

54 Cohen, "Indian Rights and the Federal Courts," *Minnesota Law Review*, Vol. XXIV (Jan., 1940), 145, 155.

55 18 U.S.C. 3401, as amended by act of July 7, 1958, 72 Stat. 348, authorizes United States commissioners specially designated for that purpose by the court

4. By Non-Indians Against Non-Indians (on Reservations)

Unless some federal or Indian interest is affected, state law, both criminal and civil, governs non-Indians in relation to other non-Indians or their property on a reservation. For instance, the state possesses exclusive jurisdiction over a non-Indian who murders, robs, or assaults another non-Indian in the Indian country.[56]

5. By Indians (on Reservations) but Involving No Victim

Offenses not involving a victim or victims are usually subject only to federal and tribal jurisdiction, not to that of the state. A state may not punish an Indian who on a reservation highway drives in a manner which outside the reservation would be un-

to try and sentence persons committing petty offenses in places of exclusive or concurrent jurisdiction. They can grant probation. Any misdemeanor for which the penalty does not exceed six months' imprisonment or $500 fine or both is a petty offense (18 U.S.C. 1).

56 Cohen, *Handbook of Federal Indian Law*, chap 23 and *Federal Indian Law*, 985–1051. Public Law 280, 83 Cong., 1 sess.; act of August 15, 1953, 67 Stat. 588 as amended, 18 U.S.C. 1162 and 28 U.S.C. 1360, extended state civil and criminal laws, with limitations, into Indian country in California, Minnesota (except Red Lake Reservation), Nebraska, Oregon (except Warm Springs), and Wisconsin. Among other measures that extend state authority over Indian country are: act of June 8, 1940, 54 Stat. 249, 18 U.S.C., sec. 3243, which confers concurrent criminal jurisdiction on Kansas; act of May 31, 1946, 60 Stat. 229, which confers concurrent jurisdiction on North Dakota over Devil's Lake Reservation. The Supreme Court of North Dakota nullified this federal law by ruling that the state did not consent to assume jurisdiction and, therefore, its courts had no jurisdiction, despite the federal law, to try an Indian for assaulting an Indian in Indian country. See *State* v. *Lohnes*, N.W. 2d 508 (1954).

Act of June 30, 1948, 62 Stat. 1161, granted Iowa concurrent criminal jurisdiction over the Sac and Fox Reservation; act of July 2, 1948, 62 Stat. 1224, 25 U.S.C. Sec. 232, granted New York exclusive criminal jurisdiction over all Indian country; act of September 13, 1952, 64 Stat. 845, 25 U.S.C. 233, granted New York jurisdiction over civil actions involving Indians, with limitations protecting Indian land tax exemption and fishing and hunting rights. The tribes could publish the tribal laws and customs they wish to preserve, and the New York courts were required to apply such laws.

In 1954, legislation terminated the Menominees, Klamaths, mix-blood Utes of the Uintah and Ouray Reservation, a large number of western Oregon tribes, Alabama and Coushatta, and four bands of Paiutes in Utah. All 1954 termination laws are in 68 *Statutes at Large* and 25 U.S.C., chap. 14. Act of February 15, 1929, 45 Stat. 1185, 25 U.S.C., sec. 231 (state health laws); act of August 9, 1946, 60 Stat. 962, 25 U.S.C., sec. 231 (compulsory school attendance laws); *United States* v. *McBratney*, 104 U.S. 622, 1882; *Draper* v. *United States* 164 U.S. 240, 1896; *New York ex rel Ray* v. *Martin*, 326 U.S. 496 (1946).

lawful, even though the Indian is on a highway built and maintained by the state on Indian land over which the secretary of the interior had given the state an easement.

A case in 1958 held that an easement does not extinguish Indian title; consequently, a state has no jurisdiction. This decision was based on the New Mexico Constitution, which disclaims all right to land owned or held by an Indian or Indian tribes, the title of which has been acquired from the United States or any prior sovereignty.

Jurisdiction has been likewise disclaimed in Arizona. A Navaho Indian pleaded guilty to drunk and reckless driving on U.S. Highway 66 (built and maintained by Arizona on an easement granted the state by the secretary of the interior), but the Arizona Supreme Court decided that the state has no jurisdiction to try a tribal Indian for any crime committed in Indian country (18 U.S.C. 1151).

6. By Non-Indians (on Reservations) but Involving No Victim

The jurisdiction in such cases is uncertain and needs to be clarified by statute. Traffic offenses constitute the bulk of these cases. An obvious contradiction exists when Supreme Court decisions hold that a state has sole jurisdiction to try a white man for murdering another white man on a reservation, even if that state's constitution expressly disclaims jurisdiction over Indian land.[57]

Courts

The courts adjudicating an Indian problem may have to determine whether federal, state, or tribal law is applicable. The general principle is that federal legislation prevails and, in default thereof, Indian customs rule, but in the absence of either code the court will turn to state law.[58]

---

[57] United States v. McBratney, 104 U.S. 622 (1882); Draper v. United States, 164 U.S. 240 (1896); New York ex rel Ray v. Martin, 326 U.S. 496 (1946); Williams v. Lee, 358 U.S. 217 (1959). See Cohen, Handbook of Federal Indian Law, 365, and Federal Indian Law, 324.

[58] W. C. Rice, "The Position of the American Indian in the Law of the United States," 16 J. Comp. Leg. (1934), 78, 92; Cohen, Handbook of Federal Indian Law,

Tribal Governments

A. FEDERAL COURTS

Whenever possible, Indians and tribes use federal district courts for their litigation. The reason is that in federal courts the juries are drawn from a wide area and are, therefore, apt to be without local prejudice, and the judges are understanding and not subject to political pressure. Federal courts have a limited jurisdiction. They require that the plaintiff and the defendant should be residents of two different states, or that the case arise under the Constitution or laws or treaties of the United States. Moreover, if jurisdiction is to be based solely on diversity of residence, the amount involved must exceed $10,000, exclusive of interest and costs. Congress has also conferred authority on federal courts to try specific kinds of cases (such as suits by Indians for an allotment), to condemn land belonging to tribes named in the statute, and to permit tribes to establish their title to land.[59]

To remove a case from a state to a federal court, diversity of citizenship and the jurisdictional amount must be present. That a party is an Indian or a tribe does not alone give the federal court jurisdiction, unless there is specific statutory authority. Indian Reorganization Act charters did not confer citizenship on tribes, although individual Indians are citizens. Tribes cannot, therefore, satisfy the diversity of citizenship required of the individuals involved if federal courts are to have jurisdiction. Federal corporate charters authorize tribes under the Indian Reorganization Act to sue and be sued, limitations being placed on levies to satisfy a judgment. Indian groups under the Indian Reorganization Act generally have the capacity to bring their own cases.

379 and *Federal Indian Law*, 363. Applicable tribal ordinances as well as custom should be applied. The necessity for proof arises out of the general rules of conflict of laws that the tribunal applies its own laws if "foreign" law, otherwise applicable, is not proved.

59 28 U.S.C. 1331, 1332; 25 U.S.C. 345; act of May 10, 1926, 44 Stat. 498 (condemn land of New Mexico Pueblos); act of July 1, 1892, 27 Stat. 62, 64 (condemn Colville Reservation land); act of June 7, 1924, 43 Stat. 636 (title to New Mexico Pueblo land) ; Cohen, *Handbook of Federal Indian Law*, chap. 19, and *Federal Indian Law*, 326, 341–42; *Martinez* v. *Southern Ute Tribe*, 249 F. 2d 915, C.A. 10 (1957); same case 273 F. 2d 731, C.A. 10 (1960); *Iron Crow* v. *Oglala Sioux Tribe*, 231 F. 2d 89, C.A. 8 (1956); *Arizona* v. *California*, U.S. (still pending as of the date of publication of this book) .

This right is of great importance, permitting Indians to appeal to courts to protect their property even against capricious federal officers.

Suits by the United States on behalf of a tribe are practically always commenced in federal district courts, which have jurisdiction of suits in which the government is a plaintiff. The government has the right to intervene in an action between two states begun in the United States Supreme Court and to present Indian tribal interests for adjudication. If the United States-tribal relationship is terminated, Indians will be limited to state courts with local juries. This eventuality they fear.

B. STATE COURTS

Professor Ray A. Brown, the legal expert on the Meriam Survey staff, stated:

> The Indian, whether tribal and a ward of the Government or not, may, except where specially restricted by Act of Congress, make contracts, acquire and dispose of property, and sue and be sued in the State or Federal courts.[60]

The types of cases in state and federal courts to which Indians have been parties are these: habeas corpus to gain release from custody of an army general; breach of contract; and suit on a promissory note. An Indian has been allowed to bring his own suit in a state court and in a federal court, to compel state officials to allow him to vote and to issue him a common carrier's permit, and a hunting and fishing license previously denied because the applicant was an Indian. An administrator appointed by a state probate court for a reservation Indian could sue in state court for the Indian's wrongful death. A state court has jurisdiction over a civil action to recover damages caused by a collision on Standing Rock Reservation, both parties being members of the

---

[60] *Felix v. Patrick,* 145 U.S. 317 (1892) ; Cohen, *Handbook of Federal Indian Law,* 162, 379, and *Federal Indian Law,* 341, 540; Ray A. Brown, "The Indian Problem and the Law," *Yale Law Journal,* Vol. XXXIX (Jan., 1930) , 307, 314; Jerry Angle, "Federal, State, and Tribal Jurisdoction on Reservations in Arizona" (Tucson, University of Arizona, 1959) ; Laurence Davis, "Criminal Jurisdiction Over Indian Country in Arizona," *Arizona Law Review,* Vol. I (Spring, 1959), 62, 78.

Standing Rock Sioux Tribe, notwithstanding the disclaimer of jurisdiction over Indian territory in the state constitution.[61]

In 1959 the Supreme Court of the United States decided the Williams case, in which a non-Indian licensed as an Indian trader (as required by federal law) sued a Navaho couple to collect money owed for goods sold on credit. Plaintiff and defendants lived on the Navaho Reservation in Arizona, where the sale was made. The Arizona Supreme Court approved a judgment against the Indians. However, the Supreme Court of the United States unanimously reversed the Arizona decision. The basic policy established in 1832 by Chief Justice Marshall that Indian tribes are dependent nations in whose territory state law does not apply has remained, although it has been modified where essential tribal relations are not involved and the rights of the Indians are not jeopardized. When Congress wishes a state to exercise civil or criminal jurisdiction over Indians on a reservation, it has expressly granted the jurisdiction. Moreover, the 1868 treaty emphasized that internal affairs should be left with the Navaho government.

Opinions differ regarding the implication of court decisions. A former attorney for the Navaho tribe found that the Williams case "did not change the legal status of Arizona Indians one iota. . . . In the absence of Congressional legislation, a State has no jurisdiction." Another commentator at the University of Arizona found that "state civil jurisdiction in cases involving Indians, arising in Indian country, is much more restricted than previously thought."[62] The attorney general of Arizona used the decision to question the right of Indians to vote. The Supreme Court of Colorado, in ruling that a state court has no jurisdic-

61 Cases collected in Cohen, *Handbook of Federal Indian Law*, 163, 379, and *Federal Indian Law*, 363, 541: *Porter* v. *Hall*, 34 Arizona 308, 271 (1928), p. 411; *Harrison* v. *Laveen*, 67 Arizona 337, 196 P. 2d 456 (1948); *Trujillo* v. *Garley*, No. 1353, U.S.D.C. N.M. (1948), unreported; *Bradley* v. *Arizona Corporation Commission*, 141 P. 2d 523 (1943); *Begay* v. *Sawtelle*, 53 Arizona 304, 88 P. 2d 999 (1939); *Trujillo* v. *Prince*, 42 N.M. 337, 78 P.2d 145 (1938); *Tenorio* v. *Tenorio*, 44 N.M. 89, 98 P. 2d 838; *Vermillion* v. *Spotted Elk*, 85 N.W. 2d 432 (1957).

62 Davis, "Criminal Jurisdiction Over Indian Country in Arizona," *Arizona Law Review*, Vol. I (Spring, 1959), 63, 78; Angle, "Federal, State and Tribal Jurisdiction on Indian Reservations in Arizona," 15.

tion over a divorce action between two reservation Indians, declared: "We think [the Williams case] controls the instant action. . . . The test is not whether a State has disclaimed jurisdiction, but whether Congress has authorized such a jurisdiction within the State."

The New Mexico Supreme Court in June, 1961, held that a state court has no jurisdiction to try an ordinary automobile-collision damage case between two reservation Indians when the accident occurred in Indian country. The court relied on the Williams rule and its own prior holding (in *State* v. *Begay*), that the state has no jurisdiction over a traffic offense committed by an Indian on a state road on the reservation.

Similarly, the Juvenile Court of Washington has no jurisdiction to declare Indian children dependent, deprive their parents of custody, and make them wards of the state subject to adoption when the children are members of a tribe living on a trust allotment. Nor does jurisdiction exist to place an abandoned Indian child in the custody of the juvenile probation officer when the child is a member of a tribe residing on the reservation.

On the other hand, North Dakota has terminated parental rights and transferred custody of Indian children to the state when the enrolled Indian parents living off the reservation have abandoned children outside a reservation and when there is no showing of tribal membership of the children or of any tribal law on the subject. The court found no conflict with federal law.[63]

C. TRIBAL COURTS[64]

Except for limitations set up by federal statute, a tribe may vest its court with jurisdiction to try all kinds of civil actions;

[63] *State* v. *Superior Court,* 356 P. 2d 985, Washington (1960); *In re* Colwash, 356 P. 2d 994, Washington (1960); *In re* Holy-Elk-Face, 104 N.W. 2d 308, N. Dak. (1960); Letter of Feb. 11, 1959, from attorney general of Arizona to Senator Robert E. Morrow; *Whyte* v. *District Court of Montezuma County,* 140 Colorado 334, 346 P. 2d 1012 (1959), cert. den. 363 U.S. 829; *Valdez* v. *Johnson,* 68 N.M. 476, 362 P. 2d 1004; See *Your Food Stores* v. *Village of Española,* 68 N.M. 327, 361 P. 2d 949 (1961).

[64] The tribal courts of the Oklahoma tribes have been abolished, therefore, the tribes in that state are omitted entirely from the discussion.

and in some classes of litigation the jurisdiction is exclusive, as the Williams, Whyte and Valdez cases show. The tribal courts thus have the jurisdiction to adjudicate cases involving property, torts, and family law (including divorce, adoption, and guardianship), to decide the validity and meaning of wills, and to determine heirship, except for regular allotments. Unless they reject cases by outsiders, tribal courts have jurisdiction of all suits between tribesmen and those brought by non-members against tribesmen or the tribes. State courts have jurisdiction in this field only if Congress grants it. Tribal courts, on the other hand, have jurisdiction unless it has been curtailed by Congress.

Civil judgments of a tribal court are recognized and given effect by outside courts. A Circuit Court of Appeals case held that such judgments were on the same footing as a judgment of a court of a territory and, therefore, entitled to the same faith and credit. In 1950, Arizona recognized the validity of and gave effect to a divorce decree granted by a Navaho tribal court on the basis of the rule that a divorce valid by the law where it is granted is recognized everywhere as valid.

Moose Dung's case in 1899 (Minnesota) illustrates the importance of tribal law. A treaty allotted land to Chief Moose Dung. After his death his eldest son and sole heir by tribal usage leased the tract. Later a second lease was made with rentals going to six descendants and with Moose Dung, the younger, getting only one-sixth. The secretary of the interior decided the first agreement to be invalid and approved the second one, pursuant to a Congressional resolution specifically authorizing its approval. The Supreme Court, however, held that inheritance was controlled by tribal custom and not by the law of the state or by any action of the secretary of the interior. It held that

> Rights under that lease could not be divested by any subsequent action of the lessor, of the Congress, or of the executive department.[65]

65 *Jones* v. *Meehan*, 175 U.S. 1 (1899); under the General Allotment Act, allotments now descend according to state law. The court has also held that whether action taken in the name of a tribe is in fact tribal action should be determined

Most Indian Reorganization Act tribes, following the pattern for Courts of Indian Offenses in the federal Code of Regulations, provide that their tribunals shall enforce the pertinent United States statutes, the rulings of the Department of the Interior, and any ordinance or custom of the tribe not prohibited by federal legislation. Typically, where matters were not covered by federal law or tribal custom and the habits of the tribe provided no guidance, they turned to state laws.

A tribal judgment can be enforced outside the reservation only by bringing a suit on it in a state court—an expensive and time-consuming process, which diminishes the effectiveness of tribal courts. They are important because in some civil cases some litigants, non-members as well as members, have no other courts for redress. Provision should be made for recording tribal judgments in a county office and for making them enforceable.[66] All the tribal codes and the secretary's law-and-order regulations require the tribal courts to deliver any offender to federal authorities when the federal court consents to exercise its jurisdiction.

Some tribes hire an outside professional lawyer as the tribal judge. Other tribes, including the Navahos and the Utes, have conducted programs to educate judges and court personnel. But in most tribal courts the judge is not a trained attorney, indeed, professional lawyers are excluded from most of the tribunals. Secretary Udall has amended his regulations to allow professional lawyers in the fifteen courts of Indian offenses, but he could not change the rules of the more than fifty independent tribal bodies, which continue to maintain their ban against lawyers.

---

by the customs of the tribe. An agreement by lawyers with the "captain" of a tribe was void when the tribal custom required such agreements to be made by the council. See *Pueblo of Santa Rosa* v. *Fall*, 273 U.S. 319 (1927).

66 Cohen, *Handbook of Federal Indian Law*, 275, 382, and *Federal Indian Law*, 369, 471; 25 Code of Federal Regulations, sections 161.38 to end; civil codes of various tribes; Davis, "Criminal Jurisdiction Over Indian Country in Arizona," *Arizona Law Review*, Vol. I (Spring, 1959), 63, 78; Angle, "Federal, State and Tribal Jurisdiction on Reservations in Arizona," 15; *Stanley* v. *Roberts*, 59 F. 836, C.C.A. 8 (1894), app. dism. 17 Sup. Ct. 999 (1896); *Raymond* v. *Raymond*, 83 F. 721, C.C.A. 8 (1897); *Begay* v. *Miller*, 70 Arizona 380, 222 P. 2d 624 (1950); Indian Law, sec. 52, chap. 26 of *Consolidated Laws Service* (1950).

Judgments of tribal courts usually can be appealed within the tribal system, either to a court of several judges or to the elected council sitting in an appellate capacity. However, the absence of any procedure by which a litigant can obtain an outside review of an important tribal judgment has aroused complaint in some tribes. The Kennedy Task Force found much criticism of the courts, and the tribes which continue to maintain their own judicial system will find it necessary to make constant improvements.

Tribal courts in many, perhaps most, tribes show weaknesses. But the problems are as diverse as the tribes themselves, the ability to deal with them varies widely, and the situations can better be met by local agreements than by outside edict. Some of the states and the counties, on which the burden would fall if state law should be extended, are themselves inadequately financed and inadequately prepared to maintain justice in the Indian areas. The Navahos, a large and wealthy tribe, spend more than $1,000,000 a year to preserve peace and order, support seven judges who, although not lawyers, are experienced in their work, and maintain a large police force, modern equipment, and jails. At the opposite pole are tribes which expend little or nothing and have insufficient equipment and facilities and poor enforcement. The Kennedy Task Force heard, as this Commission has, complaints about poor courts, law enforcement, badly prepared judges, inadequate rights of appeal, favoritism, infringement of civil liberties, outmoded detention facilities, absence of proper quarters for female and juvenile offenders, and the practice of refusing to allow attorneys to represent persons on trial.

Some of the law enforcement problems high-lighted by recent court decisions demand resolution either by Congress or by agreed transfer of the matters to the states. As a rule, it is unsatisfactory to exempt from state jurisdiction Indian traffic violators on reservation state highways. Who can tell at a glimpse whether a speeder is a tribesman? In off-reservation allotted land where the ownership is checkerboarded, it is even impracticable to determine whether the offense occurred on or off an allotment. To complicate matters further, it is not clear whether non-Indian traffic violators on the reservation should be tried in a federal or a state court. The cross-commissioning of officers, although apparently working fairly well in some regions, is at best a makeshift.

Clarification of jurisdiction is also called for in other respects. To limit enforcement of contracts to tribal courts tends to restrict the credit which Indians so badly need for development. It is not evident that any Indian interest is protected by denying a state court authority to try a reservation automobile accident case or to enforce a contract to which an Indian is a party. The Williams decision is a narrow one; but state courts are interpreting it broadly to deny their jurisdiction over cases such as automobile accidents, which they would otherwise adjudicate. Contracts and tort lawsuits are transitory actions, which, in general, can be brought where the defendant can be found. The same rule should apply to cases arising on the reservation. At the very least, the state jurisdiction should be concurrent with the tribal.

III. Recommendations

The national policy, which for more than one and one-half centuries has sanctioned the maintenance of tribal governments, should be abandoned only when a majority of a tribe so desires, and the form of government desired by the majority of the tribe should be recognized. The authority of these bodies in local affairs should not be curtailed unilaterally by the United States except in one respect: federal law should require that tribal actions safeguard basic civil rights and provide for the appeal of civil rights cases to federal and state courts.

By governing themselves, Indians acquire, among other things, knowledge of and experience in the laws and procedures of the greater community. When it is to their advantage, they should adopt the good features of these other governments. The costs of tribal rule should be met, where feasible, by an equitable system of taxation of the members and others rather than exclusively from the collective tribal resources.

The tribes should install modern fiscal controls and so manage their common properties as to insure that all members participate fairly in the benefits.

Legislation should allow tribes otherwise exempt to consent to being sued, subject to limitations specified in tribal ordinances.

Judges should have greater and continuing training, hold office for longer terms or during good behavior, and be removable only for sufficient cause upon notice and hearing by the legislative branch.

Federal judges should appoint more United States commissioners, conveniently located near reservations, with authority to try and sentence petty offenders in the Indian country.

Public Law 280 should be amended: first, to necessitate agreement of a tribe before a state assumes responsibility for the civil and criminal causes specified in the act; second, to provide in express terms that with tribal consent a state may take over jurisdiction piecemeal as to subject matter and to area; and, third, to require any such state to meet minimum standards in rendering services to Indians, which standards should not fall below the highest maintained within the state.

Provision should be made for recording tribal judgments in county offices and the judgments of tribal courts should be made enforceable through the state judicial system.

3

Economic Development

I. INTRODUCTION

THE ECONOMIC POSITION of the Indians is less favorable than that of any other American minority group.[1] In most Indian communities the pattern is one of bare subsistence, with the result that some of the nation's worst slums are to be found on Indian reservations.[2]

Obviously, Indians cannot solve their problems isolated from the mainstream of American life; and, clearly, their prospects for economic advancement are geared to those of the national and local economies. But avenues open to Indians for improvement are often blocked, as they are to millions of other Americans, by a lack of assets by which to make a living. In addition, Indians are often faced with the extremely complex problems caused by the juxtaposition of basically alien cultures.

Most reservations in sparsely settled areas are poor in fertile soil, minerals, timber, water, and jobs. Even total utilization of such resources as are present would not, in many instances, supply an adequate income for all reservation residents. The Gila River Indian Reservation, for example, contains an adequate amount

[1] *1950 United States Census*, Special Report, P-E, No. 3B, Vol. II, "Characteristics of the Population" (Part I), United States Summary: Family Income of Reservation Indians by State, Agency, and Reservation (Washington, G.P.O.).

[2] Lauren K. Soth, "Farm Policy for the Sixties," comprising chapter 9 of the Report of the President's Commission on National Goals, *Goals for Americans* (Washington, D.C., Judd & Detweiler Press, Inc., 1960), 207–22.

of arable land but insufficient water. In many instances, a single economic resource incapable of properly supporting an entire community must nevertheless serve that community.

Even if all reservations were rich in natural resources, many difficulties would remain. Indians often lack training for managerial work or responsible positions. Like many rural whites, the untrained Indian finds work only as a laborer. Moreover, only a few Indian workers have known the stability resulting from their own or their parents' regular employment. Another handicap lies in the basic concepts of some Indian cultures. Even in agriculture, traditional with groups like the Pueblos of New Mexico, modern methods are directly contrary to general Indian customs and beliefs. Modern agricultural development rests on research, improving seeds, use of fertilizer, on new ways of performing old tasks, and on an increased control of environment. But to the Indian cultures, which typically stress ancestral customs based upon a need to work in harmony with nature, such modern practices are often alien. The historical experience of the Indian has, in general moved outside of traditions of science and technology; yet the individual must acquire an ability to make sound judgments in distinguishing between the scientifically valid and the deceptive in order to co-operate with a highly technical and competitive society.

At the same time, there is a wide difference among individual Indians and between tribal cultures. This diversity constitutes another major difficulty in achieving general economic balance for improvement. A "typical reservation" or a "typical Indian" does not exist; therefore, no single rule applies. Some groups such as the West Coast Salish adjusted easily to modern ways. They have always been good businessmen, believers in keeping busy. Having themselves developed ways of making life more comfortable, they have had no prejudice against the white man's tools. If his device was superior, they adopted it; if traditional methods served better, those methods were maintained. Some of the aboriginal Salish techniques, such as their fishing gear, have been used by the white fishing industry.[3] The community-centered Pueblos of New Mexico, on the other hand, have been slow to acquire new ways, their resistance only solidifying in the face of pressure used to induce them to move more swiftly.

Variations within tribal communities spring from many factors: individual degrees of personal isolation or of contact with others; amenability to outside thinking; native intelligence; emotional retention of Indian values; and one's respective generation.

The breach between Indians and whites was not originally so great. When the first white settlers landed in America, they found the natives living in huts quite as comfortable as the newcomers' own improvised cabins. The whites learned from the Indians methods of farming and hunting, without which they probably could not have survived. The aborigines also contributed many unfamiliar foodstuffs now basic to modern life—corn, white and sweet potatoes, beans, peanuts, pumpkins, and other things such as tobacco.[4]

The newcomers, for their part, imported a novel set of political and social institutions and a language with which to keep abreast of new European developments. Although these innovations made little difference at that time, they were the basis from which evolved today's urban-industrial, highly complex, and interrelated systems. Their later confinement on reservations rendered the Indians even more out of touch with these dynamic changes, so that the gap between the two races widened. And conditions will only become worse unless adequate steps are quickly taken to help the Indian (and persuade the white man) to bridge the gap.

If the Indians' economic status is to be improved, first—whatever the actions taken—the means of improvement must be related to Indian concepts, aspirations, and values. Since the In-

3 Marian W. Smith, "The Indians and Modern Society," *Indians of the Urban Northwest* (New York, Columbia University Press, 1949), 7–8.
4 Felix S. Cohen, "Americanizing the White Man," *American Scholar*, Vol. XXI, No. 2 (Spring, 1952), 179.

dians will bear the final responsibility for carrying out plans for utilization of reservation resources (including the human), their interest and co-operation must be enlisted at every stage of all programs.

Some Indian farmers and ranchers have already taken on managerial jobs; and reservation employment can be increased by the development of whatever natural resources are present, by construction of irrigation projects, by new land uses, by the improvement of range, trails, and water supplies for cattle, by the establishment of simple industries and emphasis upon arts and crafts, by the opening of curio shops, and by the establishment of attractive science recreation areas. Moreover, to a limited degree, factories may be induced to locate on or near some reservations. Such developments are taking place or are now planned in many Indian communities and impressive progress is being made.

Indians in their twenties and thirties desiring to leave reservations are given training and encouraged to seek jobs in urban areas (see below, "Employment Assistance"). Until the Indian has learned to operate in the major culture he is not able to choose his way of life. If he desires leisure, which was his cultural heritage, and is content with part-time work on the reservation, this decision should be made by him only after he has had other possible alternatives from which to choose. A decision to earn less money and work only part time is one which may face quantities of American citizens in the 1970's.[5]

Tribal economic programs need ample time for successful development. The notable Navaho program originated in 1946 with a plan prepared at the request of Secretary Krug.[6] Sixteen years later, with the tribe's expenditures for the last decade having approximated $100,000,000[7] and the B. I. A.'s from 1954 to

[5] Gerard Piel, *Consumers of Abundance; An Occasional Paper on the Role of the Economic Order in the Free Society* (Center for the Study of Democratic Institutions, June, 1961).

[6] Charles A. Collier, director, Navajo Program Group, *A Ten-Year Program for the Navajo* (mimeographed), Dec. 1947.

[7] *The Navajo Yearbook, 1951–1961,* Report VIII (1961).

1960 having reached \$121,314,000 (a grand total of well over \$200,000,000[8]), the benefits have not yet touched all tribal members.[9] Another essential is genuine co-operation and help from many sources—the federal government, which bears the chief responsibility; the states involved; the Advisory Board on Indian Affairs, established by Secretary Udall in 1961;[10] and private groups sufficiently informed to act with knowledge and judgment. Unless such help is given and such measures are taken, the Indians face a grim future.

II. PRESENT RESERVATION ECONOMY: PROBLEMS AND POTENTIALS

Although it is essential to develop Indian economy, a lack of relevant statistical and other information makes it impossible to analyze in any detail the present conditions among reservations. In addition, there is no uniformity between similar sets of B. I. A. data. This lack reflects the government's narrow interpretation of its obligations, which stresses governmental trusteeship and administrative functions to Indians but ignores, except by occasional enlightened commissioners, comprehensive, long-term planning.

When Professor Peter Dorner began his study for the Commission in 1958, he asked the Washington office of the B. I. A. for basic reservation data on population, employment, income, and the like. The reply was as follows:

> While we do have some limited information here on population and enrollment for some of the reservations, we are certainly a long way from having information across the board in all the categories that you mention. The point, of course, is that the Bureau normally compiles only those statistics which are needed in connection with the performance of its functions. Thus, we have rather complete statistics on realty, education, forestry, and other specific

8 Communication from Walter Olson, assistant area director, Gallup Area Office, B. I. A., Jan. 12, 1962.

9 Telephone communication from Walter Olson, July 26, 1962.

10 87 Cong., 1 sess., Proposed Advisory Board on Indian Affairs, *Congressional Record*, Vol. 107, Part 10 (July 24, 1961), 13207–208.

categories of our work. But since data of the type you list are not actually required for the performance of our regular statutory functions, they simply do not get compiled in any systematic or comprehensive way.[11]

Available data establish a broad general pattern: a growing population but a young one, a decreasing and already inadequate land base (made additionally unprofitable by the broad problem of fragmented ownership), high unemployment, low incomes, and other characteristics typical of underdeveloped peoples and areas. For example, the 1960 census affords interesting data on approximately 90 per cent of New Mexico's Indians, who live in six of the state's thirty-two counties. Indians account for from 93.6 to 99.2 per cent of the non-whites in the six counties. The census shows that two-thirds of the non-white population fourteen years old or older in those counties are not considered in the labor force; that only 27.5 per cent of the labor force was employed in 1960; that 72.2 per cent of the families had 1959 incomes under $4,000, with the median family income in one county being only $870.[12]

Population and Land

The total number of Indians in the United States (exclusive of Alaska and Hawaii) increased about 161,000 between 1938 and 1960, according to the United States Bureau of the Census. During the same twenty-two years the "on-reservation" Indian total grew only about 30,000 (see Appendix, Table 2). More than half of all Indians are under twenty, compared with slightly more than one-third of the white population;[13] and on some reservations from which large migrations have occurred, the Indian percentage of those under twenty is even higher: 53.8 per cent in

[11] Communication from Leon Langan, assistant to the commissioner of Indian affairs, Washington, D.C., to Professor Peter Dorner, July 30, 1958.

[12] Margaret Meaders, "Some Aspects of Indian Affairs in New Mexico,"*New Mexico Business* (Bureau of Business Research, University of New Mexico, 1963).

[13] *Health Services for American Indians*, U.S. Dept. of Health, Education, and Welfare, Public Health Service *Reports*, No. 531 (Washington, G.P.O., 1957), 1.

the Aberdeen area of the Dakotas and Nebraska in 1957,[14] and 58.6 per cent of the Many Farms Navahos.[15]

Over the decades the amount of land included in the reservations has dropped sharply. In 1887, after having surrendered almost all their territory east of the Mississippi and vast areas in the rapidly developing West, the Indians owned about 138,-000,000 acres.[16] (By 1858 the United States had already acquired Indian land estimated at more than 581,000,000 acres.) By 1960 the Indian holdings had shrunk to about 53,000,000 acres.

A. Employment

For reservation Indians of working age the pattern has long been one of intermittent or seasonal employment, combined with reliance on welfare payments of one kind or another. Unemployment rates of 30 to 50 per cent and over have not been unusual.[17] Congressman Lee Metcalf reported 81.5 per cent unemployment on the Tongue River Reservation and 90 per cent on the Rocky Boy Reservation.[18] On the Turtle Mountain Reservation in North Dakota, it is reported that "unemployment faces the bulk of the employable laborers during six or seven months of the year."[19]

A 1955 study estimated that on the Standing Rock Reservation 59 per cent of the manpower was not then being used and that 29.5 per cent of all families were receiving over 50 per cent of their income from welfare payments.[20]

[14] Peter Dorner, "The Economic Position of the American Indians: Their Resources and Potential for Development," Ph.D. dissertation, Harvard University Library (Feb., 1959), 25.

[15] The Navajo Yearbook, 1951–1961, Report VIII (1961), 325.

[16] M. Wilfred Goding, "The Management of Tribal Lands," Land: The Yearbook of Agriculture, 1958 (Washington, U.S.D.A.), 96–102.

[17] Dorner, "The Economic Position of the American Indians," 96–99.

[18] 85 Cong. 2 sess., Congressional Record, Vol. 104, Part 14 (Aug. 15, 1958), 17901–902.

[19] Indian Relocation and Industrial Development Programs, Report of a Special Subcommittee on Indian Affairs of the Committee on Interior and Insular Affairs, House Committee Print. No. 14 (Oct., 1957).

[20] Cultural and Economic Status of the Sioux People, 1955, Standing Rock Reservation, North and South Dakota, U.S. Dept. of Interior, B. I. A., Missouri River Basin Irrigation Project Report No. 151 (Billings, Mont., Feb., 1957).

Until twenty years ago, on most reservations and in other parts of the nation, the major dependence was upon subsistence agriculture; during the last two decades there has been a shift to wage work.

In 1957 the Employment Service in Arizona reported 5,048 Indians in agriculture, but 4,491 in non-agricultural work. When farm jobs and unskilled industrial occupations were considered together, they accounted for almost 65 per cent of the employment, compared with only 24 per cent for the non-Indian civilian workers.[21] Nearly 23 per cent of the total family income among the Navahos in 1955 came from railroad work (apparently not reported by the Arizona State Employment Service); seasonal agricultural wages contributed only about 6 per cent.[22] Railroad unemployment compensation accounted for 8 per cent. In 1960, railroad wages comprised 4.7 per cent of all personal cash income and 5.5 per cent of earned cash income, with the unemployment compensation accounting for 3 per cent of total cash income and 3.5 per cent of total earned cash income.[23]

Many Oklahoma Indians have moved to cities and are doing well financially,[24] but a large number of the rural tribesmen still have low incomes. Of the family heads of rural Cherokee households reporting unemployment in 1952, 45.3 per cent were in unskilled labor; 4.5 per cent were in semi-skilled; 5.5 per cent were in skilled; 4.5 per cent were in professional; and 40.2 per cent were self-employed.[25]

On the Turtle Mountain Reservation, as well as at Fort Totten and some Minnesota reservations, many job opportunities for seasonal labor have been lost as a result of mechanization of potato planting and harvesting in the Red River Valley. Within five years the number of potato workers needed in the valley

[21] "Sixth Annual Report on the Expanded Employment Services to Reservation Indians in Arizona," Arizona State Employment Service (Phoenix, Feb., 1958).

[22] *The Navajo Yearbook of Planning in Action,* Report V (1955).

[23] *The Navajo Yearbook, 1951–1961,* Report VIII (1961), 228.

[24] "Status of Indians in Two Cities and Two Counties in Oklahoma," Muskogee area office, B. I. A. Summary of 1950 Census data.

[25] "The Rural Cherokee Household, Study of 479 Households Within Fourteen School Districts Situated in the Old Cherokee Nation," Muskogee area office, B. I. A., June, 1953.

area has dropped from approximately three thousand to three hundred. Especially affected are those Indians accustomed to working with seasonal crops now using mechanical equipment like cotton, sugar beets, potatoes, and other vegetables.

In communities like Isleta, San Felipe, and other Río Grande pueblos, the Indians live at home and commute to Los Alamos, Santa Fe, or Albuquerque, where they have stable jobs. When they are laid off, they still have a place to live and can, if they wish, continue their ceremonial and social life. But in isolated reservation areas with no work available within commuting distance, a desperate need exists for developing a nucleus of economically successful Indian operators of farms, ranches, and small commercial undertakings.[26] Such enterprises would provide members of the rising generation with examples of success among their own people. To increase work opportunities, it should be consistent government policy to engage qualified Indians for all jobs.

The General Timber Sales Regulations (approved April 10, 1920) specify that in all timber contracts "Indian labor will be employed by the purchaser at the same wages as other labor and in preference to other labor not already in his employ whenever the Indian labor seeks employment and is competent." The solicitor general has held this specification to be valid even in states that have fair employment practices acts. He has also declared that preferential-employment clauses in Indian contracts do not violate the President's order requiring federal contracts to prohibit discrimination.

In addition, the lease for minerals, except oil and gas (Form 5–159, October, 1957) contains a clause that in the case of the Laguna Pueblo uranium operations of Anaconda Copper and Mining Company has given preferential employment to Lagunas.

B. Welfare

Welfare payments constitute a very important source of Indian income. Such payments come from several sources. The

26 Dorner, "The Economic Position of the American Indians," 103.

B. I. A.'s Welfare and Guidance Service, which includes social services, had a budget in the fiscal year of 1965 of $12,214,500. The service is responsible for general assistance, child-related aids, and miscellaneous relief to Indians unqualified for assistance from public agencies. The child-welfare program provides institutional, foster-home care, and adoptions for needy youngsters.[27]

Another source of support is the federal program for distribution of surplus agricultural products, an important source, as demonstrated by the fact that such commodities given out at Pine Ridge, South Dakota, in fiscal year 1958 had a wholesale value of $309,306. Surplus commodities have also become important in the Navaho economy. During 1960 they received foodstuffs valued at over $353,249.

State welfare assistance was summarized in 1957 by a House committee from a questionnaire—that thirteen out of the twenty-one states answered. Six states offered general assistance, and all twenty-one provided old-age assistance, aid to the blind, and help to dependent children. The minimal annual expenditures for all such programs in the twenty-one states was estimated by the committee to be approximately $18,782,773.

Not all states have assumed responsibility for Indian welfare. One alleged reason is the tribesmen's tax exemption; but in Nebraska the Indians pay land taxes, yet received no state welfare services in 1956.

As should be expected, Indian welfare payments are disproportionately high, compared with those going to the general population. A questionnaire sent to twenty western states by this Commission during 1959–60 revealed that comparable data on Indians was reported only by Minnesota, Montana, North Dakota, and Oklahoma. In these states more than three times as many Indians per hundred received assistance as did other per-

27 *Department of the Interior and Related Agencies Appropriations for 1966,* Hearings Before a Subcommittee of the Committee on Appropriations, U. S. Senate, 89 Cong., 1 sess., on *House Report 6767* (1965), 637, 652. (Hereafter cited as 89 Cong., 1 sess., Senate Hearings on *House Report 6767,* Appropriations for 1966.)

sons.[28] Where Indians comprise about one-twentieth of the population, they receive more than two-fifths of all the aid extended to dependent children.[29] In 1955 more than one-sixth of all individual incomes of the Navahos came from welfare or unemployment compensation.[30] The reliance on welfare payments for support is general among economically depressed minority groups.

C. THE SHRINKING LAND BASE

The need for creating employment and developing Indian property is rendered more imperative by the fact that a growing reservation population is coupled with a diminishing land base. The B. I. A. estimated in October, 1960, that the United States had in its care about 52,398,565 acres (exclusive of Alaska), both tribal and allotted. This acreage represents what remains of the once vast Indian domain, the heaviest losses in recent times having occurred between 1887 and 1934, and during the 1950's (see Appendix, Table 3).

In 1958, James E. Murray, chairman of the Senate Committee on Interior and Insular Affairs, reported that:

> During the past 4 or 5 years there has been grave concern over the increasing alienation of Indian lands from trust status . . . . The major apprehension is that decreases in Indian land base will seriously impair the effective use of Indian tribal and individual trust land in terms of economic land units.[31]

Accordingly, Senator Murray induced the secretary of the interior to declare a suspension of sales of Indian land while the Senate Committee studied the problem.[32] The investigation dis-

[28] Edward Threet, Report on Indian Welfare for the Commission on the Rights, Liberties, and Responsibilities of the American Indian (1960) (Commission files).

[29] "The Sioux, Our Unknown Neighbors," Sioux Falls (S. Dak.) *Argus-Leader*, June 2–20, 1957 (Anson Yeager series reprint).

[30] William H. Kelly, "The Changing Role of the Indian in Arizona," Agriculture Extension Service *Circular 263* (Tucson, University of Arizona, June, 1958), 3.

[31] 85 Cong., 2 sess., *Indian Land Transactions,* Memorandum of the chairman to the Committee on Interior and Insular Affairs, *Committee Print.,* XVII (Washington, G.P.O., Dec., 1958).

[32] *Ibid.,* I.

closed (1) that an alarming amount of individual Indian land
(2,595,414 acres) had been completely removed from trust status
and government responsibility from 1948 to 1957, and (2) that
the largest losses had occurred on reservations in areas containing the most allotments—those under the area offices of Billings,
Muskogee, Minneapolis, and Sacramento (see Appendix, Table
3). An additional 421,000 acres had been taken for public purposes. The over-all shrinkage of 2,174,518 acres led Senator
Murray to say:

> . . . individual Indian trust land alienation is climbing at a
> potentially disastrous rate . . . . The magnitude of these removals
> raises a question as to whether the Indian Bureau has exercised
> its authority wisely in granting so many applications for sales and
> patents.[33]

There is substantial evidence that many Indians want to keep
their land undivided, but there is also evidence to the contrary.
For example, the Klamath people in Oregon voted in 1958 to
fragment their holdings.[34]

The wisdom of allowing sales should be determined on the
basis of whether a particular piece of ground contains needed
water, could contribute to land consolidation, or could promote
better use of the surrounding area for grazing. And in every case
the final decision should rest with the tribe concerned.

D. Heirship Land and Tribally-Owned Land

The system of tenure determining ownership of Indian lands
is immensely complicated. The terms "fractionated" and "fragmented" heirship apply quite accurately. For example, a single
heirship case on the Wind River Reservation involved the interests of 104 heirs—Indians (enrolled and not enrolled, resident
and nonresident, minors, competent and incompetent) and non-
Indians, with seven unprobated estates which would eventually
add twenty-two more heirs. It is not at all unusual for at least
five persons to own interests in a single small tract of land.

[33] *Ibid.,* XVIII.
[34] *Klamath Tribune* (Chiloquin, Ore.), Vol. III, No. 4 (April, 1958), 1.

Chiefly responsible for creating this situation were the General Allotment Act and similar laws, which provided that the federal government should divide tribally-owned land among tribal members, the United States to hold the plots in trust until the Indians gained the white man's sense of individual, private ownership. Unfortunately, the authors and proponents of such legislation failed to foresee that partitioning an owner's land following his death would often prove impractical. Indians may own parts of allotments in their own or other reservations, and for an heir to work a single tract, he needs the approval of all his fellow owners. Many times a tract is too small, too poor, or too arid for efficient use even in its undivided whole. Also, the patterns of inheritance of allotted lands are determined by state laws instead of by tribal laws. Furthermore, only under special circumstances can superintendents lease heirship land (25 U.S.C.A. 380). Therefore, the heirship system adds little to the Indian purse, but it does increase Indian economic problems and adds to the burden and expense of B. I. A. record-keeping.

The Indian Reorganization Act in 1934, as already noted, prohibited further allotments on the reservations to which it applies (48 Stat. 984); and executive orders extended the trust period in the case of tribes not adopting the Act.[35] But not even these measures prevented an increase in the number of heirs. The accompanying table indicates the heirship status of Indian-owned land.

Of the more than 6,000,000 acres in heirship status, about 1,500,000 are used by non-Indians; 45,000 are leased to the tribes; and about 500,000 lie idle, mainly because of the difficulty of making leases or of subdividing property among the owners.[36] One of the obstacles to leasing land was the limitation of the term of the lease, which has recently been extended, in some instances to ninety-nine years by Public Laws 86–326 and 88–167.

It is significant that on the San Carlos and the Navaho reserva-

[35] 86 Cong., 1 sess., *Indian Heirship Land Survey*, Part 1, Memorandum of the chairman to the Committee on Interior and Insular Affairs. *Committee Print.*, U. S. Senate (Washington, G.P.O., Dec., 1960), 2, 3.

[36] *Ibid.*, Part 2, x.

Heirship Status of Indian-Owned Land

Total heirship land (acres)	6,222,754
Number of tracts	40,787
(approximately half of these tracts are owned by five or more heirs)	
Type of land (acres):	
Irrigated	211,344
Dry Farming	869,037
Grazing	4,381,109
Forest	405,312
Other	209,225

tions, where the land was never allotted and is still almost all in one block, the members of both tribes make use of all the soil. In the Plains states, where the government-allotted land is owned individually and inherited according to state law, consolidation of land holdings requires a complicated and expensive court procedure and may be practicable only if carried out as an area-redevelopment project. In contrast to the complications developed by the allotment policy, Pueblo land that is still owned by the tribes and is under the administration of tribal governments can easily be consolidated into larger, economically useful, modern ranches. Proposed regulations of the secretary of the interior allow for consolidating 69,700 acres of tribally-owned land in central New Mexico. This is to be accomplished through the Bureau of Land Management, which can, with secretarial approval, exchange public lands within and without the reservations for non-Indian holdings, while the tribal councils can exchange their land with that of inholders.[37]

In contrast to the secretarial regulations used in consolidating tribally-owned tracts, complications flowing from the Allotment Act are too costly and too complex for one tribe alone to handle. A good example of an unsuccessful effort to combine heirship land is that of the Rosebud Sioux. In 1943 the Sioux Council

37 Dept. of Interior news release, April 2, 1962.

formed the Tribal Land Enterprise to purchase and merge land into economically profitable units (1,920 acres for grazing, or 480 acres for farming, or some combination of the two), and then to lease the land to tribesmen. Owners then received Tribal Land Enterprise certificates in exchange for property they turned over to the tribe to administer. When grazing fees or rents were collected each certificate holder received his proportionate share.

By 1959 a total of 312,668 acres—the majority purchased from single owners—were under Tribal Land Enterprise management, and only nine of the multiple-heirship tracts offered for sale had been purchased, since the tribe could not afford the excessive cost of clearing titles. Consequently, the effort to solve the heirship problem was of little account.[38] Spending money for consolidation of tracts may not be warranted in the case of tribes renting land to others that they themselves might use. In December, 1958, the B. I. A. granted the Rosebud Sioux half a million dollars for land purchases at a time when they were leasing 600,000 acres of tribal land to non-Indians.[39]

Many reservations will be unable to solve their economic problems until they can cure this evil of fragmented ownership. A bill known as the "Fractional Interests Act of 1966" has been introduced into Congress. House Record 11113 (September 16, 1965) provides that when trust or restricted allotment of Indian land, or a fractional interest therein held by a person after the date of this act is less than a specified amount, or the average net income accruing from the land is less than a certain sum, the land shall descend to one person who shall be a member of his family, the highest priority being given to the closest relative. In addition, a "Fractional Interests Acquisition Fund," to be established by the Treasury, shall be available for the secretary to use in purchasing interests from owners who desire to sell. If this bill passes, it may give the secretary of the interior sufficient latitude to attack the heirship problem.[40]

[38] Carl K. Eicher, "Constraints on Economic Progress on the Rosebud Sioux Indian Reservation," Ph. D. dissertation, Harvard University, 1960, pp. 93–95.
[39] *Ibid.*, 130.
[40] As of October 15, 1965, hearings had not been held on *House Report 11113*.

Economic Development

Present Uses of Natural Resources

Indians with adequate capital and training often lack the experience necessary to make commercial use of their own lands (through farming, ranching, mineral, or timber operation—whatever the area offers), and even if heirship-land problems were solved and irrigation improved, indications are that only approximately one-half of the reservation Indian families could obtain incomes comparable to those realized from similar white ventures.[41] At the present time, however, resources have not been developed to anything like their full capacity.

Indians are presently using less than half of their irrigated farmlands and only about three-fourths of their rangelands, with the remainder either being leased to non-Indians or left idle. In 1961 the B. I. A. estimated than on major reservations, totaling about 1,129,464 acres, approximately 378,000 acres not then in use could have been developed for irrigation.[42]

Even agricultural Indians like New Mexico Pueblos are abandoning farming. Indians are lured from using their arable lands fully by ready and "easy" money offered by nearby employers or white renters, insufficient funds to purchase machinery, develop water, or expand acreage for better cultivation, or by inadequate training in handling larger units. Additional deterrents include high production costs, lack of credit, marketing competition from chain stores, absence of personal encouragement, and the bitter contrast between the hard life of the "small" farmer and the relatively easy life of the wage worker. These influences are exerted upon all small-scale farmers—Indians and non-Indians alike. The B. I. A. has been attempting to enlarge the size of farming units in the Río Grande Valley. In the early days, when land was plentiful, Pueblo Council officials assigned tribally-owned surplus land to newly married couples, a use right that continued in the family. Individuals thus acquired a vested interest in the holdings, which upon their death were divided

41 Dorner, "The Economic Position of the American Indians," 286–88.
42 Communications from Evan L. Flory, chief, Branch of Land Operations, B. I. A., Washington, to Professor Peter Dorner, Feb. 6, 1962.

equally among the children. As the population increased and surplus land dwindled, the agricultural units became smaller. In order to consolidate uneconomical tracts, the tribal councils, in accordance with their own rules or customs, exchanged land among members. At Isleta, New Mexico, 1,067 acres of land tribally and individually owned was developed by the B. I. A. First the land to be subjugated was identified by a map from an aerial photograph. If several fields were to be combined into one unit, ditches reshaped or realigned, or undeveloped land subjugated, the tribal council first approved the changes. In this way the holdings of many persons were increased.

In Sandia, near Albuquerque, the tribal council cancelled all assignments on the 1,148 acres that were subjugated, and then reassigned land in economical units to potential farmers. However, when the land was ready to plant, only eighteen men applied for farms, and over 1,000 acres were leased to people outside of the Pueblo.[43]

The fact that Indians are turning away from their land does not constitute proof that they do not want to farm or raise livestock, or that they cannot be trained or conduct such operations efficiently. Mr. Willard W. Beatty's comment in 1955 supports no such view,[44] and other observations confirm his. At Cheyenne River, Mr. Beatty found that enough families were interested in livestock operations to make possible utilization of their lands under the reservation rehabilitation program. Reportedly, at Standing Rock more people want to stay on the reservation than

[43] Communication from Melvin Helander, area land operations officer, B. I. A., Gallup, N.M., Feb. 6, 1962 (Commission files).

[44] George A. Dale, *Education for Better Living*, (B. I. A., 1955). Comment in Preface (p. 4) by Willard W. Beatty, formerly chief, Branch of Education, B. I. A. It was at this time that the curriculum was changed from an emphasis on academic subjects to vocational agricultural training. This change seemed desirable since, as Mr. Beatty points out, the Indians were not leaving the reservations and yet were using only about one-third of their lands. "Discussion of the entire problem with old hands in the Indian Service was not very hopeful," says Mr. Beatty, "for it tended to be their conviction that 'you can't make a farmer or a cattleman out of an Indian,' which was another way of recording their conviction that an education was pretty much wasted on an Indian anyhow. In spite of this, the vocational program of the Oglala Community High School, Pine Ridge, was broadened in 1936 to include cattle raising and irrigation farming."

can reasonably be provided with the opportunity to do so. During a study of the Sisseton-Wahpeton Sioux, "62 per cent expressed the wish to become independent farm operators."[45]

Undoubtedly, large sections of irrigable land remain idle because of water shortage, but in other areas adequate water is available, but the acres have not been developed, as in the Colorado River Reservation and the six middle Río Grande Valley pueblos (Cochiti, Santo Domingo, San Felipe, Santa Ana, Sandia, and Isleta). Only about half of the estimated 20,242 Pueblo acres susceptible of cultivation are irrigated, and in 1957 only 6,000 were being farmed.

A. FARMING

Reservation farms are run by individuals and by tribes. On the Gila River Indian Reservation, approximately 12,000 irrigated acres in the Pima-Maricopa community are operated as a tribal farm and about three-fifths of the tribesmen own ten-acre allotments of irrigable land.

Indian farms vary greatly in size. Most are smaller than the 80-acre unit considered the minimum size capable of profitable cultivation through the most intensive, several-crops-a-year methods.

Faced with many handicaps, Indian farmers obviously have small chance of equaling the production of white farmers. On the Blackfeet Irrigation Project in 1954 Indian per-acre figures contrasted sharply with those achieved by white farmers: 56 per cent less wheat, 25 per cent less barley, and 61 per cent less alfalfa hay. On the White Swan Irrigation Project during the 1948–56 period the average per-acre crop values showed these disparities: Indian operations, $89; white operations on Indian land, $126; white operations on non-Indian land, $222.[46] The same situation obtains on all irrigation projects on reservations under the area office at Phoenix except on the Colorado River Reservation,

[45] Thomas S. McPartland, *A Preliminary Socio-Economic Study of the Sisseton-Wahpeton Sioux* (Vermillion, S. Dak., University of South Dakota Institute of Indian Studies, Dec., 1955), 28.

[46] *White Swan Project, Yakima Indian Reservation* (Portland Area Office, B. I. A., March, 1956), 80.

where the 1957 per-acre values were about the same for both races.[47]

The problem of instituting equitable utilization of Indian farm lands has not yet been solved. If only a few Indians benefit from land programs the question arises as to whether a tribe should spend funds to acquire and enhance land values by cultivation and then allocate large areas to a few tribesmen without charge.[48] The answer seems to be that only by paying fees can the individual user equalize the benefits from land and water and provide dividends to other tribesmen not using those resources.

B. RANCHING

Indians utilize more of their grazing than farm land. During 1964, Indians used 88 per cent of the forty million acres of range and owned livestock valued at $63,739,244, with an annual gross value of about $24,500,000.[49] In size and productivity of ranching operations they lag behind non-Indians. Ranch operations in the mid-1950's show that a minimum of one hundred head of beef cattle are required for a family income of $3,000 to $3,500; at present operation costs, such a herd would yield only $2,200. But, in 1953, fifty-four Indian ranches on the Crow Reservation in Montana had an average of only forty-eight cattle. On the Fort Peck Reservation in 1947, 76 per cent of Indian ranches had fewer than one hundred head (all cattle expressed in terms of mature animals); 84 per cent of the ranches in 1952 and 80 per cent in 1957 possessed fewer than one hundred head of cattle. Over 50 per cent of all Indian ranches in North and South Dakota run fewer than one hundred head of cattle, and only 666 families out of 4,679 on the Dakota reservations owned herds of any size in 1957.[50] In 1952 the total number of Navaho families was reported as 14,949, and scarcely more than half had grazing

47 Annual Irrigation Crop Report, supplied by the Phoenix area office, B. I. A.
48 Cohen, *Handbook of Federal Indian Law,* chap. 9; *Federal Indian Law* (1958), 746.
49 89 Cong., 1 sess., Senate Hearings on *House Report 6767,* Appropriations for 1966, Part I, p. 667.
50 Dorner, "The Economic Position of the American Indians," 28–29.

permits. Only 445 families earned more than $1,500 that year from farming and stock raising.[51]

Unlike farming, cattle raising is frequently managed by associations. Private operation requires intensive, sustained effort and the dispersal of families, which is not in the Indian tradition and therefore requires a difficult cultural adjustment. Moreover, an Indian's small landholding may reap so meager an economic reward that he comes to associate the idea of private ownership with hardship and inefficiency.

Among the Pueblos, where livestock is an important source of income, a variety of organizations have been created to coordinate the activities of individual ranchers. Originally, the war chief had charge of all range and agricultural land, but in some villages he has been replaced by sheep and cattle officers. The duties of the supervisor are similar. He allots range, issues permits for each livestock owner to run a specified number of animals, sees that the various pastures are used at appropriate seasons, decides the time for dipping the animals, cares for all equipment, and collects fees for and oversees the use of disinfectants and vaccines. He plans and supervises roundups, classifies and advertises animals to be sold, and invites buyers to the sales.

Examples of a cattle trust, a tribal herd, and a cattle association are found at Isleta and San Carlos. The Isleta cattle trust operation was organized in 1934.[52] Trustees were nominated by the tribal council and appointed by the commissioner of the B. I. A. The trustees borrowed money for administrative expenses and for herd maintenance. They received 1,500 head of Hereford cows and 85 registered bulls from the Federal Emergency Drought Relief Program, which they culled to 864 cows and 64 bulls. The trustees had the power to run the herd as a private operator, except that they were required to stay within a budget approved by the commissioner of Indian affairs and

[51] William H. Kelly, *Indians of the Southwest—A Survey of Indian Tribes and Indian Administration in Arizona* (Tucson, Bureau of Ethnic Research, Dept. of Anthropology, University of Arizona, 1953), 91.

[52] *United Pueblos Quarterly Bulletin*, Vol. I, No. 4 (July, 1940).

to return one yearling for each animal given by the government. They kept half of all their net profits for maintaining the animals, for improving the range, for economic development, and for contingencies; the other half was paid to the tribal council. By agreement part of the range was assigned to this cattle trust. During the 1940's the herd brought an annual income of $9,000 to $10,000. As range practices were improved, the calves increased in weight: in 1935, calves had averaged 255 pounds; in 1939, they weighed 495 pounds each and won prizes at the New Mexico State Fair.

At first the United Pueblos Agency gave the trustees technical advice on range management and help in preparing and operating within a budget. However, during the 1950's B. I. A. extension employees paid little attention to the business of the trust. The Indians, too, lost interest, the herd became badly managed, and the treasurer embezzled funds. Meanwhile, individual owners complained that drought and overgrazing had made their own ranges inadequate. The trustees had developed good wells and grass on their assigned range and would not let cattle belonging to these malcontents forage on the trust range.

Unfortunately, 1959 brought the end of the operation. Tribal politics, the desire of individual owners to use the range assigned to the trust, the new policy of termination, a mistaken belief that the operation was contrary to free enterprise, and the advice of some B. I. A. employees led Commissioner Emmons to dissolve the trust in 1959.

The advantage of such an association was its initial efficiency. The trust provided high-caliber management and on-the-job training for tribal members. Family incomes were increased for the members who could live at home and work, the tribal council received greater returns, and the people gained an occasional per capita payment.

The Apaches on the San Carlos Reservation have tribal as well as association cattle herds.[53] Their land is ideally suited to

53 Harry T. Getty, "San Carlos Apache Cattle Industry," *Human Organization,* Vol. XX, No. 4 (Winter, 1961–62), 181–86.

this business, since their entire 1,853,841 acres are in one block.[54] In pre-Spanish times, Apaches lived by hunting, cultivating maize and other foodstuffs, and collecting edible roots and plants. By 1890, after they had been forcibly settled on their reservation, a few individuals began to accumulate animals from the live cattle received as rations. Since most of the reservation was leased to white cattle operators, the Indians ran their livestock on desert land located along the Gila and the San Carlos rivers.

In 1923, Superintendent James B. Kitch came to San Carlos. He proposed that the Indian cattle industry should use the entire reservation, but the idea of terminating white operators' leases met with strong opposition. The B. I. A. in Washington was skeptical about the Kitch plan, and reluctantly allowed the Superintendent to try it. Mr. Kitch utilized the basic Indian unit of social organization—the extended family. As each section of the range was vacated by a white permittee, it was assigned to one or more related families. The cattle on the newly assigned rangeland, although owned by an individual of a kin group, belonged in practice to all its members. This co-operative ownership simulated the old pattern of sharing.

With Kitch's encouragement, the kin groups were formally organized into associations, which adopted constitutions and by-laws signed by all participants and appointed boards of directors. There are now eleven such livestock associations among the San Carlos Apaches.

In addition to the association herds, the Apaches have two tribal herds, one of registered animals for the use of the San Carlos ranchers and the other composed of income-producing animals. With one exception, the manager-stockmen have been Indians. These herds provide not only employment, but for young Indians hope and incentive as well. A man wishing to start in the cattle business may file an application to enter one of the associations. Once approved by the board of directors, the tribal council, and the superintendent, he has his name placed

[54] *United States Indian Population and Land* (Dept. of Interior, 1960), 7.

on a waiting list, with preference given to married men with families.

When the new member's turn comes, if he has no capital with which to purchase stock he may take twenty head of breeding stock either from animals in two tribal herds or from branded maverick (wild) cattle belonging to an association. Within seven or eight years he must return twenty-two head of cattle—twenty to replace the original grant, two as interest on the investment.

Owners must help in dehorning, spraying, and vaccinating cattle and with the work of the roundup. If an owner himself cannot contribute time or money, he must send someone in his place or be fined. The tribal council charges a small fee for each animal sold. The auctioneer's percentage and the cost of feed at the shipping pens are prorated to owners; the remainder is used by the individual to pay his grocery debt. Relatively few Indians operate on a cash basis, and credit at tribal stores is based on the net income of individual owners. Since a man's children cannot inherit his cattle, upon his death they are sold.

The supervision and administration of the entire San Carlos Reservation cattle industry, once in the hands of a federally employed extension agent, now is the responsibility of a committee of Indians, mainly members of the tribal council. Since the spring of 1955 the clerical work once handled by the B. I. A. has been done by tribal employees.

During 1950 the Indians brought in specialists on range and cattle management who recommended combining some of the eleven associations, reducing the cattle to the carrying capacity, controlling breeding, purchasing blooded bulls, building additional fences, hiring a general manager, and collecting grazing fees from all owners of cattle.

Almost seventy years have passed since a few individual Indians began to accumulate cattle, and almost forty years since Superintendent Kitch commenced his systematic effort to build an Indian cattle industry among the San Carlos Apaches. But Indian folkways, the kin-group pattern, the Apaches' generosity, their sporadic activity, and community living instead of isolated family living on the range have all prevented efficiency equal to that of most white operations.

In 1956 only six Indian cattlemen were operating on a basis comparable to that of successful white ranchers. Of the 713 permit holders, 24 per cent had no cattle; 36 per cent had herds inadequate to support their respective families; and 40 per cent had herds that provided only a barely adequate income. Some herds were decreasing in size. Such is the record of one cattle industry, which is largely Indian owned.

Other Indian groups have designated local businessmen to assist them with plans for development of cattle operations. For example, the Ute Indians in March, 1962, appointed a ranch commission to make policy and to supervise all enterprises on the reservation. They chose the president of the Utah Cattle Growers Association, the manager of the Roosevelt Branch of the First Security Bank, and a local white rancher.[55] With such expert advisers the Indians should gain an insight into how to operate their own programs.

C. Mineral and Timber Operations

The mineral wealth on Indian reservations is unevenly distributed. In 1955, this total income was $29,973,932—45 per cent of which was received by six reservations (Navaho, Jicarilla, Blackfoot, Wind River, Fort Peck and Fort Berthold). The Oklahoma Indians got another 45 per cent, two-thirds of which was paid to the Osage people. Thus, 90 per cent of all 1955 mineral income belonged to the people of six reservations and to the Indians of Oklahoma.

There has been a marked increase in such income in recent years. Oil and gas royalties, rentals, and lease bonuses paid to the Navahos in 1960 totaled $11,688,646. Income from other minerals that year came to $694,683 from tribal property and $212,900 from allotments.[56] Total oil and gas revenues during fiscal year 1964 amounted to $66,000,000 for all reservations.

55 "Ranch Commission Appointed; Ute Enterprise Expansion Set," *The Ute Bulletin*, March 24, 1962, p. 1.
56 *The Navajo Yearbook, 1951–1961*, Report VIII. (1961).

The Jackpile uranium mine in New Mexico paid approximately $1,750,000 in royalties in 1958 to the Laguna Pueblo tribal council and paid wages to some four hundred Laguna and Acoma truck drivers, miners, engineers, supervisors, laborers at the mine, and millworkers in Grants, New Mexico.[57] The Anaconda Copper Mining Company, which operates the mines, reduced employment substantially in 1962. This presented new problems to Laguna residents of this 250-year-old town, because wage earners had adjusted to a higher standard of living.

Minerals are developed by outside firms, and when explorations are fruitful, tribal councils receive a rental fee in addition to bonuses and royalties. Much of the income from minerals and timber is used to support tribal governments or to provide services which the B. I. A. supplies free to those without resources, and therefore it means little to individuals in the tribe, except as employment opportunities.

Timber as a resource is found on only a few reservations. During the ten years from 1950 to 1960 almost one-quarter of all Indian income from timber was received by the Klamaths of Oregon. During 1961 the Klamath and Menominee federal trusteeship was terminated; consequently the B. I. A. no longer keeps records on these tribes.

During 1962 approximately 546,000,000 board feet of lumber were cut, bringing in cash receipts of over $8,000,000. The estimated volume of lumber to be cut during fiscal year 1966 was 870,000,000 board feet at a calculated sale price of $13,000,000. This should create approximately six to eight thousand man-years of employment. The B. I. A. manages leasing and provides knowledge and skills in forest management.[58]

Tribal sawmills exist on the Navaho and Red Lake Reservations. Where there is no tribal sawmill, the timber is put up for bid, usually by the B. I. A., and the contract awarded the highest bidder. The contractor is not always obliged to hire Indian labor.

[57] *Albuquerque Progress* (Albuquerque National Bank,) Vol. XXV, No. 3 (May–June, 1958).

[58] 89 Cong., 1 sess., Senate Hearings on *House Report 6767*, Appropriations for 1966, Part I, pp. 666–67.

At the town of Navajo, New Mexico, a $7,500,000 sawmill is turning out 150,000 board feet of ponderosa pine lumber a day. Considered a model plant, the giant facility of the Navajo Forest Products Industries supplies jobs for about five hundred tribesmen, and an annual payroll of around $1,700,000. It will soon be processing 200,000 board feet a day cut from Navaho forests estimated to hold in 1960 2,000,000,000 board feet of merchantable virgin timber.[59]

D. SUMMARY

A few families have achieved relatively high incomes. Some members of these families have been well educated and are employed in skilled occupations in nearby towns. On every reservation a small number prosper in agriculture or ranching. But the overwhelming majority, largely dependent on seasonal work and welfare, are incredibly poor. Those who work steadily are employed as unskilled laborers or in inefficient farming and ranching operations.

There are, however, examples of improved farming and ranching techniques among Indians that suggest means by which others can achieve levels of productivity that are already commonplace to non-Indians. As first measures, the heirship tangle must be unraveled, idle and rented lands should be utilized, better training provided for managers, and necessary capital obtained. And, basic to all, planning is needed to chart a new course.

III. FUTURE DEVELOPMENT

Planning

The B. I. A., in trying to grapple with the Indians' problems, relied until 1960 on improving health and education, expanding relocation, and promoting industrial development. But such measures are insufficient. Formal education alone has not been able to overcome the influences of poverty, idleness, and unstable homes. Many Indians, young as well as old, are unqualified for jobs. Native languages and customs provide formidable barriers

[59] *The Navajo Yearbook, 1951–1961*, Report VIII (1961), 183–85.

between the Indians and the urban, industrial, and scientific culture by which they are surrounded. Greater preparation is required on and off the reservation. Half-measures that fail to meet financial, managerial, and land-tenure needs only confirm or reinforce Indian self-doubt. Funds and staff must be sufficient for planning and carrying a program of economic development to completion. Plans must provide for consistence and continuity, even though B. I. A. administrations change. Economic development requires a simultaneous attack on many fronts, a generous investment, and the discovery of high-priority enterprises through individual reservation studies.

Indian Water Rights

The water rights of Indians in the arid, western appropriation states[60] for tribal and allotted lands differ from the rights of non-Indians in their origin and source, their nature, their extent, their priority, and their permanence. Indian rights are derived from aboriginal ownership or from the United States through treaty or by federal law, and not from state law, which is the common source of such rights when held by others. Indian tribes generally have the right to sufficient water from all sources in their reservations for irrigation and for stock, domestic, and related uses. The water right (a vested property right appurtenant to Indian land) is implied and need not be expressly stated in the treaty, statute, or executive order. The priority is fixed by the date the reservation was established.

Because of the wide differences among state law systems, to transfer jurisdiction of these Indian rights from federal to state law would present unusually complex and novel legal, administrative, and practical problems, many of which cannot be foreseen. To make such a transfer without adequate protection

[60] The appropriation law is variously recognized in all seventeen Western states. The riparian doctrine is recognized in varying degrees in seven of them, repudiated in eight, and not clear in two. Riparian rights are repudiated *in toto* in Arizona, Colorado, Idaho, Montana, Nevada, New Mexico, Utah, and Wyoming. Where riparian rights have some validity, the two systems are recognized concurrently—called the California Doctrine. *Water Resources Law* (Vol. III, Report of the President's Water Resources Policy Commission, 1950), 155–56.

would place the Indians' water rights in jeopardy and lead to long, expensive litigation. It is too late for Indians to seek any rights by complying with state law, because all major streams are fully appropriated.

The general rules for determining Indian water rights are clear, but applying them is difficult. Often the amount of irrigable acreage in a reservation is not known, and only experts can determine what kind of land can be successfully irrigated. Moreover, the total amount of water in the river or stream system, its availability for use, the amount to be diverted for Indian use, and the quantity and priorities to which other users on a river are entitled must be determined. These often depend on judgments based on extremely complicated facts. The amount of money available to the Indians to employ engineers, soil experts, historians, economists, skilled lawyers, and others to protect their rights, and the background and predilection of a judge may determine what happens to the Indian rights after termination.

Indian rights are reserved rights and legally do not depend on beneficial use,[61] nor do they derive from or depend upon compliance with state law, a typical expression of which is Article XVI of the Constitution of New Mexico:

> Beneficial use shall be the basis, the measure and the limit of the right to the use of water.

Judge Rifkind's Report in *Arizona* v. *California* (1960) sharply points up one consequence of this difference. Although the Indians had never used so much water beneficially, Judge Rifkind allowed them to divert 717,148 acre feet from the Colorado

[61] The water rights of the terminated tribes are excepted from this statement. The Klamath Act postponed application of Oregon's abandonment law for fifteen years from termination. It is doubtful that reserved rights, for which uses could have been developed at any time since the 1864 treaty, would be protected by a fifteen-year deferment of forfeiture for non-use. The other terminations of tribes in arid states provide that nothing in the act shall abrogate their water rights, but state law is made applicable. The meaning of this is not clear. Indian water rights are vested property rights, and applying state law may impair them, thereby raising constitutional issues. Questions will inevitably arise over ownership, use, and control of the Menominees' lakes and streams even though Wisconsin is a riparian and not an appropriation state.

River. Only the doctrine of reserved rights enabled him to award the Colorado River tribes enough water for the 107,588 acres in question.

A similar example is afforded by case of the Pueblos of Cochiti, San Felipe, Santo Domingo, Santa Ana, Sandia, and Isleta, which have more than 20,000 acres of irrigable land, but only 8,000 or 9,000 acres under cultivation. Therefore, if state law applied, they would have abandoned, as a minimum, water rights for more than 12,000 acres, or roughly 36,000 acre-feet of prime water rights worth between $7,200,000 and $10,000,000. State laws vary regarding the length of non-use which results in forfeiture of rights: in New Mexico, four years; in Arizona, Idaho, Nevada, Oregon, and Utah, five years; and in the Dakotas, three years. But although the reserved rights of Indians cannot legally be lost by non-use, practically they can be lost if the Indians do not have legal help. This is shown by the history of the Pima-Maricopa Indians.

The ancestors of the present-day Pima Indians—the Honokam —used water from the Gila River since prehistoric times. Velarde, a missionary, as early as 1716 found these Indians effectively handling large quantities of water for agriculture by means of canals.[62] By the late nineteenth century many white farmers were using the water from the Gila River and its tributaries and depleting the amount of water that reached the Gila River Indian Reservation.

Congress, by an act of 1924, authorized the construction of the Coolidge Dam, which provided in part:

> That the Secretary of the Interior, through the Indian Service, is hereby authorized to construct a dam across the canyon of the Gila River . . . for the purpose, first, of providing water for the irrigation of lands allotted to Pima Indians on the Gila River Reservation, Arizona, now without an adequate supply of water, and, second, for the irrigation of such other lands in public or

[62] Paul H. Ezell, "Is there a Hohokam-Pima Culture Continuum?" *American Antiquity,* Vol. XXIX, No. 1 (1963), 61, 63.

private ownership, as in the opinion of the said Secretary, can be served with water impounded by said dam *without diminishing the supply necessary for* said Indian lands. . . .

The dam was completed in 1929. Congress required the Department of Justice to bring an action in the U.S. District Court of Arizona to determine all water rights on the Gila River. This decree *(U.S.A.* v. *Adams, et al.,* No. E 59, Globe Equity, 1935) established the rights of the Pima Indians to water in the Coolidge Dam sufficient to irrigate 35,000 acres of their land. This right stemmed from their aboriginal rights to water (priority immemorial)—rights based on 1916 use of water. These rights were limited to 60.6 per cent of the first 300 second-feet, 51.7 per cent of the second 300 second-feet, and 56.1 per cent of all water in excess of 600 second-feet. The remainder was to go to the white farmers.

The practical result of this distribution of water rested upon the amount of land which could be cultivated. The Indians have never used all the appropriated water because they lacked the money to purchase heavy equipment and the knowledge to practice commercial agriculture. However, the white farmers by the use of water in the Coolidge Dam and deep wells (from underground water of the Gila River) have developed approximately 200,000 acres of irrigated land. So there is a continual shortage of water on the Pima-Maricopa Reservation in spite of the Indians' legal right to reserved water.

Indian land should not remain undeveloped. Water should be used to the fullest extent, not only as a source of income but as a practical protection of their rights. The need for more water for municipal, industrial, domestic, livestock, and agricultural uses is increasing so rapidly that surplus water is not likely to go unnoticed for long, especially in the semiarid West. The old observation that nothing is more dangerous to Indian land than a rich mine applies equally well to unused water rights. It is easier to "justify" taking Indian water if the Indians are not using it.

Extension and Managerial Training

To improve farm management, Indians need both their present techniques and brand-new methods. To this end there must be a large, adequately paid, well-trained staff working closely with Bureau planners; and there must be extension workers stressing new skills.

Private decisions are increasingly inadequate in today's complex situations. Therefore, extension specialists must emphasize the importance of making sound group decisions—concerning watersheds, conservation, rural zoning, co-operatives, brucellosis control, economical water use, and the like. Extension agents must now be prepared to teach about and assist with the management of tribal and individual business enterprises. The complex of industrial-urban extension and development, coupled with a rapidly expanding population, is blurring the line between formerly distinct urban and rural problems. Because of new and improved highways farmers can hold jobs in cities and urban workers can move to the country. New subdivisions in rural townships require borrowed funds for additional school buildings; water, sewage, and other services must be provided, and recreation facilities are needed. Industries settling in rural areas create problems of water allocation, irrigation restrictions, factory wastes, and water pollution.

Private decisions cannot settle such matters. Solutions require negotiation and planning by leaders or selected representatives of the various interests and analyses of claims and counterclaims as a basis for wise decisions.

Since the 1930's, when agricultural extension and home economist workers first became available to Indians, the effort has been too feeble to be effective. Extension men were burdened with the Bureau's loan funds and were made responsible for reports so voluminous that 25 to 60 per cent of program time was absorbed by paper work.[63] Moreover, the B. I. A. has not

[63] 80 Cong., 1 sess., *Hearings Before the House Appropriations Committee* (1948), Dept. of Interior, Part I, Bureau of Indian Affairs: testimony by Mr. A. C. Cooley, director of B. I. A. Extension Programs, p. 1449.

provided the same ratio of extension workers to Indian farmers as that provided for non-Indian farmers and so they could not possibly give the Indians the necessary time or education.

Howard W. Gorman, member of the Resources Committee of the Navajo Tribal Council, discussing the Colorado River irrigation project, testified:

> We of the Navajo Tribe realize that we cannot just take our people off the sheep ranges and put them down on the Navajo Indian irrigation project, hand them a shovel, and then forget about them. The Bureau of Indian Affairs took some of our Navajo people off the sheep ranges to 80-acre assignments on the Colorado River Indian Reservation at Parker. The Bureau planted alfalfa on these assignments, and our people had nothing to do but cut it. They did this the first year, the second year, and the third year, each year getting a smaller crop. The fourth year the alfalfa did not come up, and our people who had been sheepherders all their lives did not know what to do. Most of them came back to the sheep ranges.
>
> This is not going to happen on the Navajo Indian Irrigation Project.* Realizing that an inexperienced person cannot succeed as an irrigation farmer, the Navajo tribe on March 25, 1956 established a farm training school on 1200 acres of recently developed irrigated land near Shiprock, New Mexico.[64]

At Shiprock in 1956 the Navahos inaugurated an experiment in agricultural education involving 1,200 acres of land, based on a management plan devised by a commercial company and administered by a board of directors chosen from the Resources Committee on the Navaho tribe. The board can limit the size of

* The Navajo Irrigation Project will consist of 110,630 acres at an estimated cost of $135,000,000 at January 1959 prices.

[64] 85 Cong., 2 sess., *Hearings Before the Subcommittee on Irrigation and Reclamation of the Committee on Interior and Insular Affairs*, U.S. Senate, on *Sen. Bill 3648*, a Bill to Authorize the Secretary of the Interior to Construct, Operate, and Maintain the Navajo Indian Irrigation Project and the Initial Stage of the San Juan–Chama Project as Participating Projects of the Colorado River Storage Project and for Other Purposes (July 9 and 10, 1958): statement of Howard W. Gorman, member, Resources Committee of the Navajo Tribal Council, Window Rock, Ariz. (as presented by Paul Jones), pp. 103–105.

the class (eleven members in 1959), choose trainees, dismiss misfits, and appoint their own farm manager. The Bureau supplies a vocation specialist and classroom teachers, who give instruction in the use of fertilizers and machines and in welding, carpentry, English, arithmetic, and handling money. Farming techniques are taught on the job, and the wives of married trainees are taught child care and home economics.

Tribal appropriations for this venture were $230,000 in the fiscal year 1957, $160,900 in 1958 and $214,000 in 1966. Single trainees receive $110 a month in cash, plus $70 deposited for savings. Married trainees receive $140 a month in cash, plus $40 in savings and an additional amount for each child. Families live in modern two-bedroom houses; single men reside in a dormitory. At the end of the training period each trainee will have accumulated money with which to buy machinery, seeds, and other necessities to start him in farming. Unsuccessful farmers must return their savings to the tribe.[65]

Several reservations have their own tribal rehabilitation programs. The Cheyenne River cattle project, commenced in 1956, had approximately 11 per cent of the participating Indians drop out within two years. Interviews with Indian cattlemen revealed that half wanted more technical assistance. The tribal council had hired five members as cattle-operations field agents, selected without regard to their knowledge of livestock and range management. Had they been well trained, their number would have been adequate for the ranches they served.[66]

The Southern Ute tribe, with about eighty-five farmers in 1958, was assigned part-time service by the La Plata County (Colorado) extension office. The tribe and the B. I. A. paid 80 per cent of the salary of the assistant county extension agent, and 50 per cent of the salaries of a home demonstration agent and

---

[65] *Navajo Farm Training Project, Shiprock Subagency,* January, 1957 to July, 1958 (mimeographed).

[66] *Present Status and Projected Future Needs of the Cheyenne River Rehabilitation Program,* as of April 15, 1958, U.S. Dept. of Interior, B. I. A., Missouri River Basin Irrigation Project, *Report No. 157* (Billings, Mont., June, 1958), 3.

an office secretary. However, the tribe wants full-time services of an extension agent and a home demonstration agent.[67]

The need for farm vehicles and machinery is obvious, but practices like fertilization, use of hybrid seeds, timely planting and harvesting, and irrigation, marketing, and conservation are harder to "sell." The Indian must have either a notion of cause-and-effect relations or else complete trust in his teachers and exemplars. Transferring important concepts from one culture to another demands an extension agent with keen awareness of Indian philosophy and experience.

The present B. I. A. policy of contracting extension work with the Department of Agriculture has not been altogether successful and has created duplication of effort. In the fiscal year 1965, the B. I. A. received $1,494,900 from Congress and gave $769,000 to fifteen states (through Johnson-O'Malley contracts) to be turned over to the land-grant colleges.[68] This money went for approximately ninety extension workers who counsel with individual Indians, families, and organized groups on farming, livestock raising, home management, 4–H clubs, and community development and improvement.

The state agricultural extension agents have no background in or special knowledge of reservation conditions and because of that often cannot supply the needed help. Duplication of administration and of other services simply increases program costs.

Industry

All Indian communities would profit greatly from successful industrial development, but on many depressed areas the human and physical resources are inadequate to support manufacturing plants.

Even an established industry may fail, one reason being a

---

[67] "Progress: A Report to the Commissioner of Indian Affairs," Southern Ute Tribe, Ignacio, Colo., Jan. 1, 1958, pp. 40, 42.

[68] 89 Cong., 1 sess., Senate, Hearings on *House Report 6767*, Appropriations for 1966, p. 669.

lack of factual data to permit adequate planning. This was pointed out in the controller general's report in 1958.[69]

Beginning in the 1960's, professional planners have been given contracts by the B. I. A. to make feasibility studies. Determinations are based on analysis of finances required, cost-benefit ratios, layouts, sources of investment funds, operating capital and credit, adequacy of raw materials, transportation facilities and costs, markets and marketing manpower requirements and availability, management, and operating plans. Detailed schemes are also outlined for land use, public facilities, and improved utilization of existing reservation resources. Seventy-five studies on the feasibility of establishing diversified reservation industries were made during 1964.[70]

A total of fifty-six industrial plants, including those in Alaska, have been located on or near reservations. Except for six plants established prior to 1960, the remaining fifty were developed after that date, and half were located on reservations during 1964. The fifty-six plants employed a total of 2,363 people, of which 1,385 were Indians. As of September 30, 1964, six plants have closed and seven are under construction, leaving forty-three in active operation.

The industries represent a wide variety of manufactured materials. To cite a few examples—cheese and milk products are produced at Selfridge, North Dakota, near the Standing Rock Reservation, and by the Sioux Dairy Co-operative at Mission, South Dakota; electronic components are made in the Laguna Pueblo in New Mexico; wood products are manufactured by Indians on the Coeur d'Alene, Lac Courte Oreilles, Yavapai, Cherokee, Blackfeet, Ute Mountain, Navaho, Umatilla, Santo Domingo, Fort Apache, and Jicarilla reservations; tufted carpets are produced at Anadarko, Oklahoma; electric meters and parts are made on the Lac de Flambeau Reservation in Wiscon-

[69] *Administration of Withdrawal Activities by the Bureau of Indian Affairs,* Report to the Congress of the United States by the Comptroller General of the U.S. (1958), 40.

[70] U.S. Dept. of Interior press release, January 15, 1965.

sin; and metal products are manufactured by the Turtle Mountain Steel and Supply Company at Rolla, North Dakota.[71]

Industries, in combination with employment assistance, which has helped disperse Indians on overcrowded reservations, have advanced the economic level of tribesmen remaining on reservations where the upswing has been going on for a couple of decades, as, for example, the Cherokees of North Carolina. But among groups as yet unaware of the promise of concerted effort and with unsolved heirship and other problems, neither the help of employment assistance nor a few new industries have had time to make perceptible changes.

An example of a reservation where the economic development program has, as yet, made little impact is the 2,300-square-mile Pine Ridge Reservation in South Dakota. It consists mostly of rangeland, and has a population of approximately 8,000, with a mean annual family income of almost $900. Two industries on which the Sioux may rely for jobs are the Manderson Tent Project, established during 1963, which employs 8, and the Wright and McGill Company, established in 1961, making snelled fishhooks, which employs 160 Indians. These payrolls have not made much of a dent on a group in which half the work force was unemployed and in the lean months of February and March one-third of the population was on welfare. Sioux still live for the most part without electricity, half of the houses are without wells, some people have to haul water fifteen miles, and indoor plumbing and telephone service is rare.[72]

The picture among the Eastern Cherokees living on eighty-eight square miles of federal land located in North Carolina is more promising. These people, with a population of about 5,500, had an average annual family income in 1946 of less than $1,000. Today it is more than $2,700.

[71] *Department of the Interior and Related Agencies Appropriations for 1966,* Hearings Before a Subcommittee of the Committee on Appropriations, U.S. House of Representatives, 89 Cong., 1 sess., (1965), 787–89.

[72] James Ridgeway, "More Lost Indians," *The New Republic,* Vol. 153, No. 24 (Dec. 11, 1965), 19–22.

The upswing commenced about twenty years ago when the Cherokees formed a co-operative and the federal Arts and Crafts Board provided a full-time director. Oconaluftee Village was built as a replica of an ancient Cherokee town and a museum of Cherokee Indians was established, both as tourist attractions.

Then in 1950, in connection with the Cherokee Historical Association, an offspring of Western North Carolina Associated Communities, the three groups wrote and presented a yearly pageant, "Unto These Hills." This drama attracted tourists by the thousands to the reservation. The demands created by the influx of transients resulted in the Cherokees' borrowing money and establishing motels and services. Employment on the reservation improved, but the Cherokees decided seasonal work was not enough. In 1956 the council, by dint of an abandoned dairy barn offered for a low rent and financial assistance from the B. I. A., persuaded a leather craft plant to move to Cherokee.

The plant started with five employees making moccasins. Eight years later, "The Cherokee, Inc." expanded to four other buildings and now employs 135 Indians with a payroll of $300,000. It is the largest manufacturer of Indian arts and crafts in the world.

In 1959 a manufacturer of comforters and other quilted products was attracted to the reservation by a building the Indians constructed with money borrowed from the B. I. A. and an on-the-job training program offered by the Bureau. They now employ 125 Indians and 70 non-Indians, with a payroll of almost $500,000 annually.

During 1963 with the administration's renewed interest in the welfare of Indian tribes, two new industries have been established on the reservation. One firm manufactures woman's hair accessories and employs 40 Indians; the other company makes modern furniture and has a payroll of 8 Indians. In addition, a building (constructed from funds borrowed from the B. I. A.) has been leased to a rug and placemat manufacturer anticipating the employment of 35 additional Cherokees.

Officials of the Cherokee tribe believe they have been successful because they offer businesses buildings, on-the-job training, and workers both dependable and capable. Other important factors are attributed to the help of local and state people and dedicated superintendents. Less important, but compelling, was the attractive mountain environment and excellent industrial sites.[73]

Arts and Crafts

The traditional Indian crafts are a means of identification—both for the individual and for the tribe—supply a device for obtaining admiration, and often give the white man his first appreciation of Indian culture.

Within any cultural group, arts and crafts constitute one of the most satisfying means of expression. For Indians, to whom English is a borrowed and an awkward tongue, their paintings, their silverwork, their jewelry, their pottery, and their weaving provide a stabilizing force during the difficult days of cultural transition.

If an Indian craftsman is a highly skilled "career artist," he can make a comfortable living, for the intrinsic beauty of his work often commands high prices. If he is even moderately good, he can supplement a meager cash income by making and selling jewelry or pictures.[74]

The adaptation of crafts from production for utility to production for artistic appeal came about slowly. Today there are many examples of artistic creation—the distinctively beautiful jewelry of the Zuñi silversmiths and the black-on-black pottery of San Ildefonso are widely known and admired. Both resulted from the Indian's native ability, coupled with a professional awareness of the market for such products.

Fifty years ago C. G. Wallace opened a trading post on the Zuñi Reservation and taught the Indians to substitute turquoise-on-silver for their ancient art of inlaying turquoise-on-bone.

[73] Carol F. White, "Cherokees Cite Tourism for Improved Living Standards, Job Opportunities," *E. S. C. Quarterly,* Vol. XXII, Nos. 1–2 (Winter–Spring, 1964).

[74] Dorothy Dunn, honorable Associate of Indian arts, School of American Research, Santa Fe, "Training and Evaluation of the Indian Artist," March 9, 1960 (mimeographed).

99

Gradually the designs became more sophisticated, and today many silversmiths earn a good livelihood at home.

About the same time, E. L. Hewitt, directing archaeological excavations near San Ildefonso for the School of American Research, employed the skill of a native potter, María Montoya Martínez, and the ability of her husband, Julián, to duplicate a potsherd decorated with a prehistoric design. Out of the project developed a career that brought renown and prosperity to María and Julián and, eventually, some measure of rehabilitation to the entire pueblo.[75]

It is estimated that Navaho handicrafts worth between $7,000,-000 and $8,000,000 are sold in or shipped from Gallup, New Mexico, each year.[76] The comparable value in 1939–40 was only $80,000.

A skill can also be introduced inexpensively but successfully. In 1939 an Oklahoma Choctaw community—in which the average annual cash income per family was only $48—was taught to card, spin, and dye wool, a craft previously not practiced there. Subsequently, a group of Cherokee Indians using this wool were taught to weave the fiber into fabrics and rugs. Eventually the more adept workers were able to earn $2.50 a day—a long jump forward from that annual per-family income—and the initial investment had been only $200.

Much of the credit for the development of Indian craftsmanship is due the Indian Arts and Crafts Board, established within the Department of the Interior in 1935 and for many years headed by Réné d'Harnoncourt. The Board developed native arts in various ways, but no program was more important than its promotion of art in government schools. Under Board sponsorship Miss Dorothy Dunn developed an excellent department of art at the Santa Fe Indian School—one including fine collections of traditional art, traveling exhibits, and student appreciation of Indian art. Many of Miss Dunn's former students have

[75] Alice Marriott, *Maria: The Potter of San Ildefonso* (Norman, University of Oklahoma Press, 1948).

[76] "Economy of Gallup," McKinley County Chamber of Commerce, Gallup, N.M., March, 1962.

achieved notable careers, five receiving the *Les Palmes Academiques* Medal and the title *Officier d'Academie* from the government of France.

To facilitate the sale of student work and make cash available for additional raw materials, the Arts and Crafts Board encouraged the forming of the Tesuque Arts and Crafts Guild in the late 1930's. The result was a flourishing business for the young craftsmen.[77] Unfortunately, during the term of Commissioner Glenn Emmons the B. I. A. abolished the guild, and gave little or no encouragement to art work at the school, so it declined. Reorganized during the 1960's, the school now has the expressed purpose of training students of Indian descent in any or all of the arts—traditional and otherwise.[78] It is staffed largely by professionals who can recognize economically feasible work, not easily reproduced by machinery, and acquaint the Indian with the luxury market. The school has already made notable contributions in the fields of choreography, painting, and sculpture.

The Board's requested 1966 budget of $365,000 would permit on-the-job training of Indian managers, experimental production, traveling exhibits, prizes for exceptional work, and collection of specimens of traditional crafts for the museums supervised by the Board at Anadarko, Oklahoma, and Rapid City, South Dakota,[79] and cover the operation of the Blackfeet Museum at Browning, Montana.

In summary, Indian arts and crafts are important to both the Indian and the white man. They provide a cultural anchor for the tribesmen, a living for some, rehabilitation for others, and a sense of artistic achievement for many. They make the white man more sensitive to Indian history, and they also make a genuine aesthetic contribution to our civilization. But if the skills are to survive, they require that the artist have freedom of expression, a capital investment, and time. They are slow growing and difficult to evaluate and so must not be prematurely

[77] "Trust Indenture for Conduct of Pueblo Indian Arts and Crafts Market," Feb. 28, 1941 (Commission files).
[78] Dept. of Interior news release, April 26, 1962.
[79] 89 Cong., 1 sess., Senate Hearings on *House Report 6767* (1965), 676.

written off as failures. They cannot provide the spectacular profits compatible with American economic expectations; moreover, they require protection against periods of depression which follow whenever Indian designs are successfully copied for machine production.

Recreation

The development of commercial recreation sites on tribal and government-owned land under B. I. A. supervision offers—from Florida to California—real possibilities for increased Indian income. Many tribes are already operating recreation programs, other development projects are under way, and a number of others are being planned. Fishing is one of the most popular outdoor recreational activities in the nation; and in 1960 some Indian tribes retained title to 3,600 lakes and ponds and 6,000 miles of rivers and streams, plus 27,000,000 acres of hunting land—all suitable for tourist development by tribes. Three-fourths of the sites and acreage are in the West.

In addition, reservations contain the potentials for 125 improved camping areas that will accommodate 10,000 persons a night; 790 other camp sites with a per-night capacity for about 4,000 campers; 781 picnic areas that can serve almost 11,000 persons at a time; and 13 winter-sports sites, which might accommodate 2,800 enthusiasts at once. More than 1,000 improved boat-launching facilities are also available.

Picnicking, water sports, tribal ceremonies, and museums attracted some two million visitors to Indian land in 1960. The industrial division of the New Mexico development reports that the Navaho tribe may some day be able to realize $3,000,000 annually through developing reservation recreation.[80]

Employment Assistance (Relocation)

The Branch of Relocation in the B. I. A., created in the 1950's, enlarged its activities during the 1960's and is now known as

[80] *Indian News* (news letter of the New Mexico Commission on Indian Affairs, Santa Fe), May, 1962, p. 6.

Employment Assistance. Today finding jobs for Indians is, perhaps, the least of its activities. Vocational and remedial training preparatory to entering a trade school and courses designed for reservation Indians as an introduction to city life occupy a large part of the time of the field staff. In addition, the clerical force compiles lists of available positions, studies the market for jobs which, because of automation, are becoming obsolete, and seeks new jobs where Indians might be used to advantage.

Assimilated reservation applicants, who wish work and have been found, after screening, to be qualified in experience and education are given money for transportation to the job location and given living expenses until they have found a position and received their first paycheck. After this, the staff follows them for about a year should they need help in adjusting to the new environment. Indians in this category are, however, usually conversant with state or federal employment agencies and can find their own work. But most Indians need additional education and assistance.

Over the years, experience has shown that many Indians lack the training to be eligible for a job. Vocational education is available under Public Law 84–956 (August 3, 1956), which was passed to fill this need. It includes authority for tuition, subsidy for travel, living expenses while attending an accredited institution, or for apprentice training, or on-the-job instruction for a period not to exceed twenty-four months. This law was amended in 1959 to provide that Indians did not need to reside on trust property in order to qualify for its benefits. The success of the program led Congress to raise the amount from time to time from the original $3,500,000 to $15,000,000 in April, 1965 (Public Law 89–14).

Indians lacking the education to matriculate in a vocational school or without the experience to adjust to city life have the choice of pre-vocational training or on-the-job training and, if necessary, orientation courses. Pre-vocational education for Indian men and women is being undertaken through the joint efforts of the Employment Assistance of the B. I. A., the Department of Labor (Manpower Training and Development Act, Public Law 87–415), and state education and employment agencies in Washington, Arizona, and California.

In Seattle typical pre-vocational classes concentrate on remedial reading, arithmetic, and the communication skills for about four hours a day; during another two hours students get experience in metal work, wood trades, food preparation, clerical skills, health services, or horticulture. During the twenty-week session an attempt is made to teach basic education, acceptable work habits, regular attendance, punctuality, and some insight into the different trades the pupils might follow on entering vocational schools. Wives of married trainees are given instruction in child care and homemaking. Pre-vocational training has been a success for those Indians with determination; others have had to be sent home if they did not, on their own initiative, drop out.

On-the-job training from January through September of the fiscal year 1965 included approximately 717 Indian workers—an increase of 10 per cent over the total for the entire preceding year. Companies with contracts for training Indians are located in Oklahoma, Minnesota, North Dakota, New Mexico, North Carolina, Arizona, Wisconsin, and Montana and include the manufacturing of garments, precision products, jewelry, leather goods, modern hair accessories, electronic parts, and lumber and related products, as well as fabricating aluminum culverts, and the extrusion of plastic pipe.[81]

Orientation courses for Eskimos and reservation Indians unfamiliar with the manners and customs of life outside their villages have been started in Seattle, Washington. The three-week course is based on the assumption that the quickest way for students to adjust to modern life is to let them use up-to-date conveniences. At the same time the Indian's appreciation of contemporary city living may motivate him to excel in his trade so that some day he may be able to afford similar luxuries for his family.

81 U.S. Dept. of Interior news release, Sept. 27, 1965.

The training center is, therefore, located in a modern motel. Seven furnished apartments are rented for the trainees and their families and a couple of additional apartments serve as office space. All the accommodations have carpeted floors, draperies, an all-electric kitchen, private bath, and living rooms.

It is too early to evaluate the results of the orientation or pre-vocational training courses. However, methods of teaching have been developed and are being studied by psychologists, psychiatrists, linguists, and other specialists so that improvements are constantly being made. There still remains much that needs to be explored about the motivation of the reservation Indian when he comes in contact with the demands of a highly techno-logical society.

Economic Opportunity Act (78 Stat. 508)

Maximum Indian self-sufficiency may be advanced through programs under the Office of Economic Opportunity and administered by Indians, while the B. I. A. assists applicants to fill out forms and offers advice.

Title I (A and C) establishes job corps, provides full-time work experience for unemployed youth, and promotes part-time employment for needy students. Under this Title, three conservation centers have been established and seven are under construction on Indian reservations. Indians as well as young people from all over the nation receive a second chance at schooling and training in skills. More than 18,000 Indian boys and girls from seventy-one Indian communities in twenty-one states have work in hospitals, schools, libraries, and other government and nonprofit agencies where they earn $1.25 an hour while completing school.

Title II (A) of the act provides incentives for urban and rural communities to combat poverty by mobilizing their resources and establishing projects relating to health, education, employment training, child welfare, and old-age care. Sixty-eight proposals have been submitted by Indian communities, and twenty-nine have been approved. Following are three of the many successful projects: the $265,000 Northern Cheyenne Community Action Program, South Dakota, which stresses education; the first Community Action Program in Montana, which includes pre-school training, health education, remedial reading, and pre-college training; and the Santa Clara, New Mexico, Community Action Program, called "Operation Head Start," which was cited by the Office of Economic Opportunity as one of the nation's best pre-school programs.[82]

Reports indicate that hundreds of individual Indians have applied for small loans under Title III. Nearly two hundred unemployed Indian adults have enrolled in work experience projects under Title V.[83] These programs originate locally and are presented to the Washington Office of Economic Opportunity.

IV. COST OF ECONOMIC DEVELOPMENT AND SOURCES OF CAPITAL

Cost Estimates

A 1958 cost estimate by Peter Dorner of a ten-year program of economic development for the American Indians came to approximately $1,947 per capita for the reservation population, or a total of $600,000,000, which at 1965 levels would be more nearly one billion dollars. The estimate included none of the functions now performed by the Bureau with present annual budgets.

The budget did include costs of establishing farm and ranch units (with allowances for equipment and livestock), land consolidation, elimination of the heirship problems, and managerial training for established farmers and ranchers. Also included were housing, training, and other rehabilitation investments, as well as welfare costs for that portion of the reservation not able to be accommodated under the development program or existing Bureau services. The assumption was that the B. I. A. and

---

[82] *Indian Affairs* (news letter of the Association on American Indian Affairs, Inc.), No. 61 (Dec., 1965).

[83] U.S. Dept. of Interior news release, Oct. 11, 1965.

tribal policies would remain consistent, assuring co-operation for a sufficient time to carry through a plan.

Two tribal budgets support the Dorner estimates: In addition to regular B. I. A. money for administration, the budget for the Navaho tribe from their own resources plus money appropriated by Congress for the ten-year rehabilitation program, 1951–60 (Public Law 474), amounted to $190,496,738.[84] Assuming an average population of 90,000, the per capita figure is about $2,117. The Cheyenne River Reservation (population, 3,284) estimates an expenditure of $6,895,000 over ten years—$2,100 per person over and above regular Bureau programs and expenditures.[85]

The total estimated $600,000,000, or one billion dollars, could not be allocated to all tribes at once. Some reservations are neither ready for nor desirous of economic development. The Indians themselves must take the responsibility for initiating, approving, and carrying out programs.

Sources of Capital: Tribal and Individual

During fiscal year 1962 approximately three hundred Indian tribes, bands, or identifiable groups had some six hundred accounts in the United States Treasury, totaling $64,506,982.[86] These monies came from Indian resources, from condemnation of land for dams, right-of-ways, or takings for other public purposes, money awarded June 7, 1924, for loss of land under an Act to Quiet Title to Lands Within Pueblo Indian Land Grants, and from the Indian Claims Commission (60 Statute 1049, August 13, 1946), etc. The funds are used largely to finance services normally provided by local governments. They are subject to the provisions of tribal constitutions, by-laws and charters, and resolutions of Indian governments, bands, or groups, and are used

---

84 *The Navajo Yearbook, 1951–1961*, Report VIII (1961).

85 *Present Status and Projected Future Needs of the Cheyenne River Rehabilitation Program*, as of April 15, 1958, U.S. Dept. of Interior, B. I. A., Missouri River Basin Irrigation Project, *Report 157* (Billings, Mont., June, 1958).

86 *Interior Department and Related Agencies Appropriations for 1963*, Hearings Before a Subcommittee of the Committee on Appropriations, U.S. Senate, 87 Cong., 2 sess. (1962), 158, 160.

to finance tribal programs, enterprises, or businesses. When the funds are divided among the many tribes, very few have adequate liquid wealth for economic venture.

Moreover, these funds are not unrestricted, but are programmed under permanent, annual, and indefinite authorizations. Permanent authorizations are made available to Indians under acts of Congress; annual authorizations require yearly Congressional approval; indefinite funds are made available through the Department of the Interior Appropriation Act, under the heading "Tribal Funds." Before any of these monies can be used, the tribes are required to prepare budgets for approval by the Bureau.

About half of the $190,000,000 for Navaho economic betterment during the decade 1951–60 came from Congress. At least two factors are making it increasingly difficult for tribes to acquire sufficient capital: rising equipment costs and the replacement of small family farms by large ranches. The Indian farmer is barely competitive with the "small" white farmer. He can scarcely hope to hold his own against a very large commercial operation.[87]

Frequently such capital as the Indians do have comes from awards for lands taken by the government, filed under the U.S. Court of Claims or the Indian Claims Commission (see Chapter Two, under "Treaties and Agreements"). In addition to claims filed under the Claims Commission for past damages, Indians have received money for land taken for public purposes. The Lower Brulé Sioux Indians in South Dakota were paid for individual and tribal lands occupied by the Big Bend Dam and Reservoir. The Act of Indemnity provided that a portion of the award should be expended for improvement of the economic and social conditions of enrolled tribal members and a portion invested in industrial development.[88] Such measures to insure that all of the money will not be divided among the members of the

---

[87] Piel, *Consumers of Abundance.*
[88] 87 Cong., 1 sess., *Congressional Record,* Vol. 107, Part II (August 7, 1961), 14769.

A Hopi weaver works at his loom in the time-honored tradition
of his ancestors.

This elderly Michigan Potawatomi couple supplement their income with the beautiful hampers woven by the lady of the house.

Bureau of Indian Affairs

This Mesquakie Indian lady who resides on the Sac and Fox Reservation in Iowa obviously enjoys the beautiful beadwork she is doing.

Bureau of Indian Affairs

The Navaho silversmith employs crude tools and age-old methods
in the creation of exquisite jewelry.

Bureau of Indian Affairs

A member of Wisconsin's Bad River Chippewa community puts the finishing touches on a magnificent ceremonial drum.

Bureau of Indian Affairs

A modern haircut is given to this Navaho boy under the approving
eyes of his family, dressed in traditional costume.

Bureau of Indian Affairs

Navaho tribal enterprise—the tourists.

Neighbors' helping hands speed the erection of a Mutual Help House Program home on the Apache Reservation (San Carlos-Bylas Project). The homeowner exchanges his labor hours on his new home for credits toward the purchase price.

Bureau of Indian Affairs

tribe for per capita payments have on the whole proved of little long-term benefit.

Federal Sources of Indian Capital

Until recently Indians needing credit usually turned almost automatically to the B. I. A. The Bureau administers a revolving loan fund, authorized by Congress June 18, 1934 (48 Stat. 986; 25 U.S.C. 470), which is available to tribal Indians or to those of one-quarter or more Indian blood and to Indian organizations. The amount appropriated under this authorization for twenty-seven years (1934–61) was $17,799,666.[89] From 1934 until June 30, 1952, 77.3 per cent of all loans from this fund were under $1,000 and were largely for emergency subsistence. The amounts and kinds of loans made during this period demonstrate the inadequacy of the Bureau's policy on economic development.

On August 8, 1961 (Title 25 U.S.C., Amendment 91.6), a regulation reduced interest rates from 6 per cent to 4 or 5 per cent for farm expenses, and permitted Indian co-operatives and tribal enterprises rates of from 2 to 5 per cent. On June 26, 1963, another amendment increased interest rates on certain types of loans and permitted forty years as a maximum period of maturity on interest money. There is a bill pending in Congress to increase the fund from $27,000,00 to $62,000,000 in line with the recommendations made by President Kennedy's Task Force on Indian Affairs.[90] During the fiscal years 1963 and 1964, the amounts of $5,900,000 and $6,700,000 were advanced, and these new loans stimulated tribal investment of $25,000,000 and private investment of $100,000,000. Applications for Bureau loans as of the middle of 1965 exceeded by $42,000,000 the available cash balance. Money from government and commercial sources will always be required to provide the larger capital needs of a resource-development program.[91]

---

89 *Annual Credit Report,* Fiscal Year Ending June 30, 1961, U.S. Dept. of Interior, p. 7, n. 8.

90 U.S. Dept. of Interior news release, June 17, 1965.

91 William Schoenfeld, "A General Review of Credit Policies and Procedures of the Bureau of Indian Affairs with Recommendations" (Corvallis, Oregon, Jan-

The federal government has become deeply involved in planning for economic development among non-Indian citizens, especially in depressed areas with high unemployment rates. Programs providing vocational training, improved labor-market services, and other special area assistance—all of which are available to Indians under certain conditions—are listed (see Appendix, Table 4).

Private Sources of Indian Capital

The policy of encouraging Indians to borrow from commercial agencies has not been a success. There are many reasons for this. Since most Indians have little capital, men in the credit business have assumed that adequate financing is available to Indians through government sources and have felt no special obligations to them. Moreover, Indians have been reluctant to approach them.

The Plains Indians are not expert in handling cash, and their long experience in the cattle business has made them wary of borrowing large sums of money at 6 per cent interest. Not having permanent work, they have been unable to establish a credit rating or to acquire collateral.

During the calendar year 1957 the Rosebud and the Yankton Sioux Indians borrowed $271,500 from national and state banks and $59,800 from the Farmers Home Administration. Affluent ranchers took the largest share of the loans. One rancher alone borrowed $83,000; another, $23,000. Trading posts were the next largest borrowers. Operators of small herds or farms—the people most needing help—were unable to borrow from commercial lending concerns.[92] Moreover, even good managers of family-size ranches or farms may go broke if they must borrow on a future harvest.

The Committee on Federal Credit Programs in a report published February 11, 1963, recommended more credit for Indians

uary, 1953 [mimeographed]), 143; Dorner, "The Economic Position of the American Indians," 172.

92 Eicher, "Constraints on Economic Progress on the Rosebud Sioux Indian Reservation," 125.

so as to increase the amount of financing from private sources. Accordingly, Congress has been asked for authority to establish an Indians' loan guarantee and insurance fund of $15,000,000 to guarantee up to 80 per cent any loan made to an Indian organization to finance tribal enterprises or to loan money to an individual Indian; and to insure up to 15 per cent of the total loans against individuals or against a small tribal enterprise.[93]

V. Responsibility of the Indians

A basic need in successful economic development on reservations is strong motivation. Another is capable Indian leadership. A third is the use of methods and the development of institutions that can fit Indian thinking and encourage Indian choices.

One difficulty in the way of meeting the first need has been pointed out by Hagen and Schaw (in relation to the Sioux), the frozen attitude of "hostile dependence" of many Indians:

> . . . by being completely passive, by leaving in the hands of the white society complete responsibility for their problems, they would remind the white of his incapacity to solve the problem he had so arrogantly set out to master.[94]

To overcome some of the difficulties, Indian leaders must be well paid (and given generous budgets) and must have sufficient official tenure to originate and execute plans; they must have an appreciation for both cultures—their own and that of the dominant society—and enough personal prestige to achieve the support of dissident factions; they must possess mature judgment, patience, and enough courage to move into those areas of Indian life not covered by contracts, rules, laws, or Bureau regulations, in which the community can exercise its own discretion; and they must know enough tribal history to relate new problems to old ones so that the new can be understood. The concepts involved in long-term economic plans may be entirely beyond the compre-

93 89 Cong., 1 sess., Senate Hearings on *House Report 6767,* Appropriations for 1966, p. 670.

94 E. E. Hagen and Louis C. Schaw, *The Sioux on the Reservations* (Center for International Studies, Massachusetts Institute of Technology, 1960 [multilith]), chap. 6, p. 9.

hension of many Indian communities. Bridging the gap between the expectations of the old culture and the demands of modern society is not easy.

Among conservative tribes no action may be possible, even with capable leadership; and the Indians' predilection for unanimity, of great use in building group coherence and value when decisions were few and time unlimited, may be a severe handicap. Individual members are likely to be *against* much, but *for* almost nothing. Tribesmen, varying greatly in language ability, in educational level, and in understanding of a money economy, may expect and want their council to make decisions for them.

Some Indians want to maintain the tribal unit; others want to dissolve it and divide its assets. But no matter what the variety of attitudes, *Indians must assume the final responsibility for their own development.* Until people learn to decide between alternatives and to weigh a proposed plan against the labor and deprivations involved in changing values, those people may not know what they really want.

Obviously, therefore, to achieve community development among Indians will require "an unselfish and understanding leader who can face failure without bitterness." And such a leader must be equipped to direct the five steps in community development pointed out by Gordon Macgregor:

> (a) discussion of recognized needs and problems by members of the community with advisers; (b) exploration of internal and external causes of these needs and problems, so the sources of social, psychological, and economic difficulties may be recognized; (c) planning and decision making by the community on undertakings to be assumed and priorities for their initiation; (d) mobilization of internal resources and leadership, and then determination of needed outside technical assistance and consultation; and (e) a mechanism whereby one undertaking leads to a series of related activities directed toward both economic and social growth.[95]

95 "Community Development and Social Adaptation," *Human Organization,* Vol. XX, No. 4 (Winter, 1961–62) , 241.

VI. RECOMMENDATIONS

The economic goals for Indians should be (1) the development of their community and individual resources and (2) the attainment of professional, managerial, and vocational skills comparable to those of their white neighbors, so as to enable Indians to integrate with the non-Indian community on a basis of economic equality. In order to be able to make practical judgments and choices in matters pertaining to their own lives, Indians must also understand the white man's method of trial and error and his point of view. To reach these objectives, money and effort are essential. The longer the delay, the greater will be the cost in achieving the aims and the longer the continuing large annual outlays of the B. I. A.

Not only should the B. I. A. make available, at the request of any tribe, competent technicians to aid in economic planning, but it should also encourage Indians to request such help. Planning in itself is educational, and action should arise out of a reasoned consideration of alternative courses. To be effective, the procedure requires continual fact-gathering—not for the piling up of studies, as sometimes seems to be the purpose, but to get something done. The information gathered should be such as can be disseminated to tribal members, who can then understandingly participate in the subsequent process.

In order to use reservation land effectively, the problem of scattered tracts, small assignments, and multiple ownership of allotted holdings should be solved. The efficient use of such land requires merging. In addition, limitations on length of leaseholds should be liberalized to permit terms of leases long enough to satisfy the economic requirements.

In some regions this means that, to prevent disintegration of the land base, the tribe must obtain control of such small plots for reassignment or rental in larger units.

Tribes should have preferential right to acquire allotments being sold by their Indian owners.

Codes should be adopted for clarifying and making secure tribal and individual rights and duties in the land.

If money for consolidation of land is not available to a tribe, the United States should advance funds.

Before the trust status of an allotment is removed, the area in question should be examined with respect to its control of water, access to other areas, and its affect or domination of other land. The pros and cons should be presented to the tribal council for a decision.

Opportunities for more employment need to be made available on almost every reservation. Economically justified work programs should include irrigation, reforestation, recreational sites and enterprises, and projects for attracting tourists. Money required for training people to qualify for jobs should be justified in part in terms of the salutary effects on young people rather than solely on short-run considerations of resource allocation and efficiency.

Land should be developed not only for the sake of those who intend to remain on the reservation, but also as a steppingstone for those who want to strike out for themselves in the larger world.

Untrained Indians should receive instruction that emphasizes the mental and the manual aptitudes in demand in modern industrial society.

Goals of the agricultural extension service for Indians should be designed to fit Indians' needs. The program must be closely integrated with each step in the planning of economic development.

Intensive managerial training in the conduct of farms and ranches, and adult education in government and business organization should be provided for those who are to operate the reservation resources. They should also be prepared to take over the management of tribal and individual business enterprises such as sawmills, fisheries, stores, and recreational facilities. This is especially important since substantial accomplishment may serve to retain on the reservation the more acculturated and better educated members of a tribe, who now frequently leave for lack of attractive opportunities at home.

Emphasis should be placed on training in the management of money, on the importance of saving, and on the relative value of commodities, as well as on ways of locating jobs and of adjusting to many aspects of city living.

Priority should be placed on finding employment for tribesmen near their reservations. Field employment offices (Employment Assistance) should be continued, with increased appropriations for training and job finding. Each office should keep abreast of current opportunities in the labor market and, in turn, should inform Indians about possible openings and the required qualifications. Records of the resulting successes and failures should be kept as a guide to future action.

Contracts which Indians make for developing their reservation resources should invariably include clauses granting preference for employment to Indians, and the courts should strictly enforce these provisions.

Arts and crafts should supply occasional or full-time work, and in some tribes, these can provide artists with pride and status. Where appropriate, creative skills, along with possible merchandising methods, should be taught in the schools to prevent these skills from dying out.

Recreational facilities and industrial employment opportunities on and near the reservation should be systematically developed. Such resources as timber, minerals, agricultural products, fisheries, etc., together with financial inducements and trained personnel, should be used to attract private industry.

Grants, long-term and short-term loans, and guarantees of loans should be made by the United States both to tribes and to qualified Indians needing capital. Only such help will render possible investigation, planning, and the adequate development of resources, recreational opportunities, and productive business enterprises. Provision for social overhead (roads, schools, conservation, etc.), while vital, is insufficient for implementing programs of economic development.

Most Indians have insufficient collateral to qualify for a loan under present lending standards. This collateral barrier must be lowered, and credit should be advanced on terms other than those of loan companies or banks. The Bureau should increase its activity in the lending field, and Indians should be brought into contact with other federal lending agencies. Where Indian tribes have wealth, they should supply capital to their members. Whether the money lent has been used profitably must be evaluated not only by repayment returns but in terms of Indian rehabilitation.

The Indians themselves have a responsibility for initiating programs. Moreover, tribesmen equipped with the necessary skills should assume the responsibility for management and operation of reservation projects.

In all functions Indians should be given increasing responsibility for their own affairs, but not far beyond their capacity. If they undertake burdens too great for their capability, their failure will delay orderly economic development and foster frustration.

Tribal governments often need to be enlarged to strengthen the administration of economic projects.

The economic functions of a tribe should be kept separate from its political activities and to this end should be lodged in federally licensed corporations. The directors of the enterprises should have staggered terms and need not all be members of the tribe. A primary purpose, however, should be to train Indians as soon as possible to administer their own undertakings. These bodies should establish stable policies for the development and management of resources and for the equitable sharing of the benefits among the members.

The United States has a bounden duty to assist tribes if Indians are to progress from their present poverty to a decent standard of living. But no plan, however well financed and expertly guided, will succeed unless its goals coincide with the values and aspirations of the tribesmen concerned and command the support of those who make and carry out decisions.

4

Bureau of Indian Affairs

I. INTRODUCTION

THE BUREAU OF INDIAN AFFAIRS occupies a unique position among federal bureaus. No other department in the government has sufficiently broad functions to fulfill federal obligations to Indians or to carry out the necessary administrative measures. Many federal agencies concentrate on a single aspect of government services or activities. The Area Redevelopment Administration deals only with economically depressed areas; the Office of Economic Opportunity deals primarily with poverty; and the Farmers Home Administration deals with farmers' homes. But the B. I. A. deals with all the diverse aspects of an Indian's life except (and this exception went into effect only in July, 1955) his medical services. Frequently one program may encompass several branches within the B. I. A. and, in addition, one or more divisions of the Interior Department, other federal departments, and independent agencies or private businesses; but it is almost always a co-operative venture with the B. I. A. Because of the scope of the B. I. A.'s activities, incongruities and inconsistencies in theory and in organization exist; and many proposals have been made to assign to other bureaus or agencies some of its programs. But, so far, no better pattern has been found for co-ordinating the many different facets of the services needed for Indians.

This chapter deals with the main purposes of the B. I. A., its present and future organization, and the need for keeping its services under one head, but turning over to Indians more responsibility for their own affairs.

II. PURPOSE

The B. I. A. has three main functions. The first is to protect the resources of the Indians. The second is to conduct administrative or housekeeping activities—building and maintaining roads, small irrigation structures, wells, stock tanks, and schools. and to look after miscellaneous services (such as some welfare) not provided by the states. These two operations have, for the most part, been carried out efficiently. But the third and most important, that of encouraging and helping the Indians to develop their own potentials, has not been accomplished. And in this failure the B. I. A. has kept company with many European nations who have failed to meet the need for developing promising individuals in undeveloped colonial nations so that eventually newly formed governments might have trained leaders to achieve stable political independence.

Although B. I. A. history and the obvious relative helplessness of the Indians both testify to federal overprotection of the Indians, administrators still lack enough knowledge to enable them to blueprint methods by which to develop political power within a group, much less within the entire race. However, certain goals can be stated. First, Indian leaders must become versed in the scientific tradition of the age in order to possess tools for adjusting the shape and pattern of their own indigenous society and to allow them to participate in the life of the dominant society, while retaining the best of their own culture.

Civil servants can neither make the adjustment for them nor supply a model, since government employees are seldom independent of politics and of the pressures of a bureacracy and, therefore are frequently prevented from carrying out free, independent and constructive plans. One example should suffice. When President Kennedy's Task Force on Indian Affairs recommended that the Muskogee and Anadarko area offices be consolidated and moved to Oklahoma City for the purpose of serving the Indians more efficiently, the Honorable Victor Wickersham opposed the move, declaring that it would curtail Indian services. As a token of local opposition, he published fifty-eight telegrams addressed to Secretary Udall. In this instance, substantial payrolls in both Muskogee and Anadarko would have been lost to Oklahoma City so the offices were not moved.[1] Such is the pressure that local residents can put on the B. I. A.

III. THE STRUCTURE OF THE B. I. A.

Indian affairs in 1775 were under the jurisdiction of the Continental Congress. When the United States Constitution was adopted, the states ceded to the federal government the power of regulation of commerce with Indian tribes, which by statute and judicial decision was broadened to the management of Indian affairs. The agency set up for the administration of Indian affairs was established in 1824 under the War Department. Later, in 1849, it was moved to the Department of the Interior, where it is today. The B. I. A. incorporates functions characteristic of the executive, the judicial, and the legislative.

The central office of the B. I. A. is in Washington and is directed by the commissioner of Indian affairs, who is charged with the final responsibility for fulfilling federal obligations to the Indians. As of October, 1965, he was assisted by a deputy commissioner, an associate commissioner, four assistant commissioners, two assistants to the commissioner, and an information officer. The deputy commissioner carries out appraisals and reviews fiscal operations, inspects central and field offices for possible weaknesses, and supervises three divisions, each under an assistant commissioner: (1) Administration (Branches of Budget and Finance, Plant Design and Construction, Plant Management, Personnel, and Property and Supply); (2) Community Services (Branches of Education, Employment Assistance, Law and Order, and Welfare); and (3) Economic Development (Branches of Agricultural Assistance, Credit, Forestry Manage-

---

[1] *Congressional Record,* August 2, 1961, pp. A6002–A6005.

ment, Industrial Development, Real Property Management, Real Estate Appraisal, and Roads).

The fourth assistant commissioner is liaison officer with the solicitor's office, the office of the secretary, the Bureau of the Budget, and the Congress on matters of legislation. The associate commissioner of the B. I. A. supervises management analysis, policy review, and tribal operations.

The two assistants to the commissioner act as advisers on many unrelated matters. The information officer conducts a public-information program, preparing publications, speeches, and press releases.

In the field there were 10 administrative area offices, about 60 Indian agencies and major field installations, such as boarding schools and irrigation projects, and 450 minor installations. Organization of the area offices at Aberdeen, Gallup, Phoenix, and Portland was patterned after that of the Washington office, with the men in charge known as area directors (instead of commissioners). In the large offices there were assistant area directors of administration, community services, and economic development, respectively.[2] The offices at Anadarko, Juneau, Minneapolis, Muskogee, and Sacramento had only one general assistant area director each. The commissioner, the area directors, and the agency superintendents are line officers for conducting B. I. A. operations. The staffs, both Washington and area, are consultants, planners, and advisers of the line executives.

The B. I. A. organization represents, in general, a chain of command recommended in 1954 by a survey team headed by Mr. W. R. Bimson.[3] The team's stated object was to devise an organization which, on the one hand, would give greater services to Indians and, on the other, would eliminate positions, thereby effecting substantial savings. Many practical suggestions were aimed at terminating various federal services to Indians or shifting them to other federal agencies as quickly as possible in order

[2] Release No. 544, Dept. of Interior, *Departmental Manual*, Part 130, Organization, B. I. A. (July 27, 1962).

[3] Report of Survey Team, B. I. A., W. R. Bimson, chairman, Jan 6, 1954 (mimeographed).

to reduce the size of the B. I. A. However, the blueprint dealt only with the administrative and the trustee aspects of the B. I. A., and its stress on the material aspects of the organization resulted in further emphasis of the B. I. A.'s bureaucratic characteristics.

The focusing of the 1954 report on ancillary housekeeping services left the superintendents without adequate authority or staff for independent action—a situation frustrating to large groups of Indians who were accustomed to looking to the superintendents for help. Indians not being given the responsibility needed for self-development withheld their support. Consequently this organization proved largely ineffectual.

Practices and Situations Creating Inefficiency

From 1954 through October 1965, many deterrents to across-the-board efficiency have become entrenched in B. I. A. structure and procedures. In addition, certain sins of federal omission have exerted stultifying or severely restrictive influences upon the Bureau's activities. The seemingly endless review of individual directives; the time lag—sometimes running into years—between sending opinions from the field to area offices and then getting pertinent decisions back to the field from the offices;[4] an increasingly burdensome mass of directives, statutes, charters, and the like, long in need of housecleaning; too many and too restrictive regulations; the usual maddening attention to red tape; practices discriminating (if only indirectly) against Indian employees; the several ways in which superintendents are by-passed or ignored; the relatively second-rate status of tribal employees by comparison with federal employees; the fact that tribes have no power over the selection of superintendents; the lack of legal help for Indians; the resentment sometimes aroused against the B. I. A. because of its being forced to carry out unpopular Congressional legislation—all these practices and circumstances have impeded and today continue to impede the achievement of real B. I. A. efficiency.

[4] Report to the Secretary of the Interior by the Task Force on Indian Affairs, July 10, 1961, p. 46.

The present pattern of detailed review of a single directive or order requires overstaffing, diverts attention from crucially affirmative action, and emphasizes irresponsibility, since no one person can be pin-pointed as responsible for an error. Such exaggerated time- and energy-consuming attention also plays havoc with morale, as it frustrates Indians and negates the creative talent of B. I. A. employees, who see their best ideas lost or efforts dissipated by the exhausting struggle to get their plans executed. For example, one impossible order in 1956 brought on by such repetitive review is the contract regarding the distribution of feed grains by the Commodity Credit Corporation.[5] The original aim of the memorandum was to help cattlemen in drought areas by supplying barley, corn, sorghum, or oats to their animals; the result, however, was an order impossible to execute. The exact route along which the memorandum of understanding travel cannot be traced here; but, because it originated in the Department of Agriculture and was used by B. I. A. field superintendents or extension agents, it must have passed over the desk of at least six people. Yet the final memorandum presented to the Indians for their signatures stated, among other things, that Indians who received grain should not feed it to more than twenty animal units (one animal unit being the equivalent of one horse or cow or five sheep or goats). The penalty for disobedience was a fine of the amount of the cost of the grain. One Indian said that the only way such a restricted use could be enforced on an open range where many Indians run cattle together would be to teach the cows to read and obey signs: "No more than twenty of John Smith's cows can eat the grains in his bin." The Indians laughed and signed the contract, knowing that it could never be enforced. Such regulations are made because no one person has the final authority to see that an order is practical in view of local customs, and such lack of responsibility breaks down respect for authority.

Legislation on Indian affairs not uncommonly has been en-

[5] "Memorandum of Understanding, Between the Department of Agriculture and the Department of the Interior," Disaster Relief Feed Grain Agreement, Oct. 16, 1956.

acted to affect only an individual tribe or to meet one particular situation. Over the years there has been accumulated a mass of 389 treaties, 5,000 statutes (many of which may have been repealed by implication), 2,000 federal court decisions, more than 500 attorney general opinions, numerous Department of the Interior and solicitor rulings, 95 tribal constitutions, and 74 tribal charters, besides a conglomeration of administrative regulations —confusing and often contradictory—collected in a manual which is so large that, if stacked volume upon volume, it would dwarf any person wanting to consult it. The delay and uncertainty caused by having to consult this unwieldly body of prescription and direction are costly and frustrating to all concerned, and management is so handicapped that many decisions are based on reinterpretation of laws or regulations instead of on the economic welfare or social needs of tribes.

Examples of long-outmoded statutes abound. Why continue laws governing Indian agents, when there have been none since 1908? Equally irrelevant are laws adopted to curb corruption in the Indian Service in the nineteenth century, laws which minutely specify the terms for employee appointments, compensation, and annual and sick leaves and prescribe housekeeping requirements and purchasing regulations. No legislation is needed beyond the later Civil Service enactments and the public contracts and budget and accounting acts, which apply throughout the government.

Still on the books is legislation prescribing the method of payment for wagon transportation, of prohibiting federal payments to bands of Indians at war with the United States or with the white citizens of any state or territory, and of authorizing the withholding of money due any tribe having a non-Indian captive until the captive has been surrendered to the lawful authorities of the United States. Such laws may be colorful, but they are wholly useless.

Too many regulations can paralyze the activity of sensitive and understanding superintendents, who may be penalized for violating outmoded directives instead of lauded for helping Indian groups to fashion their own advances. Hobbling regulations also prevent B. I. A. officers from meeting emergencies arising within tribes. A case in point occurred at Santo Domingo Pueblo. A member of that pueblo, who worked for the nearby Kaiser Gypsum plant and was president of the union there, was elected lieutenant governor of the Pueblo in 1961. The customs of the Pueblo forbid officials to work outside their village during their tenure of office; consequently, this member had to resign from his job. He needed a loan and he needed help in explaining tribal customs to Kaiser Gypsum so that officials would agree to rehire him when he finished his term of office. He applied to the B. I. A., unsuccessfully, for both. He had a new truck, which was only half paid for. His daughter had completed one semester in nursing at Regina Nursing School at St. Joseph's Hospital in Albuquerque (tuition $400), and another $400 was due for her last semester. The Bureau could, through the Relocation Division, have paid her transportation to and tuition at a Denver hospital; but regulations forbade giving her assistance for training if she stayed in Albuquerque. The daughter tried to get a loan from the B. I. A.'s credit division, but educational grants are budgeted, and no money remained in the fund, because—she was told—all applications are considered and loans granted only in the spring. Of course, no one could have determined in the spring of 1961 that this particular Santo Domingo Indian would be chosen lieutenant governor at Christmastime. The Bureau should not be so immobilized by restrictive procedures that it cannot help a deserving Indian and his family faced with real need.

Laws and regulations make some administrative procedures more expensive. Take, for example, the requirement that technicians and lawyers under tribal contracts must itemize the cost of each meal eaten while on tribal business, listing the tips separately, and must state the subject and the cost of every long-distance telephone call. Each voucher is first submitted to the tribe, which sends it to the area office for approval, where, upon favorable action, it goes to a field solicitor, who, if he agrees, shunts it to the superintendent, who, if he approves, returns it to the tribe for payment. And despite all this elaborate procedure the amount involved may be no more than the expense of one telephone call or a trip costing less than $25.

Some excessive and hampering regulations are promulgated by B. I. A. personnel because of their belief that some tribes do not efficiently use their money from gas, oil, uranium, or leased land. On the other hand, Indians often feel that the Bureau is not trying to help them but is attempting to force unwanted change upon them.

Red tape often frustrates even the most dedicated Civil Service employees, who may be appalled both by the intricacies and complications they meet in the Bureau and by their inability to handle crises effectively, so that they lose the desire for accomplishment. When the majority of employees in a service feel this way, the organization becomes static.

Hampering regulations and excessive red tape exist in many federal agencies other than the B. I. A., where a large number of new functions have been incorporated into an organizational pattern designed for the less complicated society of a past generation.

Senator Abraham Ribicoff, former secretary of the Department of Health, Education, and Welfare, said in a speech reported October 20, 1965, in the *Washington Star,* that the "sorry disarray" of government handling of major national problems demands a basic overhaul of executive machinery.

The purpose of amending, deleting, or changing laws and regulations concerning the Indians should be to allow them to make their own decisions over a wider range of policies and activities than is now possible, for Indians, too, have their frustrations. When tribal counselors work alongside Bureau employees, the former often are assigned to shacks. If individual Indians work side by side with white government employees, the Indians sometimes are given offices that provide the contrast necessary to assure the white man his status symbol. These frustrating practices cause friction between B. I. A. employees and Indians. Often an Indian politician hesitates to live in a modern, well-furnished house with indoor plumbing or to possess other facilities associated with the white status symbols lest his fellow tribesmen's dislike of government descend on him or lest the B. I. A., reputation for rigidity be ascribed to his own organization.

Proposals Regarding Indian Services

In 1961 the Kennedy Task Force questioned whether the organization of the B. I. A. was a suitable instrument for effectuating policy. Proposals to improve the administration of Indian affairs have been many and varied: abolish the B. I. A. entirely and summarily, with no substitute; shift all B. I. A. work to the Department of Health, Education, and Welfare; spread it among other federal departments—Interior; Agriculture; Health, Education, and Welfare; and Commerce; create an authority like the Tennessee Valley Authority to fix policies executed by a general manager; or transfer complete responsibility to the states. Sometimes this last proposal is accompanied by a recommendation to compensate the state and its subdivisions for the cost of taking over Indian services. Each state would then have its own B. I. A.

The first Hoover Commission[6] recommended that the B. I. A be transferred to the (then under consideration) Department of Health, Education, and Welfare. Such a transfer would require federal Social Security to change its regulations. For example, Social Security does not make direct payment to beneficiaries (the aged, blind, or dependent children), which the Bureau has frequently found necessary. Federal money is usually allocated to the state, and the state makes regulations for payments. Also, the regulations under which many Health, Education, and Welfare agencies are administered are not sufficiently flexible for particular Indian cases, since they are designed to fit the needs of a general population. For example, some reservation Indians do not have birth certificates, which are needed by the welfare agency before it can process the case. Many social workers are

6 "Report of the Committee on Indian Affairs to the Commission on Organization of the Executive Branch of the Government," Oct., 1948, pp. 164–69.

baffled by the Navaho idea that the woman is head of the household. The matriarchal unit is not easily summarized on the printed forms provided for families by social security and the employees cannot easily grasp the implications flowing from the relationships within such a family. New regulations meeting Indian needs and new laws giving the Department of Health, Education, and Welfare the authority now held by the B. I. A. would be needed if the B. I. A. were to be transferred to this department. The end result would probably be a duplicate of the present B. I. A.

The B. I. A. constructs or contracts for the building of reservation roads, but the location and design must be approved by the Bureau of Public Roads (Department of Commerce). To transfer the road-building function to the Bureau of Public Roads without a staff of practical engineers to supervise road building would be a mistake and would necessitate a whole new division in the Bureau of Public Roads.

The Forest Service (Department of Agriculture) is admirably organized to manage its own forests, but is not equipped—as the B. I. A. is—to educate the Indians in forest management or in the use of their own timber by developing mills and manufacturing plants.

If the Indian grazing lands were to be handled by the Bureau of Land Management, which leases public domain, the Indians would be in sharp competition with large livestock owners who lease the public domain almost exclusively. And the Indians would be under threat of losing their lands, since there is always the drive to force the United States to turn over such "public" lands to the states. The Bureau of Reclamation tried to handle Indian irrigation projects, but found most Indian-owned dams or other irrigation structures too small for its efficient operation and so failed in the effort.

The proposal to create an authority like the Tennessee Valley Authority in place of the B. I. A. would involve new legislation and would increase centralization of authority. It is hard to see how the Indians could benefit from such a change.

Fragmenting B. I. A. budget and administration among many federal bureaus would increase the number of personnel dealing with Indian problems, would involve many new legal problems, would duplicate fact-finding effort and reduce flexibility; but, most important of all, it would defeat efforts at integrated planning for total Indian well-being. The Indians, in turn, would lose the services of experienced, dedicated workers now in the Bureau and would be faced with additional confusion as they tried to work with the many different federal agencies.

After all proposals are examined, the conviction remains that the simplest method of administering services for Indians and carrying out long-term plans is to retain the B. I. A. for the present. It has the decided advantage of being already in the field; it needs only revision and redirection to accomplish the purposes which the present-day situation of the Indian demands. Constant review is necessary, however; and whenever a function can be carried out more effectively by a tribal, state, private, or federal agency other than the B. I. A., the function should be delegated to that agency—but only after consent by the Indians. To avoid conflicts of policy and objectives as well as to eliminate costly duplication of effort, the B. I. A. should see that the delegated work is co-ordinated, should make available to the agency the B. I. A.'s supporting service, and should establish minimum standards of performance.

To help with some of the problems, an Indian advisory board could be established by law to work in conjunction with the Department of the Interior, its members to have a tenure longer than that of political appointees. This board could be utilized to evaluate problems in the light of our entire society and Indian welfare.

Some of the criticism of the Bureau is unfair in that it arises from dislike of Congressional legislation, which B. I. A. is forced to carry out. The termination laws were a prime example (see Chapter Seven). Criticism also arises because of inadequate funds for important projects or excess funds for unimportant work and because of mistakes by the government in general, within or outside the Bureau. Such criticism is inevitable when only a few people understand complicated government operations.

A model for a successful working relationship between the B. I. A. and technical agencies exists today within the Department of the Interior. The B. I. A. has no petroleum engineers or geologists and so uses the specialists in the United States Geological Survey. Survey engineers set the size of Indian units of mineral land which should be offered for lease or sale, fix the dimensions of drilling units, and pass on all utilization agreements by which the owners of tracts too small for well-drilling pool their land and share the income if mineral is discovered. The engineers also collect and keep records and distribute royalties to qualified owners. No sale of Indian gas and oil or solid minerals can be made unless the United States Geological Survey approves the price and the condition of the sale, but administration remains in the B. I. A. Similar working agreements have been set up between the Bureau and other government agencies equipped to supply specialists and facilities that the B. I. A. lacks.

IV. *Possible Measures for Improving B. I. A. Services*

Policy Making

The officials who alone really know the Indians whom B. I. A. serves, who alone understand both the Indians' problems and the ways in which they would like to resolve those problems, are the very officials who have their hands tied by existing B. I. A. procedures and practices. In far too many ways superintendents are bypassed in favor of area directors—by the Indians, who take important problems to the director since he (not the superintendent) makes decisions of policy, and by Washington officials who deal with the director and his staff instead of the superintendent. Such practices deprive the superintendents of both authority and the Indians' respect and make the recruiting of good men for the position of superintendent difficult. The official who knows all facets of a local situation—the superintendent—should possess enough authority to handle local problems.

Organizational form is important in accomplishing required tasks; but no pattern, however logical it looks on paper, can substitute for individual wisdom and dedication on the part of the human beings involved. This Commission's experience has confirmed that most personnel in the B. I. A. are deeply interested in the Indians and their future. Unfortunately, as is often true in bureaucracies, the B. I. A. has tended to develop a view that the Bureau and the Indians have opposing interests. Examples exist of dedicated agents being asked whose side they are on— the Bureau's or the Indians'. Such an attitude is completely destructive to the Bureau's, the nation's, and the Indians' goal. For these reasons no system can take the place of a skillful, understanding, courageous secretary of the interior and a wise commissioner of Indian affairs, assisted by competent personnel, dedicated to show Indians that they themselves are the key to their own advancement—educationally, socially, politically, materially, and spiritually; and that they can use the key only by assuming responsibility, perhaps a little ahead of what they conceive to be their own immediate abilities.

State-Tribal Relationships

Indians and state governments are becoming mutually dependent. Indians must work closely with states, for their lives can be drastically affected, for good or ill, by state policies and programs. State legislatures may pass—and have passed—laws directly affecting Indian lives.

Aside from legal matters (discussed in Chapter Two), states are constantly promulgating new regulations affecting Indian governments. Take taxes, for example. New Mexico Indians pay four different state taxes on oil, gas, uranium, and other mineral royalties derived from tribal trust property—severance, conservation, ad valorem, and special school taxes. Moreover, New Mexico is considering levying a severance tax on timber. Arizona and Utah are considering taxes of the kinds New Mexico has imposed. So far, Colorado imposes no taxes on tribal trust property.

In general, the production of oil, gas, and other minerals from allotted lands (other than of the Osages and the Five Civilized Tribes, which are governed by other laws) is taxable under state law as is such production on other lands; and the same holds true regarding mineral output and Indian rentals, royalties, and bonuses from executive order reservations.

Also, states have a moral responsibility toward Indians as citizens with the same rights as other citizens—rights to education, welfare, health, social security, and sanitation, and to the use of state employment offices and the application of the findings of industrial development commissions. States may have services which tribal governments lack, such as special courts and rehabilitation centers for juvenile delinquents.

In some instances, the tribes and the federal government may have to compensate a state if the transfer of services is to be satisfactory. The solicitor of the Department of the Interior has ruled that if states choose, under Public Law 280 (see Chapter Seven), they can extend their law by stages into Indian domain; but even such gradual action may produce bad results. If a state can itself pick the areas over which to assume jurisdiction, the danger exists that the areas chosen will be the profitable ones, with the costly ones being disregarded. The Kennedy Task Force found that when the United States has relinquished its law-and-order services after the statute's enactment, the result "has often been inferior protection of life and property, denial of civil rights and toleration of lawlessness."

The Kennedy Task Force recommended—and the B. I. A. has the authority to effect—piecemeal transfer of jurisdiction to states, upon a negotiated agreement between any tribe desiring such a move, the United States, and the state concerned.[7] At the present time, however, such action is not immediately practical. Two reasons are paramount: first, such a transfer demands that the state legislature pass laws to provide for absorbing the reservation into the state organization; and, second, many Indian

[7] Report to the Secretary of the Interior by the Task Force on Indian Affairs, July 10, 1961, pp. 27–33.

leaders strongly object to shifting jurisdiction to states unless tribal consent is first obtained and the State stands ready to provide adequate services.

For some thirty or forty years the federal government has tried without success to transfer Indian services to states, sometimes even offering compensation. When California, Nevada, and Wisconsin were faced with the issue, their legislatures memorialized Congress to continue federal control.[8] The legislatures of New Mexico, Arizona, North Dakota, and Montana— instead of being ready to include Indians within their states' administrative framework—requested additional federal aid for Indians.[9]

Transfer of Responsibility to Indians

A transfer of responsibility from B. I. A. to tribal govern-

[8] State of California *Senate Joint Resolution No. 4* memorializing Congress and the President of the United States to refrain from terminating federal control and protection of Indian reservations, adopted in the Assembly, March 31, 1954, and in the Senate, April, 1954; *Progress Report to the Legislature by the Senate Interim Committee on California Indian Affairs (Sen. Resolution No. 115)*, Senate of the State of California (1955), 19.

Senate Joint Resolution No. 13, State of Nevada, March 10, 1955, memorializing the Congress of the United States and the Congressional delegation from the State of Nevada to forbear any action leading to the termination of the federal trusteeship over American Indian wards and properties held in trust for American Indians, passed by the 1955 session of the Nevada Legislature.

Senate Joint Resolution No. 79, State of Wisconsin, memorializing the Congress of the United States to repeal the law providing for termination of federal supervision over the property and members of the Menominee Indian Tribe of Wisconsin, *Congressional Record*, July 28, 1959, pp. 13128–129.

[9] *House Joint Memorials Nos. 28, 41, 42, and 44*, State of New Mexico, asking the Congress of the United States to increase federal payments for Indian education and health facilities in New Mexico, to increase the revolving fund for economic development, and to assist Indians in solving their economic problems, *Congressional Record*, March 27, 1961, pp. 4541–42.

House Memorial No. 2, State of Arizona, memorializing the Congress of the United States to undertake a survey of the human and natural resources of the Papago Indian Reservation, *Congressional Record*, Feb. 28, 1961, p. 2563.

House Concurrent Resolution V, 34th Legislative Assembly of North Dakota, *Federal Indian Policy*, Hearings Before the Subcommittee on Indian Affairs of the Committee on Interior and Insular Affairs, 85 Cong., 1 sess., March 27, May 13 and 16, June 17, July 1 and 22, 1957, p. 11.

Montana House Joint Memorials Nos. 14 and 6, 35th Legislative Assembly of the State of Montana (1957), *Federal Indian Policy*, as cited above.

ments would be based on the proposition that the Bureau exists for the purpose of enhancing and protecting the natural and fundamental rights of Indians. Indians own the right to grow, to appraise their abilities, and to develop and apply those abilities through trial and error, and by assuming the responsibility for their errors without suffering unreasonable punishment.

When the secretary finds tribes sufficiently competent, he should give them the supervision of regular Civil Service Bureau employees, which existing law actually grants them.[10] Besides this law, broad legislation should be enacted (with the tribe's consent) to authorize delegation of functions, exempt the United States from responsibility for Indian mistakes, and allow for surrender or return of functions to the United States if the secretary and the tribe wish.

When an Indian is able to carry out a function of government at a tribal level, he should be compensated for the work; and money appropriated for B. I. A. administration should be given directly to the tribal official. Yearly audits should be made of the books of each tribe by a certified public accountant. A means should be found of giving tribal employees tenure, security, and economic benefits comparable to those enjoyed by federal employees. Otherwise, tribes may find it increasingly difficult to secure trained and efficient employees. Almost all public servants have fringe benefits, life insurance, health, retirement, etc., which most tribes cannot match. One method of removing existing inequities would be to make tribal employees federal employees, the tribe to reimburse the government for full cost but to retain the right to supervise the employees.

Tribal officials often need to be trained in bookkeeping, and they should be given the experience of presenting their own requests for money to the Bureau of the Budget. The trust in Indian land should not be removed until Indians have learned how to handle business matters and to understand the value of money.

10 25 U.S. Code Annotated, sec. 48; Cohen, *Handbook of Federal Indian Law,* 149–50; *Federal Indian Law,* 452–54.

Certainly Indians should have the right to approve or disapprove potential superintendents before final appointment. The B. I. A. should select the man; then after a reasonable period the Indians should approve or disapprove the choice. Nothing derogatory should attach to a man's reputation if he is not selected. After Indians have had some experience in this field, they will learn what to look for and what to expect. Tribal governments should have the power to tell a superintendent to leave any time they believe he has completed his usefulness.

Flexibility and courage would be required by both federal administrators and Indians in this new administrative venture; flexibility, because the danger of applying a nationwide pattern to specific groups could lead either to underassumption or overassumption of responsibility by a tribe, which would damage the program; courage, because in trying to avoid mistakes and criticism, the tendency of the tribes would be to limit projects to those apparently certain to succeed.

Legal Representation

In states where reservations or allotted Indian lands exist, 25 U.S.C.A., Sec. 175, provides that the United States district attorney shall represent individual Indians in suits at law and in equity. However, it has been determined that this statute does not require the United States attorney to represent the tribe.

Legal aid is continually needed by Indians for help with government contracts, with commercial firms, with special problems of land and water tenure, and in daily business dealings. Counsel is more necessary today than ever before. Lawyers should be made available and readily accessible either by the B. I. A. to tribes (as they were before their transfer to the Office of the Solicitor for the Department of the Interior) or by the Office of Economic Opportunity.

Indian tribes eligible for grants from the Office of Economic Opportunity because of poverty might obtain legal counsel through this office's funds. Such lawyers would have the advantage of being independent of federal agencies. The difficulty, of course, would be finding attorneys who understand Indian rights and law.

New Authority

Finally, the secretary of the interior needs broader powers. At the present time there is considerable flexibility in administration in some areas. Through agreements the B. I. A. can draw on skills in other sections of the government; and under the Johnson-O'Malley Act of 1934, as amended (48 Stat. 596), the secretary of the interior may make contracts with federal, state, and private agencies for the education, medical care, agricultural assistance, and social welfare of Indians. The act is not broad enough to allow the secretary to make contracts for the performance by non-government personnel of some services, such as law enforcement. Therefore, the present Johnson-O'Malley Act should be amended or a new law passed.

V. RECOMMENDATIONS

The primary function of the Bureau should be an affirmative one: always to counsel and assist the Indian, not to control or regiment him.

Administration in the Bureau and the Department of the Interior should be simplified, and their legislation and regulations overhauled for greater efficiency. Outdated legislation should be repealed.

The work of the federal government in carrying out its responsibilities to the Indian people should, for the present, be continued under the Bureau of Indian Affairs and the Department of the Interior.

Policy matters of B. I. A. should be transferred from area offices to agencies, with superintendents given authority to make local decisions.

In short, the Bureau's aim should be to help the Indians become politically active citizens and to let them conduct their own affairs without supervision as soon as possible. Accordingly, it should encourage their assumption of responsibilities for different functions on a gradual but systematic basis. Tribal land

and resources should remain under the federal trust until the Indians are able to hold and manage their property and choose freedom from the trust.

Statutes, regulations, and procedures should be altered to facilitate the tribes' hiring their own technicians and counselors from universities, private professional groups, or other organizations, without the delay, the hampering restrictions, and the unnecessary supervision now encountered. If such obligation requires an amendment to the Johnson-O'Malley Law, it should be obtained.

Similarly, statutes and rules should be amended, and tribal constitutions and corporate charters should be revised to permit Indians to make their own decisions over a greater range of subjects than is now allowed.

Under the Indian Reorganization Act of 1934 the secretary of the interior is required to inform tribes falling under the law, of the appropriations he will request for their projects before he submits estimates to the Bureau of the Budget. This principle of prior tribal review, now frequently ignored by the Bureau, should be enforced and extended to all tribes.

The power of the secretary of the interior to supervise the actions of tribes and of their business corporations should be so reduced as to allow the tribes freedom to operate to the full extent of their ability. The United States, however, should not be liable for any mistakes that may ensue.

Tribes which cannot effectively govern in every department or adequately enforce the law, and yet desire to continue their governments, should agree to transfer the functions in question by degrees to the states, under proper safeguards.

Whenever a function can be carried out more effectively by an agency other than the Bureau of Indian Affairs, it should be delegated to that agency (whether federal, tribal, state, or private), but only after discussion with the Indians concerned. To avoid conflicts of policy and objectives as well as to eliminate costly duplication of effort, the Bureau of Indian Affairs should see that the delegated work is co-ordinated and should make available to the agency its supporting service and establish minimum standards of performance.

The Bureau's work, however, should be supplemented by a board of distinguished citizens, appointed by the President and advisory to the secretary to look at the Indian people as part of the totality of American life. The board should recommend policies tending to assure the Indians equality of opportunity in the dominant society and to spur them to rise to these opportunities. It should also assess programs from the standpoint of justice, and practicability, and their long-range effect. The members should serve staggered terms, be provided with an adequate staff, meet frequently, and report from time to time through the secretary to the President and the nation.

5

Education

I. Introduction

THE MAJORITY of Indian pupils today are either above the general age level for their respective classes or are below academic norms, and they drop out of school more frequently than do their non-Indian classmates. The problem is to find the method of teaching and the kind of school environment most conducive to the progress of the non-English-speaking Indian.

This chapter deals with some of the steps urgently needed to raise the present low levels of educational achievement among Indian children and to prepare them to earn a living in the dominant culture without having to reject their ancestral heritage. The chapter also considers specific deviations from the present general educational program—one apparently accomplishing what the general system does not and one encompassing aspects of both teaching and administration.

First of all, the Indian pupil needing additional help must be identified. Next, determination must be made both of the age at which he should commence school and of the curriculum best suited to his needs. Then there must be sought out and adopted the type of teacher training most calculated to enable teachers to cross cultural barriers and assist Indian children to think and to speak in English. Clarence Wesley, chairman of the San Carlos Apache tribe, says:

> . . . I suspect our schools are not beginning to tackle adequately the basic difficulties of language . . . . I suspect that this failure to

comprehend on the part of the Indian child accounts in large measure for the lessening of interest and enthusiasm for school which I am told begins for Indian children along about the fifth grade.[1]

II. Studies About the Education of Indians

Educators who point out that the Indian pupils are below grade in school work and overage for their particular class are apt to attribute this retardation to pupils' lack of preparation, inadequate motivation, low economic status, irregular attendance, unqualified teachers, disturbed and inharmonious classrooms, and inability to grasp English. Comprehending the meaning and significance of words in relation to the culture is an important, if not the overriding, difficulty Indian students have in school. A direct positive correlation exists below the level of an Indian's scores (tests designed for the general public-school population) and his experience and familiarity with the language and values of the white culture. For example, an Indian pupil receiving relatively high test scores usually speaks English as a pre-school language, and comes from a family with a relatively high educational level.

Available evidence supports the view that Indian students have about the same mental equipment as other American children. Under certain circumstances even the most gifted of any race may rank low in I. Q. tests, which reflect "normal" exposure to books, English conversation, and even material gadgets, none of which are common in underprivileged homes, Indian or not. As with other races, the I. Q. of an Indian student may be high, low, average, or simply not known. Because of his difficulty with English he rarely reaps real profit from the use of textbooks and other materials oriented toward middle-class American life. Hence, academic tests cannot be considered absolute reflections of an Indian pupil's native intelligence. Growing evidence indicates that the individual's I. Q. is not permanently fixed, but that

[1] Clarence Wesley, "Indian Education," *Journal of American Indian Education,* Vol. I, No. 1 (June 1961) , 4.

factors like emotional upsets and poor prenatal or postnatal nutrition may adversely affect the functioning of the cerebrum.[2]

Although educational tests are undoubtedly limited in evaluating children as people, nevertheless the records of low test scores with marked deficiencies in English and mathematics and high dropout rates among Indian children are supported by practically all studies. These findings were emphasized in a report made by Coombs, *et al,* which included 8,000 children, half Indian, half non-Indian, in federal and public schools.[3] *The Navajo Yearbook* reveals that a substantial percentage of pupils were one or two years retarded.[4] Off-reservation Navaho pupils living in dormitories,[5] as well as San Carlos Apache students,[6] have averages below the national norm.

Recent testing in the schools attended by the youth of Northern Cheyenne Reservation showed that 40 per cent of the students were seriously behind in reading. Of the 235 elementary pupils at the B. I. A. school in Busby, 41 per cent suffered a lag of two years or more in reading skills. At the St. Labre Mission School, 52 per cent needed remedial work in reading. Over 40 per cent of the elementary pupils at the Lame Deer public school showed a reading deficiency of two years or more. The high-school situation is even more serious.[7]

Oregon's Klamath Indian pupils have attended public schools since 1928, but have made a dismal record. Of the 373 Klamath pupils in grades one through twelve during 1955–56, 79 either failed, dropped out of school, were withdrawn, or were trans-

[2] Hilda Knoblock and Benjamin Pasamanick, "Some Thoughts on the Inheritance of Intelligence," presented at the 37th Annual Meeting of the American Ortho-Psychiatric Association, Chicago, Feb. 25–27, 1960 (mimeographed).

[3] L. Madison Coombs, Ralph E. Kron, E. Gordon Collister, and Kenneth E. Anderson, *The Indian Child Goes to School* (U.S. Dept of Interior, B. I. A., Haskell Press, Lawrence, Kan., 1958) 6, 7.

[4] Report VII (1958), 26, 27.

[5] Report to the Senate Appropriations Committee on the Navajo Bordertown Program by the Commissioner of Indian Affairs, Feb., 1965, pp. 47–53.

[6] Edward A. Parmee, "Family and Community Influences on the Attitudes of San Carlos Apache Teen-Agers Towards Education and Their Personal Futures," M.A. thesis, University of Arizona, 1965.

[7] News letter of the Association on American Indian Affairs, Inc., New York, N. Y., No. 61 (December, 1965), 1.

ferred. Of the 294 who passed, one-fifth were given social promotions only, indicating unsatisfactory work. Only 9 graduated
from high school—the largest graduating class in years, and only
1 of the 9 went on to an institution of higher learning.[8] Apparently twenty-seven years is not enough time in which to bring
Indian children up to the public school norms where the curricula are designed for the white-collar stratum of society.

III. The Indian Pupil and His Needs

The B. I. A. school census rolls enumerated 129,928 young
people who were potential pupils in the fiscal year 1964. This
count was exclusive of students in public schools where the federal government no longer pays for Indian tuition and the pupils'
names have been dropped from the Bureau's school census rolls.
The states, exclusive of Alaska, having assumed full responsibility for Indian education are California, Idaho, Michigan, Minnesota, Nebraska, Oregon (except for the Warm Springs Agency),
Texas, Washington, and Wisconsin. Indian children in schools
numbered 129,928 in the fiscal year 1964. Fifty-four per cent of
these students, ages six to eighteen, were in state schools. The
others, for the most part, attended federal schools. A break-down
of the 46 per cent for whom the Bureau may be responsible
showed that 10 per cent were in day school; 19 per cent were in
boarding school; and 6 per cent were in Mission schools; whereas
8 per cent of children were not enrolled in school because of lack
of facilities; and there was no information on 3 per cent of the
students.[9]

Many Indian students are in the upper economic brackets,
and often use the English language fluently. Some Indian parents have professional degrees and are successful in government
and industry; others with a meager education live in grim poverty in communities where English is neither spoken nor liked.

[8] "Data on Termination of Federal Supervision over the Klamath Indian Reservation," compiled by A. Harvey Wright, Oregon State Department of Education
(1956 mimeographed), 7–8.

[9] *Statistics Concerning Indian Education, Fiscal Year 1964*, U.S. Dept of Interior,
B. I. A., Branch of Education (Lawrence, Kan., Haskell Press), Table 1.

Because of the wide variation in home environments, Indian students should be divided into (1) those who have substituted the white culture for their Indian heritage and whose families can afford to give them the advantages enjoyed by their white classmates and who, therefore, can profit from public schooling; (2) those who are partially assimilated; and (3) those who either do not understand or speak English or use it only haltingly, and whose pre-school education has been mainly in the ways of an alien culture. Children in both the latter groups (2 and 3), need additional training before they are ready for the usual public school curricula.

Students Who Profit From Public Schooling

The Indian child who speaks English at home and shares in the values and customs of a technological society grasps school subjects as readily as his white classmates. If the educational level of his parents is such that he begins school without handicaps, then obviously the public school is his best choice.

Students Who Need Special Help and Their Problems

Indians reared in their own culture may not be ready for public school because they may hold a set of values, standards, and a method of reasoning entirely different from those on which the white educational system was founded. Clyde Kluckhohn,[10] Dorothea Leighton, Elizabeth R. Leighton,[11] and others showed that the pattern of Navaho thought and expression was totally unlike that of the European.

The relation between the written and spoken word often eludes a youngster since he may have been brought up without any realization that oral sounds have counterparts in symbols on a piece of paper. He may have never seen books, magazines,

10 Clyde Kluckhohn and Dorothea Leighton, *The Navaho* (Cambridge, Harvard University Press, 1956), 182–215, 246; Robert W. Young and William Morgan, *The Navajo Language* (Education Division, U. S. Indian Service, 1943), 40.

11 Elizabeth Roby Leighton, "The Nature of Cultural Factors Affecting the Success or Failure of Navajo College Students," Ph.D. dissertation, University of Arizona, 1964 (microfilm).

musical scores, or written numbers before he entered the class-room. Under these conditions, teaching him English is more complicated than teaching a French or German child who understands such relationships. Because the curriculum in the public school is based on the premise that children can speak and understand English, the reservation Indian pupil needs to learn the significance and meaning of English words as they relate to cultural concepts.

Comprehending the tenses is another problem, since the Indian's idea of time is that of something flowing through everything and, like the air, existing in abundance. The Indian does not easily envisage time broken into past, present, and future.[12] Differences in grammar and inflection are also hard for the Indian child to manage. Native grammatical categories do not, as a rule, correspond to those in English.[13] Instead of the characteristic remark of a white man, "That's for sure," the Indian paraphrasing is, "That's for sure, maybe."[14] These attitudes explain in part why an Indian is perplexed by sentences in which a predicate is either affirmed or denied.

Another fundamental difference lies in the two attitudes towards nature. The white man believes that he can, through close observation, by collecting data, and by eliminating mistakes, command nature and bend it to his will. The Indian has loved nature, wanted to know and live with it, and has as often appealed to natural forces through dance and ceremony. He focuses his attention on phenomena related to his tradition and sees in them implications strange to advanced scientific thinking.

If, as the Indian believes, nature can be propitiated by magic, he is left with a recognition of his limitations and acquiescence before the inexorable force of nature ("My environment is stronger than I").[15] Answers given in terms of magic often pre-

[12] Communication from Mrs. Howarth, University of New Mexico Department of Education, Albuquerque, N.M., Jan. 26, 1962.

[13] *The Navajo Yearbook, 1951–1961*, Report VII (1958), 430–510.

[14] *Rev. Father Leon Levasseur*, O.M.I., "Some Differences Between Canada's Indians and Her More Recent Settlers" (ed. by Harriet Rouillard), (Toronto, Indian Eskimo Association, reprint of *Cultural Encounter*).

[15] *Ibid.*

clude the building of confidence in the individual. If the Indian feels that he is the victim of external forces, he can never be sure about the future and so may come to ask: "Is any job really finished when one lives with nature? Are there not things that one must leave to nature herself? Why finish a house, when one might have to move in search of food? Why calculate accurately the distance from one place to another, when a storm may delay a trip or force an extra night's camping?"[16]

The Indian over the centuries has learned by trial and error many practical lessons, such as how to construct irrigation ditches and domesticate corn. But he has not amplified trial and error into scientific methodology and he may still explain daily occurrences by "magic." This difference in philosophy needs to be explained objectively, not as something "right" or "logical," with the implication that Indian culture is "wrong" or "illogical."

Different behavior patterns of the two cultures further complicate the problem. The Indian child, taught to be passive, may have been punished at home for aggressive behavior, whereas in the classroom self-assertion may be regarded as desirable. An Indian child probably suffers from a feeling of guilt if he tries to outdo his classmates, yet his public school teachers expect him to compete and, if possible, to excel.

For the non-acculturated Indian the public school system has other drawbacks, illustrated by the New Mexico and Navaho public schools located on Indian land. In spite of the fact that almost the entire enrollment in Santo Domingo is Indian, no Indians are on the county school board, which determines policy. The federal government pays practically all expenses for educating the Indians; through Congress it supplies money for construction, for maintenance, and for staffing. The school actually costs the county nothing. Instead, it supplies employment for some of the county's citizens.

Among the strong arguments in favor of Indians attending public schools was the advantage of a mixed enrollment, but there are practically no white children attending the Santo Do-

16 *Ibid.*

mingo school. The same handicap applies to public schools on the Navaho Reservation. Teaching in these public schools is in the hands of people who often have no training in cultural differences and who may not understand Indian problems. Both schools are good examples of pitfalls resulting from placing Indians in public schools without due regard to meeting problems of the local reservation population.

The harm done to the Indian child by trying to force him into an alien pattern is not always obvious. Because of cultural differences in explaining day-to-day occurrences, the Indian pupil's concepts may be such that he cannot understand what his teacher is trying to explain. Yet his development of imitative behavior may be so good and his quick, docile agreement so deceiving that his confusion is entirely hidden from his teacher and his classmates until he attempts to pass a written English test.

To assess his place in modern society, the Indian child must understand his own heritage. For this he needs books or other materials that stress tribal values, history, and culture. These materials should be selected to demonstrate the Indians' rich inheritance.

The Indian possesses important concepts; for example, a religious appreciation of nature, which imparts strength and teaches the worshiper how to overcome tensions so prevalent in the modern age;[17] a deep respect for individual differences, in contrast to our own struggle for homogeneity;[18] and an emphasis on conservation. Wisconsin's Menominee Indians still practice their ancient custom of planting a tree for each one cut. Ceremonial occasions are frequently marked by tree planting.[19]

In addition, recent studies in ethnoscience show other Indian conceptual contributions. Among them are the Ojibwa's measurement of space and time,[20] the Iroquois' theory of dreams, which anticipated essential features of Freud's dream theory by

[17] Communication from Diego Abeita, Isleta Pueblo, N.M., Jan., 1962.
[18] Communication from Abeita, 1950.
[19] Memorandum No. 67 to the Commission on the Rights, Liberties, and Responsibilities of the American Indian (March 26, 1959).
[20] Hallowell, *Culture and Experience.*

at least three hundred years,[21] and the study of the calendric system and arithmetic of the Maya, who independently invented a positional notation and the concept of zero.[22] Accomplishments, however, have been scattered. A systematic attitude toward factual information existed in the minds of only a few.

IV. CURRICULA

There are no safe criteria or standards on which to base judgments of the curriculum most helpful in assisting Indian pupils to adjust to the dominant culture. The B. I. A. educational policy has, except for unfinished studies made during 1938–45, and the Navaho accelerated program (geared to educate teenagers who had no schooling during World War II), followed the educational practices of the Anglo culture.

Hence, there is no body of data based on research and specifically compiled for Indian classrooms. The problem of Indian education, therefore, includes all the difficulties which are encountered in the dominant culture, plus an intangible factor of the dissimilarity between two sets of values—one without a written language or alphabet where knowledge was largely transmitted person-to-person, and the other with an elaborate system of communication.

This lack of research on which to assess the Indian's potential or to elucidate his singular needs makes it difficult to evolve plans for his education. Research is needed. In the meantime practices and policies found useful among disadvantaged groups should be tried systematically in federal schools. Francis Keppel, in October, 1964, said:

> At the very time that we have discovered that children can learn more and much earlier than we have heretofore believed possible is the companion awareness that if we would succeed in the edu-

21 A. F. C. Wallace, "Dreams and the Wishes of the Soul: A Type of Psycho-Analytic Theory Among the Seventeenth-Century Iroquois," *American Anthropologist*, Vol. LX (April, 1958), 234–48.

22 Sylvanus G. Morley, *The Ancient Maya* (Stanford, Calif., Stanford University Press, 1946); Linton Satterthwaite, *Concepts and Structures of Maya Calendrical Arithmetics* (Philadelphia, University Museum and Philadelphia Anthropological Society, 1947).

cation of the disadvantaged children, we had best start with them earlier than we have in the past.[23]

Indian children might profit from commencing nursery school or kindergarten at five years or younger. The youngest beginners accepted by the B. I. A. are children who will be six years old by the first of January in their entering year. They then spend a year in pre-first grade to learn English, and are seven or eight years old on entering first grade. Public school children usually enter school at six and go directly into the first grade. The Indian's late start places him behind his public school classmate, and this handicap occurs regardless of his potential ability.

Summer programs carried on by tribal Indians in co-operation with the Bureau and other interested groups enrolled 26,075 Indian youths studying remedial subjects, special instruction, vocational work, and classes of pre-school children during 1964.[24] Training for pre-school youngsters and summer programs were requested and administered during 1965 by tribal councils through grants from the Office of Economic Opportunity.

Continuing the school year throughout twelve months, interrupted by short vacation periods, would give more time for Indian students to learn English and basic academic subjects and would also help bring the older child up to his proper grade in school. Lengthening the school day and extending the school year is being proposed by the state education department of New York.[25]

When the student reached the modal age level for his class, he could be transferred to a public school without placing him at a disadvantage, by giving him "social promotions." Public schools should not be asked to nor should they lower their standards in order to accept Indian pupils.

Examples exist today showing that some methods appear to improve Indians' scholastic standing or shorten their classroom

[23] *How Should We Educate the Deprived Child? Occasional Papers No. 7*, Council for Basic Education, Feb., 1965.
[24] 89 Cong., 1 sess., Senate Hearings on *House Report 6767*, Appropriations for 1966, p. 651.
[25] Council for Basic Education *Bulletin*, Vol. X, No. 4 (Dec., 1965), 7.

reaction time. One innovation in B. I. A. schools concerns speech. Oral English is not considered an important subject in Anglo elementary school curricula, but speech is essential for the non-English-speaking Indian child who must know what words mean before he can use them intelligently. If he is taught the printed word first, which he memorizes as a sound, he has difficulty associating the printed word with its meaning. When conversation is an important part of the school work, Indian children's English seems to improve. Another subject needed especially by the Indian child has to do with money. This would include making out bank checks, savings accounts, and such things.

An experiment in motivation during the summer of 1965, which lasted twelve weeks under the direction of Lloyd Homme, showed that the reaction time of Indian youngsters could be shortened appreciably and their interest in English highly stimulated by appropriate psychological methods.[26]

In order to use teaching methods in the present-day Indian educational system that would be most helpful in assisting Indians to adjust to the dominant culture, a survey could be made of techniques used in teaching English, mathematics, and physiology in classrooms of Bureau schools. An evaluation of the efficacy of each method could be made by following and comparing each student's performance in those subjects, and an analysis of the accumulated information might point out the more successful methods. Certain schools could then be designated as experimental centers for the purpose of testing new and promising ways of educating Indians. The staffs for these tryout centers could be drawn from Vista or federal teacher volunteers, or from returning members of the Peace Corps—assisted by appropriate university consultants.

V. APPROPRIATIONS FOR INDIAN EDUCATION

By treaty, statute, and long undisputed practice and policy, the United States has assumed obligations for the education of

[26] Personal communication from Lloyd E. Homme, head of the Behavioral Technology Department, Westinghouse Electric Corporation.

tribal Indians and, accordingly, has operated federal schools since 1819, when a federal appropriation of $10,000 was distributed to religious groups for Indian education.[27] In 1965, Congress appropriated $66,882,000 for Indian education. This includes money to cover the Johnson-O'Malley Act of April 16, 1934 (48 Statute 596), which authorized contracts for the direct operation of its own Indian schools and also for payments contributed to thirteen states, four school districts, and one hospital for the Indians' public instruction.[28] The act contemplates that the secretary of the interior will fix minimum educational standards no lower than the highest maintained by each respective state, an important requirement permitting the federal government to set up and then to enforce standards in public schools using such money.

The other authorizations for educational monies are Public Law 815 and Public Law 874, which grant federal funds to public schools in areas where government installations or Indian reservations have drastically swelled public school enrollments. Congress allocates this money to the Office of Education in the Department of Health, Education, and Welfare, and funds are given directly to local boards, by-passing the B. I. A. and state boards of education.

VI. FEDERAL SCHOOLS

The seventy-eight federal boarding schools are vital for beginning students several years late in enrolling, orphans, those from non-English-speaking families, the academically retarded, or dropouts from public schools, or those having special problems or needing vocational training that public schools are not equipped to handle. There were 28,903 Indians in boarding schools in the fiscal year 1964. This total included elementary and high school classes; some 1,154 students were enrolled in post high school technical and vocational courses at Haskell, Chilocco, and the Institute of American Indian Art. They studied, among

27 *Indian Education,* Branch of Education, B. I. A., No. 423 (Oct. 15, 1965), 4.
28 89 Cong., 1 sess., House of Representatives Hearings on Appropriations for 1966, Part I, p. 728.

other things, business practices, electronics, auto mechanics, heavy-equipment operation, commercial cooking, and vocations related to fine and applied arts. In addition to courses given by the Branch of Education, high school students take advantage of the vocational training offered by the Branch of Employment Assistance.

During the fiscal year 1964 there were eighty-eight regular day schools, eleven trailer schools and four schools in hospitals, enrolling 10,264 children.[29]

The problem of locating day schools is centered around the isolation of many homes, while the need for providing additional facilities is constant, since the Indian school population is increasing rapidly—more rapidly than children of comparable age in the general population. Indians often live in isolated desert areas without adequate water for a school well and roads that are impassable part of the year, so that bus routes cannot be established. Consequently, it is not always possible to place schools near the homes of the children's parents.

Federal dormitories in small towns near reservations were advocated by the Bureau when public schooling was considered the answer to assimilating and educating an Indian child. During this period dormitories were constructed or rented and as many students were jammed into them as possible, regardless of the child's adaptation, the size of the recreation space, or the number on the staff. In 1960 the policy changed to one which acknowledged that all children were not ready for public school; some needed additional training.

During 1964 there were nineteen dormitories housing 4,147 pupils, some modern, some of them harking back to the era of substandard housing.[30] Prior to 1958, Manuelito Hall in Gallup was built for a motel and rented by the Bureau for a dormitory. An air picture of the grounds would be indistinguishable from that of a penal institution with its stark buildings, their outlines and the land around them unbroken by trees, bushes or grass.

[29] *Statistics Concerning Indian Education, Fiscal Year 1964*, p. 15.
[30] *Ibid.*, 31.

Manuelito Hall is laid out in the form of an "H." The sleeping quarters, each about 120 feet by 18 feet long, accommodate, by means of two tiers of beds, about sixty-eight children. The dressing, study area, and the entire space allotted for privacy is between the rows of bunks. Small cabinets at the ends of the bunks hold each child's clothes and other possessions. Strong policing is necessary to keep children within the confines of the allotted space. Without facilities to work off steam, children shinny up water pipes, thereby destroying plumbing, jump from bed to bed, breaking springs, throw balls and loose objects through windows, and engage in other pranks.

Not all dormitories are as dismal as Manuelito Hall; however, most of them are still substandard in terms of modern educational needs. A well-equipped dormitory, with necessary space for recreation and an adequate staff, might well cut down on disciplinary problems, provide pupils with a background for a good education, and be worth trying.

Indian children need to be given firsthand knowledge of many of the institutions and customs of our society. They should have a bridge to take them into the average white cultural environment, which the non-Indian knows from his upbringing and experience. As an example, dining rooms for small groups are needed so that the Indian children can be taught table manners, proper use of knives and forks, and acceptable eating habits. Space is needed for extra-curricular activities, for planning and pursuing hobbies, for quiet study areas, for small libraries, and for individual counseling.

In addition, selection methods should be upgraded with the help of psychologists, psychiatrists, and educators and follow-up studies made so the choice of pupils could be evaluated on the basis of their subsequent school record and constantly improved and kept in line with the change in the outlook of their parents.

VII. Scholarships

During 1965, the B. I. A. awarded scholarships to 1,718 students with grants amounting to an average of $700 a student.

The grants range from $50 to the entire cost of a college education, including living expenses.[31] However, the average grant is often too low for the current cost of living, and the student —already behind his classmates in his academic subjects—has to spend the time he should put on his studies in working. One of the main causes of college students leaving college after the first year was found by McGrath, et al.,[32] to be a lack of money.

To be eligible for a scholarship, an individual must have one-fourth or more Indian blood, hold membership in a tribal group served by the Bureau, be without other means of financing an education, and have scholastic ability. Grants are made primarily to residents of Indian reservations, Indian-owned, or tax-exempt land. Grants are usually restricted to undergraduate students, but some have been given to medical and law students.

Twenty-nine of the more prosperous groups have established fellowships for their young people. The Navaho tribe has a $10,000,000 scholarship fund.[33] The Jicarilla Apaches have one of $1,000,000.[34] The Laguna tribal government has used $40,000 of its assets from uranium to establish a scholarship trust fund.[35] The Blackfoot tribe of Montana has appropriated $16,000 for educational grants.[36] The Southern Utes and the Ute Mountain Utes are depositing a portion of their children's per capita payments in trust funds for their future education.[37] Indian tribes offering educational grants often demand that the graduates return to the reservations for a stated period to work with their own people.

[31] U.S. Dept. of Interior, B. I. A., news release, Oct. 7, 1965.

[32] G. G. McGrath, Robert Roessel, Bruce Meador, G. C. Helmstadter, and John Barnes, *Higher Education of Southwestern Indians with Reference to Success and Failure* (Co-operative Research Project No. 939, Arizona State University, 1962).

[33] "More Indian Scholarships Available," *Navajo Times*, Vol. II, No. 39 (Oct. 18, 1961), 1.

[34] Amanda H. Finley, *Higher Education Aids for Indian Young People* (Riverside, Calif., B. I. A. Sherman Institute Press, 1956), 19.

[35] "More Indian Scholarships Available," *Navajo Times*, Vol. II, No. 39 (Oct. 18, 1961), 1.

[36] *Ibid.*

[37] Trust agreements: Southern Utes, Nov. 26, 1954; Ute Mountain Utes, May 16, 1955 (Commission files).

Beside Bureau and tribal stipends for attending college, some twenty-nine schools of higher learning, many churches, and other groups have tuition money for Indians who wish to go to college.[38] Work-study programs (Public Law 88–452, 78 Stat. 508) are also available to Indians, as well as other students.

The present dropout rate from college is high. McGrath, *et al.*, found a total of approximately 60 per cent of dropouts among three colleges in the information reviewed. Most Indian college dropouts occur during or at the end of the first year. Academic difficulties seem to be the chief cause for not continuing college.[39]

There is an urgent need to identify students with academic promise in the early grammar grades and follow them through school so that they may get tutoring, counseling, or other special assistance as the need arises. In this way they may be able to graduate from college and continue for master's or doctor's degrees.

If more emphasis were placed upon readying the academically gifted for college, they might not be shunted into the trades, as often happens today, only because they have had inadequate college preparation.

VIII. Adult Education

Adult education is usually designed for people beyond school age who volunteer to take the training. The United States Public Health Service holds prenatal classes and clinics to instruct mothers about child care. The Agricultural Extension Service teaches farmers better methods of raising crops or conducts classes in home economics. The B. I. A. instructs native policemen about law-and-order codes or indoctrinates native judges in their duties. Some vocational on-the-job training is done by the Branch of Employment Assistance. For adult education not covered by other services, the B. I. A. Department of Education conducts classes.

[38] U.S. Dept. of Interior, B. I. A., news release, Oct. 7, 1965.

[39] McGrath et al., *Higher Education of Southwestern Indians with Reference to Success and Failure,* 13–29.

Indian parents lacking a tradition of formal education continue to have difficulty realizing the importance of having their children attend school regularly. In some tribes there are no compulsory attendance laws. In addition, a parent does not realize he should visit the classrooms and discuss his child's problems with the teacher. Also, families who must sacrifice in order to afford clothes for students must forego the wages—real or potential—a youngster might earn, and parents who have had little or no schooling themselves usually do not give their children the incentive to attend school regularly or to continue to higher levels. Such cases call for adult education. In 1964, 168 Indian communities had adult education programs at a cost of approximately one million dollars.[40]

IX. FEDERAL TEACHERS AND COUNSELORS

Teachers and counselors responsible for training Indians need special help. Unless the difficulties of the Indian child lacking a background in the majority culture are pointed out to teachers, none but the most gifted and perceptive will grasp and supply the things the child needs. In-service training programs for teachers, not only for basic subjects, but also for stressing cross-cultural problems, should be continued and strengthened. All persons in contact with the Indian school child—bus drivers, dormitory attendants, and teachers' aids—need special training.

Vacations comparable to those received by teachers in public schools and a flexible salary scale are necessary for federal teachers in order to increase the range and size of salaries and to decrease the number of transfers. In order to obtain good counselors and teachers, tribes with sufficient income could augment teachers' salaries in federal schools or could hire additional teachers for children in public schools. Salaries for extra teachers paid with tribal funds might require some adjustment of regulations by the state or the local boards of education. But even the poorer tribes might make a token payment toward their children's education, thus giving those tribes an interest in the schools.

[40] *Statistics Concerning Indian Education, Fiscal Year 1964*, p. 37.

X. Branch of Education

The Washington B. I. A. Department of Education has only staff authority, and the lack of administrative centralization is apparent in every part of the system. No co-ordination exists between the Washington office and the field, nor is there inter-communication between the area offices themselves. Consequently, several different types of achievement tests are given throughout the Indian country each year on different dates, making it impossible to get a comparative evaluation of all federal schools. Records on classroom achievements are not kept up to date and lack uniformity. Many Navaho school census cards stopped in 1961. Consequently, students cannot be followed through their school years, so that judgments can be made regarding better curricula. It is generally understood among the staff that the best pupils from federal schools are sent to public schools but confirmatory studies are lacking. Since student records are not always sent with pupils who transfer to public schools, the teacher is frequently at a loss to determine where each student should be placed in his class. Incomplete or diverse records are insufficient for an analysis by the Washington staff or its educational system. Statistics that are sent from the field to Washington are adequate only for running the Department of Education, not for evaluating the quality of education.

The B. I. A. area director of schools and his staff should work not only with federal but also with public schools within his jurisdiction, checking on the use of Johnson-O'Malley money and receiving suggestions from principals on more creative co-ordination between the two educational systems.

Tighter administration is needed in the B. I. A. Department of Education in order to have comparable record-keeping in all area offices. In this way it would be possible to carry out surveys of teaching methods, acquire statistics on the number of students needing remedial or compensatory training or those ready to be transferred to public schools, and make administrative changes as new, successful educational methods are found. Wise policy decisions need to be based on carefully collected facts which bring critical problems to a focus.

XI. RECOMMENDATIONS

Indian education should afford the individual the opportunity for realizing his full capabilities. The quality of the instruction he receives and its adaptation to his needs should be the prime consideration. The schools—federal, public, and private—which Indians attend should have the best curricula, programs, teaching methods, and guidance employed in educating white students, with all these factors being modified and augmented to meet the special requirements of Indian students.

Also, the training should have as one of its continuing objectives the discovery of pupils of special promise and preparing them to move into higher education in order to qualify for executive positions inside or outside the tribe.

To all these ends, the support of the Indian community, its neighbors, and tribal and local government officials should be enlisted.

In reaching the objectives discussed above, the B. I. A. Department of Education should consider: (1) the variations among groups, areas, and Indian cultures, and the attitudes of adjacent communities, including the existence or absence of discrimination against the Indian child; and (2) the quality of the teaching staff and its ability to cope with the special difficulties of the student and his parents and to impart knowledge without destroying the moral influences and restraints of the student's family and culture.

On the basis of the above criteria, Indian pupils should be divided into three general classes, according to their capacity and background: (1) Those who will profit from public school. In general, this group would include pupils from English-speaking, stable families which have substituted the white culture for their Indian heritage: (2) Those who will profit from a federal school. They would be pupils chosen from unassimilated families, because, among other things, they are unable to speak or to understand English; (3) Those for whom both federal and public education should be considered.

For the Indian child in the second or third group the following should be provided: early and continuous training in English; instruction in the history, culture, and accomplishments of the Indians; training in arts and crafts; teachers qualified to teach both Indian culture and English as a second language; the motivating of students of different languages and cultural backgrounds; and special subjects that Indian children require, such as the handling of money, etc.

Mission schools should be encouraged to continue to supply their share of leadership.

In no case should public schools attended by Indians be required (or permitted) to lower their standards. In making arrangements for attendance of tribal Indians at public schools, the federal government, in fulfillment of its obligations, should require that adequate standards be maintained. If standards drop, the federal government should no longer allocate money to the school. Pains should be taken by all the authorities concerned to avoid any friction that might result from the additional financial burden put on the non-Indian taxpayer by educating Indians in public schools. Despite this burden, the educational duty of the United States does not diminish the obligations of the states, under their constitutions and laws, to educate Indians on a parity with other citizens.

The problems raised by taking Indian youngsters from their homes to live in large dormitories, so as to enable them to attend public schools in cities, should be evaluated in terms of the individual's age, his emotional adjustment, and the circumstances of his home life.

Qualified teachers should have adequate compensation. Those in the federal service should have a work year equivalent in length to that customary in public schools. Not only should teachers have special training, but also all other persons in contact with Indian children—bus drivers, dormitory attendants, and teachers' aids—should have special training.

Children should have counseling through elementary grades and high school. For those qualified to attend college, suitable instruction should be given to equip them to enter college and to remain there. Counseling should continue through the college years.

Education for adults should be strengthened to include more subjects, as well as the use of television and other modern techniques, and should be extended to more reservations.

A strong parent-teacher relationship should be developed and community schools re-established. Consultation of school authorities with tribal leaders should be facilitated.

The Indian parent must see that his child attends school regularly and must encourage him to do well in his studies.

Where compulsory attendance laws do not exist in a tribe, it should take action to have such legislation enacted and enforced.

Adequate scholarships, grants, and loans should be provided by the United States to Indians needing such aid.

Among families in a low-income bracket, provision for economic improvement should go hand in hand with education.

6
Health

I. Introduction

THIS CHAPTER points out the disparity between the poor health of the Indians and the comparative good health of the average United States citizen, discusses the level of Indian health possible under present-day conditions, and outlines additional steps which need to be taken to close the gap. Many problems in Indian health stem from inadequate sanitary facilities, contaminated water, substandard housing, deficiencies of essential foods, and ignorance about when and how to obtain medical services. These conditions prevail among all impoverished rural folk in the nation, but many Indians suffer under two special handicaps: one, a culture that often ignores modern sanitary practices; and, two, lives that are spent in remote and sparsely settled areas.

Of course, these barriers to good health were more pronounced in the early nineteenth century than they are today. Horse transportation over poor roads was slow, and long distances existed between settlements. Federal responsibility for health and medical care of Indians was acquired only as an incidental part of the obligation to educate the Indians, with the care of sick Indians often depending on the availability of army medical officers.

The first Congressional appropriation that explicitly provided for Indian health was made in 1832—$12,000 for employing physicians and for purchasing "genuine vaccine matter."[1] In 1836 the government, in return for the Ottawa and Chippewa nations'

---

[1] Act of May 5, 1832 (4 Stat. 514).

ceding some of their land to the United States, agreed to make annual payments for vaccines, medicines, and services of physicians in return for the Indians' promise to remain on their reservations. This agreement was later included in other treaties. Underlying such provisions was the recognition that medical care was essential not only to insure Indian welfare but also to prevent centers of contagious diseases from menacing surrounding communities. At this time only the federal government had the authority to act in matters pertaining to reservation Indians.

By 1880 the B. I. A. had provided four hospitals and seventy-seven physicians, and by 1900 it had made its health services to Indians one of its major concerns. During the 1930's the B. I. A.'s top administrative personnel for health was supplied by the United States Public Health Service (U.S.P.H.S.). The Bureau built hospitals, clinics, and quarters for medical personnel, and secured doctors, nurses, and additional assistance through the regular Civil Service channels.

In 1955 the Division of Indian Health of the United States Public Health Service took over from the B. I. A. all remaining health activities (Public Law 568, August 5, 1954); and by 1962 U.S.P.H.S. had taken full jurisdiction over Indian health, having assumed responsibility for hospital and field health services, contract patient care, administration, alterations and construction of hospitals and clinics for Indians, community hospitals for Indians and others (Public Law 151, August 16, 1957), personnel quarters, and sanitation facilities (Public Law 121, July 31, 1959). The U.S.P.H.S. budget for these services during the fiscal year 1966 was $62,702,000, compared with approximately $15,000,000 in 1951.[2] The money for health activities alone is over one-third of what Congress estimated for the B. I. A. in 1965–66 for all other programs ($222,715,000).

These increased appropriations represented a Congressional goal, as expressed by the U.S.P.H.S., to achieve "a level of health

[2] *Department of the Interior Appropriations for 1952*, Hearings Before a Subcommittee of the Committee on Appropriations, U.S. Senate, 82 Cong., 1 sess., Part I, p. 352.

comparable to that of the general population.''[3] Whether or not such a goal can be attained with money and medical facilities alone is questionable, since improved health must go hand in hand with better education and better living conditions among the Indians.

II. The Present Situation

Detailed and accurate vital and morbidity statistics for Indians as a whole are incomplete. Therefore, in an effort to present as clear a picture of Indian health as possible, this chapter has supplemented national data with certain intensively collected regional data and a report made by medical consultants from Cornell University.[4] The Cornell team evaluated Indian medical care in the field and in hospitals among Oklahoma Indians and on the Pueblo, Papago, Pima, and Navaho reservations in Arizona, Utah, and New Mexico.

The quality of medical care given any patient depends basically upon two kinds of factors—the human (a physician's training, conscientiousness, and judgment) and the material (the quality of technical facilities available). The human element is not susceptible of precise measurement. A good diagnosis derives from a physician's judgment; his judgment is based upon his training, the thoroughness with which he seeks out all aspects of a patient's complaints, and his ability to draw reasonable inferences from the assembled data; his effectiveness can be ascertained to a degree by the manner in which the patient accepts and carries out his recommendations. The measurable factors involved (including the time available for evaluating a patient's condition) are usually less important. But in combination all these things bear directly upon the quality of medical care, and in many instances those physicians serving the Indians are handicapped. Although dedicated, they often are deficient in number and—especially those doing field work—must make do without modern medical facilities.

3 89 Cong., 1 sess., Senate Hearings on *House Report 6767*, Appropriations for 1966, p. 931.
4 See Preface.

III. VITAL STATISTICS[5]

Population Age

Preliminary studies of the general 1960 census data show that Indians as a group are young: Their median age is under twenty, whereas that for the general population is thirty. The national ratio between the sexes shows these percentages of Indian males to females: 1910—50.9; 1930—51.2; and 1950—51.7. This excess of males occurred in all races in the United States (1910—51.5; 1930—50.6) until 1950, when the census for all races showed a reversal of the trend, and proportion of males for races other than Indians dropped to 49.7.[6]

Birth Rates

The Indian birth rate is high. In 1959 there were 41.4 Indian live births for each 1,000 of the population for the twenty-four federal reservation states, which is almost twice the rate of the country as a whole (24.1); and the 41.4 may be too low, because many Indians view the birth or death of a child as a personal matter which needs no reporting. The birth rate for the Ute Mountain Utes in 1960 was 55.8.[7] When birth rates were recorded among a carefully observed segment of the Navahos, residing on what is the largest Indian reservation in the country, a six-year average (1955–60) was found to be 49.1. Of the births among 442 Navaho women (ages 15–44) in this group, 43 per cent occurred outside a hospital without a physician in attendance. Consequently, except for careful checks by the Cornell medical team, many births might have gone unrecorded. Figures collected between 1952–61 under the usual B. I. A. methods for the entire Navaho population receiving Bureau services show the birth rate to have been 42.0.[8] This rate was lower than that collected

5 The material in this section, unless otherwise specified, was taken from *Indian Health Highlights* (U.S. Dept. of Health, Education, and Welfare, Public Health Service, Bureau of Medical Services, Division of Indian Health), Nov., 1961.

6 *Ibid.*, October 1960, p. 8.

7 Samuel Johnson, M.D., Sydney G. Margolin, M.D., and Conrad Riley, M.D., "Report of Health Needs of Ute Mountain Ute Tribe" (University of Colorado School of Medicine, November, 1962 [mimeographed]), Table II.

8 *The Navajo Yearbook, 1951–1961*, Report VIII (1961), 116–18.

by the Cornell research workers, but closely approximated the national Indian rate. This high birth rate may be lowered if the Indians take advantage of family planning services, available to them on a voluntary basis.[9]

Infant Mortality (Deaths per 1,000 Live Births)

The recorded Indian infant-mortality rate is high and shows variations, depending upon the care with which data are collected (see Appendix, Table 5). The national rate among Indians for 1957–59 was 53.7, almost twice that for all races (27.1 in 1958). Selected groups of Navahos in the period 1955–59 had an even higher rate—58.5. Rates for previous years were, of course, still higher: in 1944 the figure was 135.3, three times that for all races in the United States (41.4) in 1945.

Average Age and Cause of Death and Rates by Age Groups

In 1959 the average age at death for Indians was 41.8 years in the twenty-four federal reservation states, compared with 62.3 for all races.[10] Death rates calculated by percentage distribution of age groups give an indication of general health, since groups with good health often have a lower mortality than those with poor health. Statistics show that the highest percentage distribution of deaths was among infants and children. During 1959, 21.2 per cent of Indian deaths occurred among persons less than one year of age, in contrast to 6.8 per cent of the deaths for the United States as a whole. Moreover, 4.9 per cent of the Indian deaths were in the one to four age group, whereas this age group contributed only 1.0 per cent of the total national deaths. Among Indians from five through nineteen years of age, deaths were 5.1 per cent, compared with 1.7 per cent for the comparable age group among Americans in general.

Regarding the leading causes of death, rates (per 100,000 population) for 1957–59 show Indians to be from two to eight times more susceptible than non-Indians to a large group of causes,

9 U.S. Dept. of Interior news release, June 20, 1965.

10 The 1959 average age at death for Indians in all states (excluding Alaska and Hawaii) was 41.4. *Indian Health Highlights* (1961), 11 (Table 10).

bly less afflicted by a few of the giant killers. Indi-
ironmental factors explain the variations in part.
rates for the country at large, the extent to which
ional death rates for Indians were higher was
... infections of the intestinal tract, approximately
... umes; from tuberculosis, five times; from accidents, homi-
cides, influenza, and pneumonia, about three times each; and
from cirrhosis of the liver and diseases of early infancy, two
times. The rate for all races of the United States (including Indians) was about the same for congenital malformations and
diabetes mellitus. But Indian death rates from malignant neo-
plasms, heart diseases, and vascular lesions affecting the central
nervous system were only one-half those of the population at
large—perhaps because the Indians do not live long enough to
become subject to the degenerative diseases of old age. High
death rates from specific diseases among Indians are, in general,
those which were high for the general population in the early
part of this century, when the average death occurred at an
earlier age than today.

Incidence of Disease[11]

The numbers and kinds of diseases in any population category
depend, among other things, on the individual's environment,
economic status, education, and traditional attitudes. All of these
factors in turn determine his nutrition, his cleanliness, and his
health-consciousness, as well as the availability of and the demand for medical services.

Incidence rates for selected notifiable diseases among Indians
for 1960 compared with rates for all races in the United States
for 1959 and calculated on 100,000 of the population show a high
ratio for certain diseases: ratios of twelve or over in diphtheria,
bacillary dysentery, hepatitis, and typhoid fever; of five or over
in gonorrhea, meningitis, meningococcal infections, mumps,
Rocky Mountain spotted fever, trichinosis, tuberculosis, and

11 U.S. Dept of Health, Education, and Welfare, Public Health Service, *Illness
Among Indians* (1961), 12 (Table I).

tularemia; of two in brucellosis, chicken pox, amoebiasis, encephalitis, measles, rheumatic fever, streptococcic throat, scarlet fever, and whooping cough. Tuberculosis has decreased since the 1950 discovery and use of chemotherapeutic drugs, which inhibit the growth of the bacilli. National rates, in which Indian morbidity from twenty-four reservation states is calculated together, can in turn be broken down into rates for various groups. Three-fourths (76.3 per cent) of the illnesses of the Navaho Indians are due to microbial infections, two-thirds of which occur in persons less than five or six years of age.[12] On the other hand, Indians like those in Oklahoma (who have largely adopted white ways and have ready access to medical centers) suffer more frequently from obesity, diabetes, hypertension, and pathology of the gall bladder.[13] Whether this distribution of diseases among different cultural groups is a result of the patient's own decision regarding what constitutes a condition needing medical attention or is actual incidence of the ailment cannot be determined, since most morbidity statistics are collected only for those who visit hospitals or clinics.

Trachoma

Trachoma is caused by a virus-like organism, which has recently been isolated. The incidence rates for trachoma (calculated per 100,000 of the population) among Indians for 1959 was 1,319.9; for 1960, 938.0. Today the disease can be distinguished from other diseases of the eye; hence today's diagnoses cannot be compared directly with those made thirty years ago, when many unrelated pathological conditions were diagnosed as trachoma. It is known, however, from clinical observations that trachoma has decreased since the early 1930's when it represented a major health problem among Indians.[14] There are no comparable fig-

12 W. McDermott, K. Deuschle, E. Kilbourne, and D. Rogers, "Interim Report on Indian Health to the Commission on the Rights, Liberties, and Responsibilities of the American Indian," June 20, 1959, p. 83 (mimeographed).

13 *Ibid.*, 4.

14 Meriam and Associates, *The Problem of Indian Administration,* Institute of Government Research *Studies in Administration* (Baltimore, The John Hopkins Press, 1928), 3.

ures for trachoma for all races in the United States, because the disease has almost disappeared. Today it is found mainly in foreign areas where the sanitation is poor—areas such as the Mediterranean Basin, the Middle East, and Asia.

IV. HOUSING AMONG "ACCULTURATED" AND TRIBAL INDIANS AND FEDERAL HOUSING

Some factors contributing to the poor health of Indians can be illustrated by an inspection of their homes. The following descriptions of "typical" Indian homes testify to the need for better housing in Indian country.

The Cornell medical team described a Cherokee home typical of three impoverished settlements in Oklahoma.[15] The houses were made of unpainted, irregular slabs, sometimes partially covered with tarpaper. Almost all homes had kitchens and sinks, although some depended on hand pumps for water. Where there was no well, water was often brought in buckets from a nearby brook or spring and stored by the kitchen sink. Rooms were commonly dirty and full of flies. (The B. I. A. lists a total of approximately 58,000 Oklahoma Indians—see Appendix, Table 1—but the number of impoverished families is not known.)

A typical Cherokee family consisted of one or more young women in their twenties, perhaps an elderly woman, many children and infants, and the husbands of the young women. The men, usually young, were without work and at home in mid-morning. There were some wage-earners, but the major income came from Aid to Dependent Children. Frequently, families had constructed their own homes on land to which they had neither title nor right of occupancy. The living conditions among these Indians were probably not much lower than those of poor non-Indians in Oklahoma. In contrast to the majority of Indian homes in the state, a few were owned by the occupants. These were well kept, with clean interiors, containing a stove and a refrigerator, and they had running water.

A comparison of life among the Navaho and the Oklahoma In-

15 McDermott *et al.,* "Interim Report on Indian Health," 20.

dians show significant contrasts. In Oklahoma, as a result of the Allotment Act (Dawes Act),[16] Indians have lost most of their land; and without this land, tribal structure and organization have almost entirely disappeared. On the other hand, the Navaho Reservation is intact; it has a powerful tribal organization, a strong committee on tribal health, and a vital religion, which stresses health, with many medicine men as political leaders. In Oklahoma, there are good roads and medical facilities situated near the Indian homes. Roads in the Navaho country vary from paved to impassable; they may go over sheer rock or be washed out overnight by a flash flood. In some instances, more than one hundred miles must be traveled to reach a hospital. In Oklahoma there is no language barrier, whereas few pre-school Navaho children have a knowledge of English. In Oklahoma water is often adjacent to the home, but the Navahos frequently have to haul all their water from one to five miles.

Navaho hogans are usually located several miles apart.[17] They are six-sided, windowless, constructed of logs and mud, with a mud-packed floor and a central smoke hole in the roof. Fecal contamination of the dirt floor by infants is common. The interior usually contains only one bed, so most of the family sleeps on sheepskins on the floor. Since the door does not fit the sill, the resulting aperture and the smoke hole provide ventilation. Heating and cooking may be done over an open fire or on either an iron stove or one constructed from a kerosene drum. In most cases the problem of keeping infants out of mischief is solved by securely lacing them to cradleboards, which can be carried on the back or swung from the ceiling.

Slab cabins—at first glance, an improvement over hogans—have been built in parts of the Navaho Reservation. The cabins afford some protection for food, since they may contain a table

16 See Chapter One, pp. 18–20, above.

17 The Cornell medical team described a representative Navaho dwelling from a composite of forty Navaho hogans. The number of persons living under substandard conditions is not known, but neither is the total population. The B. I. A. estimates that there are 73,614 Navahos, *The Navajo Yearbook* estimates 80,364, and the U.S. Public Health Services gives a total of 81,255. *The Navajo Yearbook, 1951–1961,* Report VIII (1961), 311–12.

and some chairs; but they are often floored with rough boards difficult to clean, and many are airtight, with windows that cannot be opened. The government housing projects, however, are of excellent construction, with adequate space for the whole family.

The Environmental Sanitation Branch of the U.S.P.H.S. Window Rock field office conducted a survey in 1962 of some 563 Navaho Reservation homes. Checks were made on water supply (source, treatment of source, storage and distribution systems, and water samples), on sewage-disposal facilities, on area sanitation (refuse collection and disposal), on insect and rodent control, and on food sanitation. Some of the dismaying facts the survey uncovered were these: 291 of the homes had no water source on the premises; of 325 water sources inspected, 90 per cent were unsatisfactory, and of the 294 storage and distribution systems surveyed, *all* were unsatisfactory; more than 55 per cent of the homes had no facilities whatever for disposing of excreta, and 84 per cent of the privies and 92 per cent of sewage-disposal facilities were unsatisfactory; provisions for refuse disposal were 98.5 per cent unacceptable, insect and rodent-control measures were 93 per cent unacceptable; and 87 per cent of the food-sanitation practices inspected were not satisfactory.[18] Housing among the Navaho Indians was comparable to that found among the Sioux. A great majority of Indian homes on the Pine Ridge Reservation are one- or two-room cabins, poorly furnished and commonly constructed of rough plank, with the roof made weather resistant by a cover of tarpaper or sod. A stove, centrally placed, supplies heat. Auxiliary buildings usually include an outhouse, a shed, and one or more tents. The tents not infrequently provide the only sleeping area for some members of the family or for relatives even in the most severe weather.[19]

Housing conditions among the Oglala Sioux are also generally

[18] *Annual Report,* Environmental Sanitation Branch, U.S. Public Health Service, Division of Indian Health, Window Rock Field Office, Window Rock, Ariz., July, 1962.
[19] Vernon D. Malan, *The Dakota Indian Family, Bulletin 470,* South Dakota State College (Brookings, S. Dak., May, 1958), 5–6.

depressing. Space is limited, ventilation poor, and overcrowding is characteristic—partly to conserve heat in the Dakota sub-zero winters.

The Public Housing Administration, since 1961, has shown an awareness of the Indian's poverty and his needs. In 1962 a mutual-help project was launched by the Bureau and the Housing Administration. Indians with incomes below the minimum requirements set by the Housing Administration contribute their own labor and land as a down payment for their homes.

These mutual-help programs are operated by a local Indian tribal authority, the Public Housing Administration, and the B. I. A. The tribes appoint their own tribal authorities; the Housing Administration gives money directly to the officials of the tribe for construction supplies for the homes, while the B. I. A. employs reservation housing officers and construction superintendents. The housing officer assists the local Indian housing authority in selecting eligible families and making application for assistance to the Housing Administration, and later helps in choosing sites for the dwellings.

In 1965 over 300 homes were either partially or entirely completed; 1,075 were expected to be started by the spring or summer of 1966; and 2,000 units of additional homes had been requested by the Indian tribal authorities. These figures are exclusive of houses which may be needed by tribes in Oklahoma. Until a recent action of the Oklahoma legislature, Indians in this state were not eligible for public housing. Secretary Udall pointed out that the housing program is a major factor in improving living conditions among 60,000 Indian families.[20] On August 10, 1965, Public Law 87–117 was signed by President Johnson. This law, among other things, provides for 140,000 units of housing for Indians and other citizens with low or moderate incomes.

Many federal agencies, however, cannot underwrite loans to Indians unless Indians have assets, employment, or other means of qualifying as good risks. Rules used in processing Indian requests for housing loans are generally wise. Experience has

[20] U.S. Dept. of Interior news release, Nov. 5, 1965.

shown that when housing is too easily financed, structures may be built in locations hopelessly removed from sources of economic opportunity. In such a case, good housing may become a trap, tying Indian families to areas where poverty with all its accompanying pains is preordained. The case of the Kootenais is a good illustration. In 1930, Congress appropriated money for eighteen cottages with running water and a community building near Bonners Ferry, Idaho. Unfortunately, the only employment in the area consisted of occasional farm work and seasonal lumbering jobs. Although Indians were the last to be hired and the first to be dismissed from all the projects, the available housing held the Kootenais as though they were chained to the area.

For many years the younger people in this group were shiftless, backward, and indifferent, and none had finished high school. Only a few of the older people could read, write, or understand English. Most of them lived on the money from intermittent jobs and welfare checks. Houses were shabby and plumbing did not work. The people lived in squalor and lawlessness and were frequently drunk. Only recently have conditions changed and some of the people been rehabilitated through three years of a community-action program by the Bureau and through moving others away from their 1930 homes.

Although adequate housing and good health frequently go together, location is also important, and dwellings should be planned in connection with work opportunities and education.

V. Hospitals

On June 30, 1961, the Division of Indian Health of the U.S.P.H.S. operated forty-five hospitals (forty-one general and four sanatoria), exclusive of Alaska, and in 1962 had $9,768,000 for contracts for Indian patient care with community and private hospitals.[21] Public Law 151 in 1957 authorized funds for construction of community hospitals, advance money to non-profit agencies or organizations for the construction of hospitals,

---

[21] *Department of the Interior and Related Agencies Appropriations for 1963,* Hearings Before a Subcommittee of the Committee on Appropriations, U.S. Senate, 87 Cong., 2 sess., on *House Report 10802,* p. 816.

diagnostic or treatment centers, laboratories, outpatient departments, nurses' homes, training and central hospitals' facilities, and contracts for patient care, all of which must meet the standards of the U.S.P.H.S.

The model for the government's advancing federal money to a nonprofit organization for construction of a hospital was Public Law 249, passed in 1949. This law authorized the B. I. A. to advance money to Bernalillo County in New Mexico for building a hospital for both Indians and indigent persons. The B. I. A. advanced $1,500,000 and Bernalillo County added $1,750,000 for the 200-bed facility.

Justifications for this hospital during the early 1950's had been based on medical-care needs of the many Indians in the region, on the availability of excellent laboratory and other medical facilities, on the presence of private doctors willing to donate their time, and on plans for a medical school, which has since been established at the University of New Mexico. The hospital was opened October 1, 1954, is supported partly by taxes, and has satisfied a real need in a state that was without any free beds until this hospital was constructed.

The U.S.P.H.S. pays for Indian patients in the Bernalillo County Indian Hospital, but its regulations prohibit admitting a reservation Navaho to the hospital unless he is a student. The Navahos suffer especially because many of them are working in Albuquerque at low-paying jobs, having been encouraged by the B. I. A. to leave their overcrowded reservation. When, however, they or members of their family get sick in Albuquerque, they must return to a hospital in the Navaho area. The man who because of an illness of several weeks' duration takes his family back to the reservation may find, upon returning to the city, that he has lost his job—one of the bad results of assigning the responsibilities for Indian services to more than one department.

To check on the quality of U.S.P.H.S. hospitals, the Cornell medical team visited thirteen general and two community hospitals in Oklahoma, Arizona, and New Mexico in 1959.[22] The

22 McDermott *et al.,* "Interim Report on Indian Health," 30–39.

team found standards high and the quality of medical care good. Airplane-ambulance service was available to transport patients with rare illnesses to centers staffed by specialists. In smaller hospitals in remote areas, housing for doctors and nurses was frequently found to be inadequate; consequently, these hospitals are often understaffed.

However, hospitals are an important part of any over-all health program; but if every Indian on the rolls of the B. I. A. census was given a careful medical examination in one of the new and well-equipped hospitals of U.S.P.H.S., was administered appropriate medicine, or was given a necessary operation, a few good meals, and sent back to live under conditions of extreme want, such services would probably not improve general Indian health significantly.

VI. Bridge Between Patient and Medical Facility

The most difficult problem before the U.S.P.H.S today in the practice of medicine among indigent people is bridging the gap between the hospital and the ill patient in the rural outpost—either getting doctors into the country or Indians into medical institutions. The basic problem among Indians is the compound problem of poverty and ignorance and that among members of the medical profession is their reluctance to practice medicine away from well-equipped hospitals.

The first step toward a solution of the problem of bridging the gap is education—education for Indian school children in good health practices and education for adults in prenatal, infant, and child care, nutrition, sanitation, and general information, so that Indians may recognize symptoms of acute and chronic illness. The second step is a matter of adjustment and must be sought among professional members of the U.S.P.H.S. and among administrative personnel: they must adjust their professional skills to the special problems connected with improving the health of an impoverished people.

Field health in the fiscal year 1965 received $11,662,000. This included salaries for a total of 4,372 hospital and 1,156 field possitions. Staff working in field clinics included sanitary engineers, dentists, public health nurses and assistants, nutritionists, social workers, community health workers, interpreters, pharmacists, and laboratory and X-ray technicians.[23] Many field clinics are staffed part-time by traveling teams of medical personnel. In addition, contracts to provide health services are negotiated with state and local health departments whenever feasible.

In Oklahoma, where the problems of health among Indians are similar to those of other indigent persons in the state, contracts for serving Indians are made between the U.S.P.H.S. and the state public health service. In other areas the field health service must often be designed to fit the needs of each particular group. A realistic field health program should be based not only on the number of Indians who use federal or state facilities, but on an estimate of those who are not but should be using the facilities.

More should be known about the economic status and the place of residence of Indians visiting clinics and hospitals. Then it could be determined whether the Indians frequenting the medical facilities are predominately the relatively well-to-do or those who live in the vicinity of the institution and whether the patients also include impoverished Indians from rural areas. Until figures are available showing use of medical facilities by income and geographical area in which the patient lives, there is no way to tell whether the Indians suffering from poverty and isolation are receiving the high caliber of modern medical care presumably at their command. These figures, in addition to birth rates and population estimates, should be used in future planning.

The adaptation of modern medicine for delivery in an acceptable form across formidable cultural and linguistic barriers is a problem of vast proportions. Its solution will require many contributory adaptations, as well as the behavioral approach by both doctors and nurses toward a variety of conditions. No a priori plan can be laid down, but two successful educational projects and a few outstanding problems will be discussed.

[23] 89 Cong., 1 sess., Senate Hearings on *House Report 6767*, Appropriations for 1966, pp. 927–1007.

An example of an imaginative approach to bridge the gap between cultures occurred when the Oglala Sioux at Pine Ridge, South Dakota, incorporated into their traditional Sun Dance pictures and charts demonstrating how to attain better health for all people. The local U.S.P.H.S. medical officer provided plans for sanitary water and sewage systems, signs and charts showing high infant mortality rates, and demonstrations on how to reduce the deaths by better care of infants, along with dental and nutritional displays. The B. I. A. helped the tribal council in planning for the safety, convenience, and entertainment of the crowd. Health education given alone would have meant little to the Indians, but, combined with a familiar ceremonial ritual, it awakened them to new medical concepts.[24] An estimated 6,000 people attended from adjacent Sioux reservations and from tribes throughout the country. Tents were pitched about a mile from the hospital for the four days of celebration.

Another project prepared the Pueblo Indians in New Mexico to use hospitals. It involved the introduction of ambulances supplied by the B. I. A. during the 1930's. Transportation enabled Indians possessing only horse-drawn vehicles and fearing modern medicine to be taken many miles to hospitals or clinics, there to receive needed services. Thus the Pueblo people learned to recognize what could be accomplished by hospital care. Today, the situation is much improved. They have an understanding of preventive medicine; jobs are more plentiful and incomes are higher; moreover, getting from one place to another is no longer a major problem in Pueblo country.

But transportation is still a serious problem among many other reservation Indians. Often they have no car or money to pay for a vehicle to a hospital, no matter what the emergency is; and the U.S.P.H.S. does not furnish ambulances, even in the most remote areas. An area officer takes the position that the U.S.P.H.S. will pay for a commercial ambulance called to a highway acci-

24 86 Cong., 1 sess., *Congressional Record*, Vol. 105, No. 165 (Friday, Sept. 18, 1959), Extension of Remarks of Hon. George S. McGovern, House of Representatives, Monday, Sept. 14, 1959, introducing an article by Will Spindler, *Shannon County News*, "Pine Ridge Sun Dance Draws Huge Crowds," pp. A8304–A8305.

dent only if a live Indian is delivered to a hospital. If an Indian dies before he reaches the hospital, the ambulance bill is not paid.[25] A contrary policy is followed among some other developing groups. For example, medical care for the Congolese is controlled by the central government, with ambulance service being a permanent part of hospital administration. Also, in Puerto Rico, where the medical school assumes responsibility for the administration of welfare and medical care of a large segment of the population, ambulance service is supplied.[26]

Some of the outstanding problems in health have to do with the lack of co-operation between federal professional and administrative personnel. Confronting physicians is the difficulty that their professional training is almost wholly hospital-oriented, and they are usually most interested in clinical work and cases demanding difficult diagnosis. To make a good diagnosis in complicated or unusual cases demands well-equipped laboratories, which are concentrated for the most part within hospitals. Serious ailments in the field are few compared with the large number of trivial ailments. Consequently, it is difficult to get physicians to work in rural areas.

The shortage of public health nurses for field work was seen when the U.S.P.H.S. contracted with the Oklahoma State Public Health Service and made available $71,000 for field nurses, but had $40,000 returned because of the impossibility of filling all the established rural positions.[27] It might be impossible to recruit a sufficient number of public health nurses for isolated reservations, such as that of the Navaho, if the plan were to duplicate the orthodox program existing in many cities today. Public health field nurses stationed in rural areas of the Indian country need help from local residents who understand the native language, are acquainted with health services, and know the people.

Co-operation between the U.S.P.H.S. and other government and private units should be encouraged. The B. I. A. maintains

[25] *Albuquerque Tribune*, Nov. 30 and Dec. 1, 1962.
[26] Personal communications from François Dresse, Harvard University Fellow in Public Health, Jan. 6, 1963, and Feb. 26, 1963.
[27] McDermott *et al.*, "Interim Report on Indian Health," 42.

roads and many telephone lines and operates crews of repairmen often needed by the U.S.P.H.S. Exigencies in the field can be illustrated by sanitary engineering projects. In 1962 the U.S.P.H.S. was given $3,620,244 (Public Law 121, July 31, 1959) "to construct, improve, extend, or otherwise provide and maintain, by contract or otherwise, essential sanitation facilities, including domestic and community water supplies and facilities, drainage facilities, and sewage and waste disposal facilities . . . for Indian homes, communities, and lands."[28]

This program has helped many communities, but at the same time it has raised the question of who will maintain electrical equipment or other apparatus on deep wells, on water, or on sewage systems. Pueblo Indian tribal governments were not asked by the U.S.P.H.S. to assume responsibility for maintaining these installations prior to their being built, and no training in repair work has been given by the U.S.P.H.S. As a result, the B. I. A. has had to get the Indians to donate labor for maintenance work on projects constructed by the U.S.P.H.S.[29] It would have been generally much more efficient, and the program would have been better understood by the Indians, if plans had been discussed with them before construction was started. In planning future installations, the government should always consult the Indians.

VII. GOALS IN INDIAN HEALTH

Within the context of the health of United States society, the goals set for the federal effort in Indian health need to be examined. Statements of policy are clear-cut, within *comparative* terms. Difficulties arise, however, when an attempt is made to define *standards*, since the quality of medical care differs in rural and urban areas in the United States. Should Indian medical care be similar to the best which exists in most medical schools

---

28 *Department of the Interior and Related Agencies Appropriations for 1963*, Hearings Before a Subcommittee of the Committee on Appropriations, U. S. Senate, 87 Cong., 2 sess., on *House Report 10802*, p. 851.

29 Personal communication from A. J. Kennedy, construction and maintenance superintendent (general), United Pueblos Agency of the B. I. A., Dec. 1, 1962.

throughout the country, or should *standards* be lower? The question of which level should be used as the "yardstick" is important. Upon its answer will depend the amount of money and effort Congress is willing to put into this venture.

The great advancements in the health of the United States population have been intimately connected with a century and a half of socioeconomic development. Indian health in every era has lagged behind the health of the well-to-do city dweller, remaining consistent with the Indian's own economic status. What the U.S.P.H.S. is now trying to do, with a mandate and generous funds from Congress, is to close the gap between Indian health and that of the general public, ignoring the economic level. Such a course may not be possible, even with today's medical knowledge, so long as the performance of the task remains in large measure a tour de force.

History has shown that the health of both Indians and other persons will improve as their economic status is raised. For the Indians such economic improvement needs to be brought about through efforts of the Bureau and of the tribes themselves.

VIII. Recommendations

The Indians should receive adequate medical care, which for maximum results should be supplemented with improved education and economic betterment. Funds allocated for hospitals, medical personnel, and general health services should bear a proper relation to those appropriated for these other purposes.

In some areas, federal, state, and local health agencies need to be co-ordinated and local specialists used. In others, a closer co-operation between the public health service and the Bureau of Indian Affairs should be established to insure that the national policy for Indian development and welfare is effective and consistent. Funds should be made available to improve roads and telephones to clinics and hospitals.

Sanitary water and sewage systems should be increased. They should be installed in co-ordination with housing and similar

ns. Pains should be taken to eliminate duplication in the
tion, operation, and administration of these undertak-

The United States Public Health Service, despite its excellent
record of performance, should adjust traditional professional
attitudes and practices to make them more suitable and acceptable to the Indian people. The doctor should treat patients not
only as individuals but also as constituent members of a group—
a group which may sharply differ both culturally and linguis-
tically from a white community. He should confer with the Indians and seek when possible to benefit from their counsel.

In view of the historic responsibility of the United States for
Indian health, the Public Health Service should not agree with
states to relinquish services without prior consultation with the
tribes to be affected.

When the tribes approve such transfer, the government should
set enforcible standards to assure the quality and continuation
of the services and prevent discrimination against Indians.

Preventive medicine and maternal and child health should be
stressed. Effective co-operation between the public health service
and schools, whether federal or state, should be obtained. Public
health nurses should be made directly responsible to the physicians in charge, and doctors, nurses, and hospital administrators
should increase their use of Indian personnel whenever possible.

The tribes, for their part, should assume greater responsibility
for health and sanitation. To this end, Indians should learn to
recognize those common diseases which demand immediate attention. Both adults and children should be educated by health
agencies to take the first steps when illness strikes.

7

Policies Which Impede Indian Assimilation

XXXXXXXXXXXXXXXXXXXXXXXXXXXXXXXXXXXXXXXXXXXXXXXXXXXXXX

I. INTRODUCTION

THE PRECEDING CHAPTERS highlight several facets of the over-all "Indian problem." So long as all these unresolved predicaments persist, the Indian problem will remain with us. This chapter demonstrates that any official policy which ignores the prevailing value systems of Indian tribes is not only doomed to fail, but to compound the difficulties already existing. To be specific—so long as levels of Indian education, health, and economy are substandard, so long as the Indian's status in practically all areas of life is uncertain, just so long will legislation or other precipitate action fail to assimilate the Indian into the majority society.

The assumption that Indians and members of other alien groups were inferior because they were simple, primitive, or savage dominated the thinking of the Western world during most of the nineteenth century. In the United States this national attitude was reflected by the Congress (which, accordingly, established policies based on this false implication) and officially expressed by the B. I. A. Under the guise of subscribing to the national attitude of "civilizing" or "assimilating" Indians, forcibly if necessary, the land-hungry people, the moralists, the super-patriots, the conformists, and even government officials exploited the Indians. Toward the end of the century, under the guidance of the emerging disciplines that we now call the behavioral sciences, a clearer view of the Indian problem and the white man's obligation began to develop.

179

The realization that conformity cannot be legislated changed the national policy toward Indians. The conviction that men and cultures differing from us and our culture must, nevertheless, be respected led to the Indian Reorganization Act of 1934,[1] which shifted the initiative in relation to Indian problems from the B. I. A. to the Indian tribes themselves. However, before the efficacy of the act could be adequately demonstrated, World War II broke out; and after the war the old attitude of trying to assimilate Indians by legislation reasserted itself, culminating in the "termination resolution" (House Concurrent Resolution Number 108, of August 1, 1953, and Public Law 280, of August 15, 1953), which has been proved capable of disrupting Indian life by depriving Indians of powers in their tribal governments and which concentrates, not on the best interests of the Indians, but on easing the burden on the federal government. The effect has been to deprive Indians of both their property and the public services for which the federal government has long been obligated.

II. BACKGROUND OF TERMINATION

The avowed purpose of termination is not new. Since the beginning of the Republic, federal policy has from time to time been aimed at encouraging Indians to adopt the ways of their white neighbors. Between 1789 and 1886 such policy vacillated between making treaties with Indian tribes as land-owning, autonomous nations and compelling them to live as wards of the government, segregated on reservations. Certain bands were virtual prisoners, forced to dwell within the boundaries of their original domain or on land given them in exchange for it. Even temporary absence from their reservations was permitted only through the use of passes.

Laws were enacted in the nineteenth century to abolish tribal existence; but most of them, for one reason or another, failed to stick. Those Choctaws who remained in Mississippi when the rest of the tribe was moved westward were terminated about

[1] See Chapter One, pp. 20–22, above.

1830,[2] the Kickapoos, in 1862,[3] the Cherokees who remained in North Carolina, in 1868;[4] and the Winnebagos, who separated from their brothers in Nebraska, took up homestead allotments about 1875.[5] Each had its tribal organization dissolved and its relation with the federal government legally severed, but today each is accorded the rights of an Indian tribe and is so recognized by the United States.

After much difficulty and many successive acts of Congress, the Five Civilized Tribes in Oklahoma were by 1906 deprived of their governments;[6] their tribal courts were abolished; their chief executives were made subject to removal by the President; and their authority was completely stripped from them, including control of schools, public buildings, and the like. One legal device alone remained: their continuation as tribal entities for the purpose of winding up their affairs. Terminating these tribes caused suffering, resentments that lasted for generations, the subjugation of a proud people, and a slowly dawning realization among some whites that this method was not the way to assimilate the red man successfully.

Until the early 1930's the federal programs were, nonetheless, based on the belief of administrators that properly executed government regulations would settle the Indian question. By that time, however, it had become clear that the destruction of Indian governments, the liquidation of tribal property, and hostility to Indian culture had been a mistake, that they had defeated rather than furthered the objective of adjusting Indians to the dominant society. The Meriam Survey *Report* in 1928, compiled under the auspices of the Institute for Government Research, pointed out these shortcomings and showed what needed to be done to achieve the desired goals. It had a profound effect. A new policy, initiated under President Hoover, Secretary of the Interior Wilbur, and Commissioner Rhoads, was expanded and galvanized into action under President Roosevelt, Secretary

---

2 Cohen, *Handbook of Federal Indian Law.*
3 *Ibid.*   4 *Ibid.*
5 *Ibid.*   6 *Ibid.*

of the Interior Ickes, and Commissioner Collier, who extended and buttressed the policy by adopting the Indian Reorganization Act in 1934. From 1934 to 1950, the period of home rule, an attempt was made to assimilate the Indian by letting him use his own culture as a springboard for his operations and as a basis for his integration.

A definite shift away from the policy of the Indian Reorganization Act occurred, however, when on February 8, 1947, the Senate Committee on Civil Service directed William Zimmerman, Jr., acting commissioner of the B. I. A., to prepare a statement outlining reduction of expenses of the Indian Office and increasing the responsibility of states for tribes within their borders. In drawing up his plans, Zimmerman did not recommend that the United States rid itself of all its Indian obligations. That move came later. In April of that year John Provinse, assistant commissioner, outlined the policy of administration foreshadowed by the Johnson-O'Malley Act of 1934[7]—namely, the transfer of some B. I. A. social services to the states and private organizations.

Between 1950 and 1960 the major controversy in Indian affairs was over whether the United States should follow a program of pressing for prompt termination of tribes without the consent of their members. Policies were confused, the secretary seeming to espouse one kind and the B. I. A. another.[8] But mandatory termination appeared to be the goal until September 18, 1958, when Secretary of the Interior Fred A. Seaton, broadcasting over radio station KCLS, Flagstaff, Arizona, surprised everyone by stating that no tribe would be involuntarily terminated.[9] Since its adoption in 1953, House Concurrent Resolution No. 108, which states that the policy of Congress is to terminate as soon as practicable, has been in effect. However, since the publication of

[7] See Chapter Five, p. 149, above.

[8] Communication from Orme Lewis, assistant secretary of the interior, to Senator Watkins, chairman of the Senate Subcommittee on Indian Affairs, March 13, 1953; Memorandum No. 67 to the Commissioners, Commission on the Rights, Liberties, and Responsibilities of the American Indian, Jan. 12, 1959.

[9] Dept. of Interior news release, Sept., 1958.

"A Program for Indian Citizens" in January, 1961,[10] the mimeographed report of President Kennedy's Task Force in July, 1961,[11] the declaration by various groups in Chicago under the aegis of Professor Sol Tax,[12] and Secretary Udall's elucidation of Indian policy,[13] the administration has emphasized the development of Indian resources.

In contrast to the frequent contradictions of policy in governmental executive and legislative branches during the history of the B. I. A., one area of stability is noteworthy. The judiciary branch of the government must enforce laws enacted by Congress, but the federal courts have, since the beginning, treated individual Indians as needing special protection and services and the tribes as dependent nations.

III. KINDS OF TERMINATION

Nobody knows exactly what termination really means— neither the Indians nor anyone else. Termination can mean, for example, that one branch of the federal government surrenders a function, as in the transfer to the United States Public Health Service of the B. I. A.'s Division of Health. It may refer to a contract made by the B. I. A. with a state or local government for special services, such as the education of Indians in public schools. It may signify the relinquishing by the B. I. A. of part of its control of property, such as is involved when Indians are allowed to negotiate their own leases for allotted land or when B. I. A. transfers a function to the tribal government, as in the transfer of irrigation works and their operation to the Navaho tribe. (These works then do not become subject to state law.) It may even mean the withdrawal from a tribe of certain services usually rendered by the B. I. A., as, for example, the Bureau's removal of a superintendent capable of advising the inexpe-

10 Commission on the Rights, Liberties, and Responsibilities of the American Indian, "A Program for Indian Citizens, a Summary Report," Jan., 1961.

11 Report to the Secretary of the Interior by the Task Force on Indian Affairs, July 10, 1961.

12 "Declaration of Indian Purpose," American Indian Chicago Conference, University of Chicago, June 13–20, 1961.

13 Dept. of Interior news release, July 12, 1961.

rienced Umatillas in retaining their land and replacing him with a man whose previous experience had been chiefly in *selling* federal land. It may mean that a state is given Congressional authorization to extend its criminal and civil laws to Indian reservations, thereby depriving the tribes of substantial powers of local self-government (Public Law 280). It may also mean the passing of laws by Congress severing the historic relationship between the federal government and the tribes, abolishing their long-existing governments, and placing their affairs and resources under control of a state. It is in the sense of the last two meanings that the word "termination" is used in this report. Termination not only is not assimilation; it is not even assured integration. Integration comes only as a race is dispersed within the general population. If Indians so choose, they can now effect such dispersal, but it must be voluntary.

Termination by Assumption of Jurisdiction over Indian Country by States (Public Law 280)

Unlike many of the earlier federal statutes which granted only judicial jurisdiction to states, Public Law 280[14] conveys legislative authority, thus giving states the right to enact measures that could vitally change the character of the communities in which the Indians live without any option on their part. A state could wipe out most tribal customs, reduce or destroy the family's traditional control, abolish customary or undocumented marriages and so make children illegitimate, change the inheritance laws, and apply a complicated criminal code to a simple people.

In Nebraska, the state and its subdivisions refused adequate policing after the United States withdrew B. I. A. law-and-order personnel from the Winnebago and Omaha Indians, although the tribesmen paid over $55,000 in land taxes and furnished a substantial part of the county budget. In 1961 the legislature at last appropriated $30,000 for that purpose.

Public Law 280 allows state, criminal, and civil legislation to supersede tribal and federal enactments in the case of reserva-

14 Public Law 280, 67 Stat., 588, Aug. 15, 1953.

tion Indians in Wisconsin, Minnesota (except the Red Lake Reservation), Nebraska, California, Oregon (except Warm Springs Reservation), and, by amendment, Alaska. The act, however, imposes certain limitations. Restricted property may not be alienated or encumbered, nor may states tax or regulate the use of the property or adjudicate its ownership in a manner inconsistent with any agreement or federal law. Hunting, trapping, and fishing rights secured by treaty agreement or statute are likewise protected; and tribal ordinances or customs, if not incompatible with state law, are to be applied in civil cases. The act further permits any other state to extend its civil and criminal statutes to Indians without Indian consent. But in order to extend its laws to the reservation, a state must amend its constitution or statutes and assume financial and other responsibilities, which few have seen fit to do.

In 1962 Public Law 280 was in all stages of adoption. Nevada, North Dakota and South Dakota have acted to extend their jurisdictions. The Nevada statute allows counties to petition to be excepted from its provisions. It is reported that every county but one has followed the tribes' wishes, even though the law does not require tribal consent. North Dakota in 1958 amended its state constitution to enable the legislature to accept jurisdiction on its own terms, but the lawmakers have yet to take action. The South Dakota law, calling for tribal referendums, authorizes counties to assume the responsibility only on the impossible condition that the United States defray the cost, which federal law does not permit.

The constitution of the state of Washington disclaims jurisdiction over Indian lands, but despite this, Public Law 280 was construed by the state as permitting state law-and-order codes to be effective on Indian reservations. This authority caused so much dissatisfaction that, on February 11, 1963, the legislature of the state of Washington passed Senate Bill No. 56. This bill provided that the state will not assume jurisdiction over Indians on tribal or allotted lands within an established reservation held in trust by the United States unless the governor of the state receives from the majority of the tribe, or tribal council, or other governing body a resolution expressing the desire to be brought under state laws. If the Indians do not accept this new law, the state still maintains jurisdiction over Indians in regard to compulsory school attendance, public assistance, domestic relations, mental illness, juvenile delinquency, adoption proceedings, dependent children, and operation of motor vehicles upon public streets.[15]

President Eisenhower, in 1953, believing the act to be a step toward complete Indian equality, approved the authority with

> . . . grave doubts as to the wisdom of certain provisions. Sections 6 and 7 . . . permit other States to impose on Indian tribes within their borders the criminal and civil jurisdiction of the State, removing the Indians from Federal jurisdiction and, in some instances, effective self-government. The failure to include in these provisions a requirement of full consultation in order to ascertain the wishes and desires of the Indians and of final Federal approval, was unfortunate.

He therefore urged that at the earliest possible time the act (Public Law 280) be amended to require both prior consultation with the tribes and concurrency of the federal government.

The Senate Subcommittee on Constitutional Rights has since 1961 conducted an extensive investigation into the Constitutional rights of the Indian, the first such study ever made by Congress. On the basis of their findings, Senate Bill 966 was introduced into Congress. It would repeal Public Law 280 and provide a feasible and equitable method of state civil and criminal jurisdiction over Indian country for those tribesmen who might elect to come under state law. Judge Lewis in a recent opinion said:

> The legal history of the status of Indian tribes under State and Federal law presents a complex and ever-changing concept of an

---

[15] Nevada Laws, 1954–55, c. 198, p. 297; North Dakota Laws, 1957, p. 792. *Senate Concurrent Resolution O;* South Dakota Laws, 1957, c. 319, p. 427. South Dakota Constitution, Art. 22, 26; Washington Laws, 1957, c. 240, p. 941. Washington Constitution Art. xxvi; Dept. of Interior news release, June 28, 1961; *States* v. *Paul,* 337 P. 2d 33 (1959).

artificial entity progressing from independent but helpless sovereignty toward a status of complete integration in the legal, economic and moral life of the people of the United States.[16]

The new concept in Indian law introduced by Public Law 280 has been further emphasized by the Kake Village case which held (369 U.S. 60; 75):

> These decisions indicate that even on reservations State laws may be applied to Indians unless such application would interfere with reservation self-government or impair a right granted or reserved by Federal law.

Integration of Indian tribes under state law is moving forward at an accelerated rate.

Termination by Withdrawal of Federal Services

From 1954 through 1960 many laws and amendments were passed abolishing tribes as political entities—to "get the United States out of the Indian business"—and shifting responsibility for Indian affairs from the federal government to the states. During these years sixty-one tribes, groups, communities, *rancherias,* or allotments were terminated. Delays were allowed in setting a final termination date for such things as federal construction of sanitary facilities and the search for a trustee to dispose of the Wyandotte Cemetery in Kansas City, for pending settlement of claims before the Indian Claims Commission, and for the distribution and adjudication of unliquidated claims of gas and mineral rights. Exceptions were made for the Alabama-Coushatta tribesmen in Texas to retain medical aid and eligibility for their children's federal education.

A. Notable Weaknesses and Undesirable Results

The policy of termination and the legislation implementing it are characterized by several glaring weaknesses. (1) The basic assumption of assimilation-by-legislation is invalid. (2) Action has been taken precipitately. (3) Indians were given inadequate

[16] *Sam Dicke et al.* v. *Cheyenne-Arapahoe Tribes, Inc.,* 304 F. 2d 113, U.S. Court of Appeals, Tenth Circuit, May 17, 1962.

information and explanation regarding all probable effects of the policy, were rushed into the situation, and were permitted no true voice in the matter. (4) Although several tribes have been abolished as governmental units, ambiguities have been written into individual termination acts, which leave many highly important jurisdictional areas unclear.[17] (5) The remaining obligations of the federal government to the Indians must yet be defined, probably by court action. For example, a terminated tribe does not know whether a state or a tribal tax should be levied on tribesmen and on persons doing business on its land. In case of a conflict, what is the proper federal action? (6) The traditional rights of a tribe to determine—in the absence of federal law—its own membership and to possess as a unit its assets in perpetuity have been transferred to federal jurisdiction. (7) The policy resulted, during the years when House Concurrent Resolution 108 was the guideline, in Congressional and B. I. A. concentration upon the withdrawal of federal services, instead of upon improving the Indian situation. It brought, in this connection, the appointment of private trustees to take over some of the federal functions (such as handling tribal resources) and the selection by the secretary of the interior (instead of by the tribes concerned) of management specialists to handle—under the secretary's instructions—whatever economic resources a "terminated tribe" may have had. (8) The legislation prohibits a tribe from spending before the termination date any tribal funds in the Treasury unless approved by the secretary.

There are other inequities wrought by the legislation, other potentially disastrous situations caused by the policy. To say the least, termination has been ill considered and weak; to say more, it has proved genuinely destructive of its own announced aim. House Concurrent Resolution 108, which the Indians believed had the force of a statute, effected some of the above far-reaching changes immediately, even regarding tribes not actually terminated by law. Once more, acquisitive white men looked toward

17 The Paiute act, 25 U.S. Code Annotated, sec. 758. The Klamath act has the same provisions, 25 U.S. Code Annotated, sec. 564–12.

At the Glen Canyon Unit, Colorado River Storage Project, Arizona-
Utah, a Navaho worker scales loose rock from a cliff
near Wahweap Creek.

U.S. Bureau of Reclamation, Photograph by A. E. Turner

Youth Opportunity Program at work in northern Idaho. This Nez
Percé youth is employed at a part-time job that will enable
him to continue his education.

Bureau of Indian Affairs

This young lady, a Snohomish Indian from the Western Washington
Agency, is a business college graduate employed by
the city of Portland, Oregon.

Bureau of Indian Affairs

Under the Navaho Community Services Program, the Navaho tribe invites and supports industries in reservation areas and supplies on-the-job training for Indian workers. These three Navaho women are preparing wire for soldering in an airplane communication system assembly plant in Flagstaff, Arizona.

Standard Oil Company (N.J.)

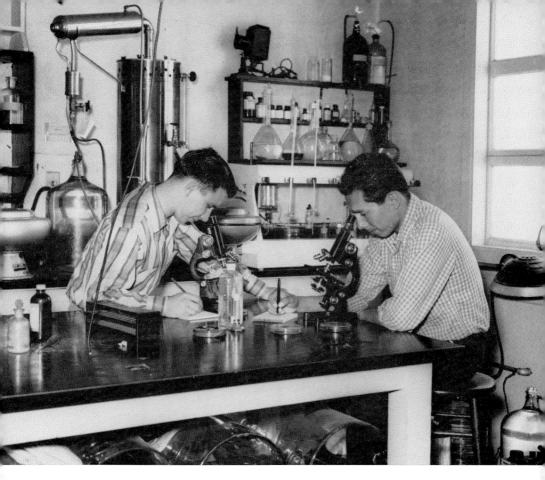

The young man on the right, a Sioux from Standing Rock Reservation, North Dakota, and a fellow student study mortuary science in San Francisco.

Bureau of Indian Affairs

Two Indian boys, a Chickasaw (left) and a Kiowa-Chickasaw, take a course in Diesel mechanics.

Bureau of Indian Affairs

Vincent Myers, Comanche Indian of Apache, Oklahoma, winner of the 1960 Interior Department Conservation Award, working on his 160-acre farm. He also leases 800 acres from other Indians, using 540 acres for crops and the remainder for pasture for livestock.

Relocation exhibit booth (Arizona), giving information on
off-reservation employment.

Standard Oil Company (N.J.)

Indian land. Once more, confusion increased regarding the status of the Indians. And the Indians themselves were seized with fear, made additionally insecure, and forced to rely for strength upon their own cultural conventions, thereby automatically accentuating every ethnic trait separating them from the dominant society.

The termination policy emphasized the housekeeping activities of trusteeship. The result was that many B. I. A. administrators became indifferent to basic Indian needs. The shortsighted policy of forcing Indians into the white man's pattern took precedence over any need to understand the effects of such a policy upon the individual. Mass transfers of students were made from federal to public schools to implement the policy, without taking into account the quality of teaching or the readiness or unreadiness of a child for the change.

The B. I. A. extension service was transferred to the Extension Division of the Department of Agriculture with the sole aim of getting rid of the Indian Service. The additional expenses involved and the compounding of administrative problems went unheeded. Land was made available for sale, with little or no thought given to the Indian's future after he had lost his land.

The historic connections between the tribes and the United States were severed by the termination acts, without a clear understanding on either side of what was involved. Special services the United States had rendered were stopped without any assurance that they would or could thereafter be provided willingly by the states or their local units. For example, the United States, as well as the B. I. A., builds roads on Indian tribal land with federal money. The western states, in obtaining their share of funds from the Bureau of Public Roads, include Indian reservations in the total land area, which is a basis for allocations. The B. I. A. also performs maintenance work. Some states or local units undoubtedly would not have money for such programs if federal support were withdrawn. Only the California termination legislation mentions roads, stipulating that they are to be brought up to standard before the federal government relinquishes its obligations.

If there had been more time for the Indians to understand and consider these termination bills, and had they then been given the opportunity to ament or reject them without the immediate inducement of cash resulting from a division of tribal funds, the Klamath and Menominee bills at least would probably never have taken the form in which they were enacted. Some states, especially those with large Indian populations, have declined to assume the responsibility to Indians without extra federal compensation.[18] If local governments are willing but financially unable to render such services, the United States should make financial arrangements with them. If the cost of service is less than taxes, adjustment should be made to forestall the realization of local profits from the transaction. There should never be any termination without federally enforcible assurances that adequate services will be continued. Court injunctions are no substitutes for schools, roads, or police protection.

Turning Indian affairs over to the states is, therefore, no solution in itself. The chances are that each state which has assumed or will assume such obligations may wind up (as have California, New York, and Texas) with a commission or division of Indian affairs. New York State, for example, which since 1787 has taken over responsibility for its Indians, has furnished special services to them. An interdepartmental committee on Indian affairs, set up in 1952 for integrating these functions, co-operates with a joint legislative committee in a continuing attempt to "find a solution for the . . . confused and paralyzing legal status of New York Indians." Actually, unless the manifold results of the termination program are more accurately foreseen and more carefully studied, the United States may end up with a multifunctional "Department of Indian Termination," costing more to operate than the Bureau of Indian Affairs.

B. Indian "Acceptance" of Termination

If termination is so patently unfair to Indians, why—one might well ask—have some tribes accepted it? Many diverse fac-

18 See Chapter Four, pp. 130–32, above.

tors have pushed tribes into such "acceptance." Near the top of the list one must place the inducement of the funds to be distributed among individual tribesmen. Perhaps the most persuasive factor, however, has been the fact that Indians have grown weary of too much supervision and resentful of what they feel to be the "father-knows-best" attitude of the B. I. A. Yet, despite their discontent, most existing tribes oppose termination because they are accustomed to a dependent relationship with the federal government and because they know they are unprepared for a clean break.

Some tribal members favor termination because they want to buy tribal land or use the reservation, but the strongest proponents are members no longer living on reservations. In some instances they presently receive nothing from tribal land, but would get their share of the proceeds if the property were divided and sold. Also, there are the selfishly interested whites—ranchers, farmers, stockmen, and speculators in oil, minerals, timber, or real estate—who are totally unconcerned with the welfare of the Indians or the moral and legal obligations of the federal government, wanting only to get their hands upon reservation acres.

C. Inconsistencies Between Testimony and Acts

The repeated assertions at hearings on the termination acts that Indians are ready for termination are all belied by the provisions of the acts themselves, which invariably set up the safeguards usually provided for persons needing guardians. In the transitional period practically every tribal action of consequence has required the approval of the secretary of the interior. Some of the acts have authorized the secretary to provide temporary education, including language, and orientation in non-Indian communities, customs, and living standards—courses which would hardly have been selected had the Indians really been ready to operate successfully in the white society. The acts have not helped individuals to meet their personal problems or the surrounding community to solve the difficulties created by the legislation.

Termination legislation when tribes were prepared for severing B. I. A. relations has caused no suffering or displacement—the bands in western Oregon, for example. In California, on the other hand, the legislature memorialized the President and the Congress, protesting the possible wholesale termination affecting seven thousand inhabitants of 117 reservations or *rancherias* on grounds that not all were ready for termination:[19]

> . . . the American Indians conveyed their property to the United States Government in exchange for the promise of perpetual Federal protection and certain other benefits; and . . . the tribes vary widely in their educational level, and social and economic development, and many of them would suffer greatly if Federal control and protection of their reservation was terminated . . . .

As a result, the final Congressional termination legislation covered only 41 *rancherias* or reservations, affecting only about one thousand people occupying 750,000 acres. (Later Public Law 85–671 was amended by Public Law 88–419 to extend the provisions of the act.) Whether these groups were satisfactorily integrated into the white culture only time will tell.

The nature of the impact of the termination acts on each reservation depended on the Indians' education, their adaptation to the white culture, the value of their resources, their leadership, and countless other factors. The Menominee and Klamath tribes, for example, both had land resources. The Menominees organized as a group to keep their resources intact, but the Klamaths divided a large proportion of their assets among withdrawing members. So that the terms of the original act could be met, Congress had to pass five amendments for the Menominee and five for the Klamath Indians.

The early history of the termination acts is instructive. At a hearing before the Joint Subcommittee on Indian Affairs in Washington on February 15, 1954, Glenn Emmons, then commissioner of Indian affairs, said that he called superintendents and area directors of the Bureau to Washington to help frame legislation. Drafts of laws were developed as a basis for discussion

[19] See Chapter Four, p. 132, above.

and were taken by the B. I. A. personnel to the groups of Indians concerned. Commissioner Emmons had explained earlier that "consultation" did not mean Indian consent to termination. He said:

> As trustee, the Federal Government must make the final decision and assume the final responsibility . . . . Naturally the time for consultation was short. But formal statements of Indian views were obtained where possible. Indians were urged to submit any additional comments they might have directly to the Congressional committees. . . . the bills were revised to incorporate all of the suggestions that were considered sound . . . . The bills are certainly not perfect. The Indians will have opportunity to present additional views at these hearings which will undoubtedly result in the development of a sound legislative program.[20]

Since Commissioner Emmons conceded that these bills were not "perfect" and implied that Indian consent was not necessary, the Indians' attendance at the Congressional hearings was, of course, all-important to them. Yet many of the hearings were held in Washington, D.C., and transportation costs were too high for most Indians to afford.

D. THREE SPECIFIC EXAMPLES OF TERMINATION

1. Paiute Termination[21]

The ill effects of hastily severing uneducated and unprepared Indians from federal services is illustrated by what happened to about two hundred members of the Shivwits, Koosharem, Indian Peaks, and Kanosh bands of the Paiutes, who owned approximately 46,000 acres of land and were among the first tribes to be terminated. Public Law 762 was passed in September, 1954, and the Proclamation of Termination of Supervision for these four groups was published in the *Federal Register* on February 28,

---

20 *Termination of Federal Supervision Over Certain Tribes of Indians,* Joint Hearings Before the Subcommittees of the Committees on Interior and Insular Affairs, 83 Cong., 2 sess., Part 1, Utah (Feb. 15, 1954), 41, 42.

21 Unless otherwise stated, the material in this section was taken from Memorandum No. 49a to the Commissioners, Commission on the Rights, Liberties, and Responsibilities of the American Indian (July 10–11, 1958).

1957. Obviously, the four bands were poor; yet, according to the evidence presented, they had received almost no services from the Bureau of Indian Affairs.[22] Testimony differs concerning their educational attainments. In 1950 a Bureau report stated that the Shivwits, Koosharem, and Kanosh were not prepared for federal withdrawal, but that the Indian Peaks band, although also not competent to manage its own affairs, was "ready for complete Bureau withdrawal as soon as the reservation is sold and the Indians completely established on individual home sites within good labor market areas."[23] Despite evidence to the contrary, Assistant Secretary of the Interior Orme Lewis wrote in 1954: "It is our belief that the members of these groups have in general attained sufficient skill and ability to manage their own affairs without the very limited special Federal assistance that they now receive."[24] The Paiutes' lack of education, their low income, the inept handling of their resources, and the fact that the final termination law (Public Law 83–762) provided that they be given instruction in English and special education to help them earn a livelihood and conduct their own affairs all testify that they were not ready for termination. And their subsequent history proves it.

A year after the Paiute termination was completed (1958), they were asked why they had not objected to termination. A Kanosh man answered that at the time of the hearings the people had not understood what was happening. According to the 1954 chairman of the Kanosh tribe, he had never been to school a single day, and many old people had very little education. Even without schooling they might have comprehended the implications of the impending law, but no one could afford either to go to Washington or to obtain legal advice. When a B. I. A. employee came to clarify what was later to become Public Law 83–

22 *Termination of Federal Supervision Over Certain Tribes of Indians,* Joint Hearings, 83 Cong., 2 sess., Part 1, Utah (Feb. 15, 1954) , 13–16, 54–56.

23 83 Cong., 2 sess., *House Report 2680, Report with Respect to the House Resolutions Authorizing the Committee on Interior and Insular Affairs to Conduct an Investigation of the Bureau of Indian Affairs,* 86–87.

24 *Termination of Federal Supervision Over Certain Tribes of Indians,* Joint Hearings, 83 Cong., 2 sess., Part 1, Utah, 9.

762, each group was approached separately, so that they never discussed together or really understood the legal implications of the act.

Soon after the passage of Public Law 83–762, Paiute land was transferred from the B. I. A. to trustees of the Walker Bank and Trust Company in Salt Lake City, about 160 miles away. The Paiutes had difficulty getting transportation to the bank and then communicating with the trust officer. An Indian Peaks man said that they finally collected enough money for gasoline to go to Salt Lake City, where they saw the trustee, but they could not understand his remarks and after a few minutes were shown out of his office. They also tried unsuccessfully to get advice from an attorney appointed by the bank and paid with Paiute money. Later the attorney wrote the Indian Peaks official that he would have samples of valuable minerals found on tribal land tested. "But," the Paiute continued, "we do not know one stone from another."

A Shivwits man said that without the tribe's consent the trustee had leased their range to a cattleman at a price of 30 cents a head each month for 100 cattle. This was $1.20 less per animal than the government's appraised value, and, in addition, their land was being overgrazed. The trustees had given the state highway department permission to repair the reservation road without the Indians' knowledge. The maintenance men had knocked down the fences, and the Indians did not know to whom they should go to get help.

Public Law 762 required the United States to reserve for ten years subsurface rights from any division or sale of tribal property and to vest the legal title in the trustee to whom property might be transferred. Thus, should profitable minerals be discovered on the land, continuing obligations of a trust nature will probably be thrust upon the United States.

Extra charges connected with public schooling entailed expenses the Paiutes could ill afford. There was a fifteen-dollar payment to the activity fund each year for each child and one dollar a week for school lunches. Many of the children in Cedar City came home during the noon hour because they had no lunch money. State services posed other problems. A man over sixty-five years of age could not get welfare payments because he had no birth certificate and could not prove his age. A Kanosh farmer could not get a loan on his farm because it was part of the land held by his tribe and owned by several people. Hospital and doctors' bills became burdens, although the Mormon church paid some of the charges.

Registering to vote, complying with state regulations for hunting and fishing licenses, or obtaining farmers' home or other loans—such important activities were all beyond the experience and understanding of the Paiutes. Without birth certificates, Social Security numbers, land deeds, and a command of English and general know-how, they are relatively helpless. This one case amply demonstrates that the policy statement of Congress "to make Indians . . . subject to the same laws and entitled to the same privileges as are applicable to citizens of the United States" (House Concurrent Resolution 108) is not accomplished by termination legislation.

2. Klamath Termination

The 2,133 enrolled Indians on the Klamath Reservation in southern Oregon had extensive and valuable holdings: 720,000 acres in forests (chiefly ponderosa pine) and 280,000 acres of range, farmland, or marsh. The act terminating their relation to the federal government (Public Law 587) was passed August 13, 1954, and the tribesmen were given their choice of taking their share of the assets or keeping the property in one block in trust for the group. In the election held to determine what should be done, 1,660 tribesmen voted for a distribution of assets while 84 voted to continue as a group.

The reservation had been set aside for these Indians by the treaty of 1864, but they had never developed the requisite skills for handling this valuable estate. At the same time they lost much of their native culture. The elders no longer counseled the young with the old adage, "Work hard so people will respect you."

Access to wealth freed the Klamaths from restraint, and the imposition on them of the B. I. A.'s economic program without their consent relieved them of responsibility. Internal stresses and jurisdictional controversies developed, which almost completely exhausted tribal, communal, and even family control. In one year five out of eight murders involved Indians.[25] With this background it is easy to see why 1,660 members voted for termination and cash.

The withdrawing members received 78 per cent of the entire property or a per capita payment of $44,000 each. As soon as it became clear that large sums of money would be distributed to Indians, many ingenious ways were developed by unscrupulous citizens to induce the Indians to part with their cash, such as exorbitant interest rates on loans made before their inheritance was received or excessive attorneys' fees. Some Klamath Indians have used their money wisely; a great number have nothing whatsoever left and may end by swelling the state welfare rolls.

In the sale of their assets tribesmen were given first choice in the purchase of land or personal property; the rest was offered to the public. The government purchased, through the Bureau of Sport Fisheries and Wildlife, 15,000 acres of land as a refuge on the flyway of migratory fowl. Eighty-four thousand acres were sold in small units without any restrictions, while 617,000 acres were divided into sustained-yield units and offered for bids. The law required the purchaser of each unit to pay at least the appraised price and to manage the land on a sustained-yield basis. Only one tract of 92,000 acres was sold to a private purchaser, the Crown Zellerbach Corporation. The remaining sustained-yield units, consisting of 105,000 acres, were bought by the government at the appraised price: one-fifth was assigned to the Frémont National Forest, and four-fifths to a new Wimena National Forest.

Four hundred and seventy-three Indians—the 84 who had voted to have their combined property handled in one block

25 Vincent Ostrum and Theodore Stern, "A Case Study of the Termination of Federal Responsibilities Over the Klamath Reservation" (1963).

and 389 who did not vote—were organized as a nonprofit trusteeship under state law. They have an executive committee of five serving as the official spokesmen for the group. They meet regularly with the officers of the United States National Bank of Portland, who administer their assets.

At the time the trust was formed, the assets of the group amounted to approximately 143,000 acres of timber, marsh, and ranch land and 206 head of cattle. Under the provision of the trust, beneficiaries were given the opportunity to terminate the trust agreement at the end of each five-year period. The first period ended in 1964. Somewhat over half the members in this group were minors in 1959 and many reached their majority by the 1964 election.[26] At this meeting the trust would have been terminated if the votes of only those present had been counted. However, it was decided to count the absentees as voting for a continuation of the trust; therefore the trust is still intact.

This trust operates on the old B. I. A. policy of paternalism—namely, to produce the maximum amount of income for the beneficiaries, with no concern for encouraging the people themselves to handle their own property. The management of the trust is solely the responsibility of the bank. Since the bank has taken over the role previously exercised by the B. I. A., some of the Indian resentments and expectations once directed toward B. I. A. are now being visited upon the bank.

These feelings were obvious at a meeting on May 4, 1963, in the Klamath County Library in Klamath Falls. Present at the meeting were a member of the American Friends Service Committee, a representative of the firm of Wilkinson, Gragun, and Barker (the Klamath attorneys), and four members of the executive committee. The fifth member of the executive committee, though absent, was represented by a delegate. There were about a dozen uninvited spectators. The Indians' discontent was centered upon the following factors: First, the failure of the bank to employ Indians to help with the forest or cattle herd. It was explained that the bank had tried hiring Indians but had not

26 Material furnished by the Portland area office, B. I. A., 1963.

found such applicants to be satisfactory. Second, the bank made too much money handling the estate. (The bank was to receive $^{39}/_{100}$ of 1 per cent of the assets, which never amounted to less than $91,000 a year; in 1962 the bank had charged the Klamaths $92,597.68). And, third, in its farm operation the band purchased equipment and then hired farmers who brought in their own machinery. (It was pointed out that the machinery purchased did not include the type of machinery rented.)

The government, however, is not clear of all relations with the Klamaths. An old claim based on loss of tribal land is pending, and there may be other suits based either on the Indians' belief that the government did not pay enough for their land or on their loss of mineral or water rights. It is too soon to tell whether termination has solved any of the Indian problems or whether there has been only a shift of problems from the federal to the state government.

Ten years after the passage of Public Law 83–587, Mrs. Marie Norris, a Klamath leader living in Klamath Falls, said: "If I had known what termination would have meant to all of us, I would have fought it tooth and nail."

3. Menominee Termination[27]

Termination of the Menominee Indians of Wisconsin (Public Law 83–399, June 17, 1954) has caused even greater confusion and disruption of tribal life than the termination of the Paiutes, although it was expected to succeed. The 3,270 Menominees on their 234,000-acre reservation in Wisconsin had long wanted independence from the federal government. For many years they had largely financed their own activities with their tribal assets, and they possessed effective leadership.

At first glance, tribal properties and on-going programs might have constituted an excellent background for the "assimilation" supposed to be the aim of termination. In truth, what appeared as resources under tribal law only compounded the Menominees'

[27] A study of Menominee Termination for the Commissioners, by S. D. Aberle, 1959–65.

problems under state law—problems rendered more bitter by the fact that although the Indians had been consulted regarding Public Law 83–399, their wishes had been given little consideration. As Rex Lee, assistant commissioner of Indian affairs, said:

> We did not feel that it was necessary for us to go back to the Tribe or the State Officials . . . and start trying to draft a new program, because we were faced with a proposal that had been approved by the Senate and approved in a Conference Committee of the House and Senate.[28]

Ignoring the Menominees' suggestions together with the tribesmen's substandard assets proved an inadequate base on which to meet the staggering Congressional demands. Public Law 83–399 made it necessary for the Menominees to transform their tribe into an entirely new political unit, fully conforming to Wisconsin's constitution and laws and offering all the usual public services; integrate tribal activities into prevailing Wisconsin systems; and create a business organization to manage the tribal forest, sawmill, and other properties. Furthermore, the act gave them only three and one-half years in which to work these miracles. When the difficulty of the situation became apparent to Congress, the deadline was extended several times.

Even though amendments delayed final settlement until 1961, the original demands were completely unrealistic, requiring as they did a full understanding of the legal, political, and practical operations of the state and its subdivisions, careful planning, gradual step-by-step action, and extensive technical, political, and legal advice. At the same time funds in the tribal treasury or from the federal government or the state for technical advice and assistance were inadequate.

The Advisory Council, the governing body of the Menominees, tried unsuccessfully to obtain B. I. A. evaluation of the reservation's recreation potentials, attempted—also unsuccessfully—to obtain Bureau approval of a contract they had worked out with Semico Corporation which would have brought in more

[28] *Termination of Federal Supervision over Certain Tribes of Indians,* Joint Hearings, 83 Cong., 2 sess., Part 6, Menominee Indians Wisconsin (March 10, 11, 12, 1954), 610.

tribal income, spent a total of three years in attacking the almost unsolvable problems, and made little headway.

The tribe in 1934 had accepted the Indian Reorganization Act, but had retained its 1928 tribal constitution. Here are examples of some of the tribe's material possessions which presented problems when they had to be operated under state instead of tribal law: The tribe had a hospital in which its members had invested more than $750,000; it had water and sewer systems in Keshena and Neopit; it had a loan fund of approximately $400,000; it operated two hydroelectric plants with power supplied by the Wisconsin Power and Light Company, but not under regulations of the state Public Service Commission; and it had a steam plant not approved by the Federal Power Commission, since approval by outside agencies under their own government was not necessary. Reservation roads maintained by the Bureau were well below state standards. This list of assets ignores the difficult problems the tribe faced of getting their children into public schools; fire protection for the forest; licensing barbers, cosmetologists, and others; state inspections of sanitation, plumbing, and electric wiring; building codes—so on and on it goes. An analysis of all the problems would fill volumes.

In addition to accommodating itself to state law, the tribal government was confronted with internal administrative adjustments. Membership rolls had to be closed at once. Jurisdiction over civil matters, previously under federal or tribal governments, was transferred to the state only two months after passage of the Menominee Act. Ownership of and tax valuations (in terms of Wisconsin assessments) on homesites and agricultural holdings on tribal land had to be determined and then the owners educated regarding taxation.

Before the Menominees' valuable assets were transferred to a business organization, financial accountings, as well as a complete plan for future operation of their land, forest, mill, and other assets, had to be made and accepted by the secretary of the interior. These adjustments were costly; yet Public Law 83–399 had stipulated a per capita distribution of $1,500, to be made from tribal funds. Later the Department of the Interior's solicitors ordered a $778 per capita payment. These payments wiped out the tribe's economic reserve.

Tribesmen were also concerned lest they should incur state and federal transfer taxes of some $80,000 in the initial distribution of property, although they felt strongly that a tax on real estate which had been acquired before Wisconsin became a state was unjust.

Finally, in 1957 tribal members established the Coordinating and Negotiating Committee (C and N). A Menominee B. I. A. employee in the Washington branch of law enforcement, George Kenote, was asked by the tribal authority to return to the reservation as chairman of the C and N Committee. He was released from his duties in the Bureau without compensation, even though the termination law authorized the secretary to provide reasonable assistance requested by tribal officials.

The C and N Committee recognized the complexity of its problem and the enormity of its own ignorance and decided to test Menominee knowledge against that of their neighbors by taking a poll regarding a single aspect of the problem, taxation. Surrounding white farmers were asked about state financing of schools, welfare, roads, and the like; and the Menominees found, to their amazement, that the farmers were as vague as they were about state government.

From the beginning the C and N Committee was seriously hampered by the general confusion prevailing on the reservation and by a total lack of understanding of the "heavy" costs entailed in the large-scale planning required. (The original C and N Committee budget of $10,000 had to be raised to $35,000 almost immediately.)

Also, the tribe was split into factions, each with its own plan: transfer of the forest to a special state-managed trusteeship like the B. I. A.'s; formation of a co-operative; continuation under the B. I. A.; management of tribal business by the Advisory Council; and liquidation of all tribal assets and division of the property among individual Menominees.

The C and N Committee set out to explore all possible legal governmental organizations, submitting the four most likely ones to a tribal referendum. A plan to set up a new and independent county won overwhelmingly, and, through legislative action, Menominee became Wisconsin's seventy-second county, its smallest and one of its poorest.

During the time the tribe was deciding on establishing a separate county, the C and N Committee, with legal help, was working on a business organization incorporated under Wisconsin law to handle Menominee assets. The C and N Committee, with the approval of the tribesmen, decided on a nine-member board of directors (three or four chosen from the tribe and the others from business and the professions—banking, manufacturing, and forestry) to run all facilities—mill, forest, utilities, etc.— seven voting trustees (four Menominees and three outsiders), with all the 3,270 tribesmen as stockholders or bondholders. Bonds maturing in twenty years were issued as a part of the equity. Restrictions were put on stockholders to keep the property intact. Stock could not be transferred for five years, but could be inherited. For the next fifteen years it could be transferred, with the corporation having first option to acquire it at the going price. Minors' shares, as it was finally worked out, would be held by the trust department of the First Wisconsin Trust Company. The plan was ready before the deadline set by the Secretary.

The sequel to the Secretary's threat to superimpose his own plan on the tribe if it failed to have a plan by July 31, 1959, was amusing. When in July the C and N Committee arrived at the Department of the Interior to see Secretary Seaton with the plan of Menominee Enterprises, Inc., the Secretary was absent. Then the question arose—to which no one knew the answers—of who besides Secretary Seaton was authorized to accept the papers. After a good deal of delay and confusion, Fred G. Aandahl, assistant secretary, finally signed for them, although he was ignorant of the plan and had not been in touch with the Menominees previously.

Eleven years after passage of Public Law 83–399 the Menominees were still making a painful but increasingly successful transition from self-reliance under tribal government to life under state laws and regulations. Whether or not they will be successful depends on their receiving adequate federal aid.

Obstacles remain: the Menominees have had to close their only hospital because it did not meet state standards. The rate of tuberculosis and diabetes is high, and there is no doctor in the county. The average family income is below poverty levels, families are above average in size, there is a high drop-out rate among school children, and welfare payments sap the county budget. There is no incorporated village in the county, no high school, no drugstore, no movie theater, no bowling alley.

The original treaty with the government gave the Menominees the right to hunt and fish on their reservation. Now that they have to obey state game laws poor families who could once have fed themselves on fish and venison go hungry during the closed seasons, leaving the game for sportsmen.

A study by the Bureau in 1965 disclosed that to provide services formerly given by the federal government was not possible since Menominee County had a budget that already exceeded its statutory taxing capacity. Most of the tax burden falls on Menominee Enterprises, Inc., which is ably managed but has to bear 92 per cent of the county's tax load. It employs 350 persons, but there is an unemployment rate of 18.1 per cent in Menominee County as compared to 3.7 per cent for the remainder of the state.

The tribal loan fund is now administered under state law, which involved long consultations with members of the banking profession and the necessity of having the Wisconsin legislature pass an act empowering the tribe to set up a five-man supervisory board of trustees.

The hydroelectric and steam plants needed a large capital outlay to make them efficient and since this was not available, the plants were sold in 1962 to the Wisconsin Power and Light Company. Although the deal was financially profitable for the tribe, much unpleasant litigation and name-calling resulted because of the shareholders' opposition to the deal and unhappiness over its consummation.

The electric facilities had to be reorganized, depreciation or amortization schedules set up, and long-term contracts with Wisconsin Power and Light modified so that the facilities could obtain state licenses.

The water and sewer facilities, after long-drawn-out hearings, studies, and uncertainties, had to be improved and each facility put on a paying basis, since Wisconsin law does not permit deficit operating or transfer of revenue from one facility to offset losses on another. Menominee Enterprises, Inc. still has to subsidize the facilities, which have been turned over to the villages but remain a tribal problem.

Public roads have been improved by federal funds amounting to about $1,200,000, and state aid is now available for maintenance. Taxes must make up the difference.

Menominee Enterprise, Inc., in spite of all its initial obstacles, is out of the red. Sales have grown each year, with the mill operating on two shifts and paying union wages. The log cut has been increased from an average of seventeen to twenty-eight million annually, the pulp and by-products production has tripled, markets have increased, and shipping capacity has doubled.

New businesses, such as small stores, bars, gasoline stations, a motel, and a laundromat have been started. Two families have become building contractors. Thirty-seven new frame homes have been built with Federal Housing Administration financing. The Menominees feel sure they can work through their problems if they can obtain a federal loan, which was requested in May, 1955,[29] even though at the present time the financial reserves of Menominee Enterprises, Inc. are depleted by taxes. Consequently, the company cannot save capital to diversify its lumber industry as its competitors have done.[30]

[29] Donald Janson, "Tribe in Wisconsin Deprived of Special Status Seeks Help in Going it Alone," *The New York Times*, Sept. 7, 1965.

[30] Communication from George W. Kenote, assistant to the president, Menominee Enterprises, Neopit, Wis., Dec. 10, 1965.

Although Congress is appropriating millions of dollars for the poverty program, it has not yet granted the Menominee poverty group $5,000,000 in long-term, low-interest loans—$2,000,000 to finance studies on the possibilities of making charcoal from bark and sawmill waste and chip board for insulation, as well as to determine the reservation's recreation possibilities and later to carry out recommendations. The other $3,000,000 is needed to supply health, education, and welfare needs.

The Menominees face overwhelming odds in their efforts to implement the precipitous revolution forced on them. For one thing, Menominee County must have a broader tax base in order to provide adequate services. What the tribe has finally achieved is far more than anyone had a right to expect.

Conclusions from the Menominee Experience

In spite of the tireless efforts of the C and N Committee to enlighten the people, most of the members resent being taxed and do not yet understand or happily accept the new governmental and business arrangements. Confusion and dissatisfaction abound. A more gradual process of termination would have accomplished the transition without leaving so many things undone, so many problems pending, and so much uncertainty and bitterness among the individuals concerned.

The most concise statement of the many difficulties characterizing the situation is that which was given in the Preamble of Senate Joint Resolution 79 of the Wisconsin legislature (1959), requesting Congress to retain federal supervision until the Indians were better prepared for termination and had voted for it:

> Whereas it clearly appears from evidence and statements of competent persons in joint hearings before the subcommittees of the committees on Interior and Insular Affairs during the second session of the 83d Congress . . . that the delegates of the tribes committed themselves to a program for withdrawal of Federal supervision on which they were not in accord because they were told by the chairman of the Senate subcommittee that if they did not so commit themselves there would be no action on their pend-

ing per capita bill providing for a per capita payment of $1500 to each member of the tribe, to which they were already legally entitled and for which there was approximately $10 million of tribe money on deposit in the U.S. Treasury; hence, such commitment from the tribe delegates was obtained by duress, was not voluntary and was against the wishes of both the tribe and its delegates . . . .

Whereas this was done contrary to the expressed wishes of the Menominee Indian Tribe that the per capita payment be dropped if it required such withdrawal . . . .

Whereas the tribe itself and the members of the Wisconsin Legislature are of the opinion that the proposed termination of Federal supervision is premature and requires more time in order that the general educational level and experience of the tribe can be further developed so that the tribe can be ready to assume such responsibilities . . . .

Whereas past experiences of independent and unprotected American Indians losing their goods, lands and resources by the device or artifice of the unscrupulous are legend and furnish a shameful pattern for what can be expected and what might happen to the possessions of the Menominee Indians if Federal supervision and control over their persons and property is unconditionally relinquished . . . .[31]

This statement spoke not only for Wisconsin, but for the Menominees themselves.

IV. WATER RIGHTS UNDER TERMINATION

The Klamath, mixed-blood Ute, Paiute, Wyandotte, and Ottawa termination laws specify that the water rights of the tribes and their members shall not be abrogated.[32] When notices of termination are published, however, the laws of states become applicable to tribes and their members, just as to other people. The Klamath Act, recognizing that the reservation's water rights had not been fully developed and would be lost under Oregon law if the water were not used for five successive years, provided that the state's abandonment law would not apply until fifteen

[31] 86 Cong., 1 sess., *Congressional Record*, Vol. 105, Part 11 (July 28, 1959), 14396.
[32] 25 U.S. Code Annotated, sec. 564m, 677t, 752, 806, 851; Public Law 85–671, August 18, 1958.

years had elapsed. Similar action was taken in the case of the California water laws. But these temporary safeguards will not adequately protect the irreplaceable and incalculably valuable water rights reserved for Indians when their reservations were established.[33] Especially imperiled are their rights to water for future development.

If the constitutionality of these laws affecting water rights is upheld, the Klamath and California Indians have obviously lost at least one valuable attribute of Indian property—the right to delay development without suffering penalty or loss. They must utilize all their water rights within the periods stipulated or lose the unused portion—a requirement not present under federal law. The abandonment laws of the states will probably apply fully where other terminated tribes are located.[34]

The purpose of reserving water for future Indian use is not consistent with state systems, which fix use as the basis and measure of water rights. Shifting property rights from one system of law to another is necessarily complicated, and all the consequences cannot be foreseen, but irreparable harm will result if termination statutes allow states, by law or administration, to curtail historic Indian rights, which because of their early priority would be impossible to replace by purchase.

The recent termination acts only guess at the length of time allowable before Indians forfeit their federal water rights. For example, the Klamath Reservation has existed since 1864, but the exact amount of irrigable land or the cost of irrigation is not yet known.[35] With all the resources of the federal government behind them, the Klamath Indians have in ninety-five years sub-

33 In the 1958 crop year, 572,944 acres of Indian land were irrigated and produced crops with a gross value of $56,305,434, and Indian hydroelectric projects added 444 new customers. *Annual Report of the Secretary of the Interior*, 1959, p. 262.

34 Typical periods for which non-use causes abandonment are, by state: Arizona, Oregon, Idaho, and Utah, five years; New Mexico, four years. *Water Resources Law, Report* of the President's Water Resources Policy Commission, Vol. III (1950), 712, 728, 745, 753, 767.

35 *Termination of Federal Supervision Over Certain Tribes of Indians*, Joint Hearings, 83 Cong., 2 sess., Part 4, Oregon (Feb. 23–24, 1954), 208–10.

jugated only about one-tenth of their land; it is unlikely, therefore, that in the fifteen years remaining before the rights are
abandoned under the state laws, they can obtain the millions of
dollars necessary for complete subjugation, can adjudicate the
rights to protect the investment, and can find time to develop
over 100,000 acres of land.

Another example is the Colorado River Indian Reservation in
Arizona and California, created between 1865 and 1876. Judge
Rifkind, in his draft report to the Supreme Court of May 5, 1960,
in the *Arizona* v. *California* case, recommended a decree adjudicating water rights for 107,588 acres, requiring a diversion from
the river of 717,612 acre-feet.[36] Yet on June 30, 1954, the total
amount of reservation land with irrigation facilities was only
35,900 acres, 2,120 of which were new lands developed in 1954.[37]
It will take years to put the 107,588 acres under irrigation. If
the federal-Indian relationship should be terminated before full
development and if Arizona's law for withdrawing water rights
unused for five years (or any other inflexible period) is applied,
the Indians will certainly lose water rights.

Federal jurisdiction should remain until the irrigable acreage
of the reservation is determined, the quantity of water required
calculated and agreed upon, and the priorities definitely fixed.
Ironclad protection against losses, enforcible in the federal
courts, should be made applicable. Although the first Navajo-
Hopi Rehabilitation Act was desperately needed, it was vetoed
by President Truman, partly—if not primarily—because it put
Indian water rights under state law without adequate protection
of Navaho rights. The wisdom of the President's action becomes
clearer as the Navaho irrigation project nears realization and
the Indians prepare to use their water for agricultural, municipal, power, domestic, and industrial purposes.

Among the many other differences between federal and state
law which might impair Indian water rights if they were subject

[36] One acre-foot of water (approximately 325,850 gallons) is the amount sufficient
to cover one acre of land to a depth of one foot.

[37] *Annual Report of the Secretary of the Interior,* 1954, p. 252.

to state jurisdiction are these: states allow "persons" to appropriate, but in defining "persons" do not include Indian tribes; some states give preference to certain uses, such as domestic; and some states allow condemnation of "inferior uses" for a "superior use." Whatever the law is, its application and administration are what count. Often the number of irrigable acres in a reservation is not known, the diversion and consumptive use has not been ascertained, and only experts can determine the amount of land that can be successfully irrigated. Also, rights on many rivers have not been adjudicated. To extend state law to Indian water rights in these circumstances would be reckless and irresponsible.

Only the federal courts should have jurisdiction of disputes over Indian water rights. State courts could be expected to be unsympathetic to reserved but unused Indian rights under their jurisdiction. No other litigation arouses such passion. It is doubtful that adequate justice could be obtained in state courts. Water suits often become a contest between high-priced experts—hydraulic engineers, geologists, soil analysts, economists, ecologists, historians, chemists, and the like. What chance would non-English-speaking, uneducated, or unaggressive Indians have to convince a state administrator, usually dependent on politics for his job, that other users with junior rights have deprived them (the Indians) of their prior water rights? How could they explain their deep conviction that their religion and their culture require them to live on their own land? How would poor tribes finance the litigation?

The minimum protection should be to withhold the application of state law to water rights of terminated tribes as long as the land remains in Indian ownership. This policy would require a federal court decree. The United States should use federal courts to retain jurisdiction and hold a case open to enforce the decree, thereby to some degree keeping Indian rights under federal court scrutiny. Such rights should not be litigated in state courts in any western state before or after termination until the Indians are financially, politically, and generally able to protect themselves. To insure justice to Indians and to fulfill the obligations of the United States, the government should see to it that no tribe owning substantial water rights is terminated until after such rights have been fully adjudicated.

V. RECOMMENDATIONS

Termination of the long-established relations between the federal government and the Indians should occur only after there is adequate information before the federal government, the Indians, the local inhabitants, and their governments as to what will happen to all four parties at interest if the tribe is terminated. This requires the solution of legal, governmental, financial, and human problems. Adequate time must be allowed for the Indians, their neighbors, state and local units, and all others who might be affected by the change to work out the necessary adjustments.

Indians should be allowed full hearings before the appropriate Congressional committees.

The government's responsibility should be relinquished only when the Indians are no longer in the lower segment of our culture in education, health, and economic status. The tribesmen must also be qualified and willing to take on additional responsibilities and be ready to take advantage of wider social, economic, and political benefits on a comparable basis with their neighbors and without discrimination.

In order that Indians may be able to make their own decisions, co-operate in the execution of a plan, and take responsibility for the results, they should participate fully at every turn. The participation should consist in working out the procedure from its earliest stages and continuing with the discussions during the maturing of the program, as well as in voting for or against the final formulation. Effective Indian collaboration in the development of a plan of termination should be a prerequisite to acceptance by Congress. The process should involve not only leaders but the tribesmen as well. Testing should determine to what extent the people affected actually know what is being planned or presented. The freedom of Indians to accept or reject a program should not be tied to offers of payment from federally held tribal funds or, in the case of favorable action, to offers of later payment. A tribe should not be terminated without its freely given consent.

Ordinarily, any per capita or other payments should be distributed in small sums over a period of time so that there is an opportunity for the recipients to learn how to handle cash before all assets are dissipated.

A termination plan should safeguard the interests of individual members whether they wish to remain as a tribal core or to withdraw when the majority rejects termination.

Final decisions affecting termination should be preceded by plans acceptable to the tribe for managing, utilizing, or dividing tribal properties. To this end, Indians should have competent and skilled assistance, paid for when necessary by the United States. The desirability and probable consequences of each plan should be discussed in advance and thoroughly understood by the Indians, the other people of the area, and the state and local officials.

Firm assurances that the plans can be carried out under state law should be obtained. If state law must be amended to permit the execution of an economic plan, the amendments should be secured before termination.

The termination measure should authorize the Indians to form a business corporation under a general federal law, so as to provide a model for all tribes instead of a particular model in the case of each state, and it should further give express jurisdiction to the federal courts in lawsuits brought by or against the corporation.

Where termination involves the disposition of natural resources and their subsequent use, Congress should give consideration to all its consequences, such as the conservation of land and wildlife, watershed protection, the economy of Indian and surrounding communities, and all other matters relevant to the national interest.

There should be no termination of federal responsibility for

Indian water rights until tribal rights and rights for allotted lands are either adjudicated or agreed upon as to quantity and priority among the Indians, the United States, the state, and other users. This should apply to water already being put to beneficial use as well as to rights for future development.

The legislation should expressly recognize that the Indian rights do not derive from the state but exist independently of state law. Legislation should insure that the federal courts have exclusive jurisdiction over any lawsuit arising as long as the land remains in Indian ownership.

If extinguishment of the trust should subject the land to local taxation, then, before termination, it should be ascertained whether it is economically feasible for the Indians to pay the taxes required by local laws. If there is doubt about this, the land should continue to be tax-exempt until Congress provides otherwise. Equitable arrangements should be made for payments by the United States and by the Indians, to the extent of their capacity, until it is determined that the land, properly used, can support taxation.

Termination legislation should in no case conflict with any existing treaty or agreement with a tribe, unless it expressly waives, in writing, the matters in dispute.

Before the United States surrenders its responsibilities, studies should be made to ascertain the ability and willingness of state and local governments to furnish services to Indians equal to those hitherto given from Washington. The relationships between the state and local governments, on the one hand, and the United States and the Indians, on the other, should be set out clearly. The state and local governments should as a minimum provide for the financing of those commitments to Indians that the federal government has theretofore met. If this cannot be done, the federal government should continue such financing or call off the termination.

Any termination act should provide enforcible standards for the quantity and quality of education, health, and other public services to be furnished by the state and local governments.

Tables

☒☒☒

TABLE 1

POPULATION AND LAND HELD UNDER TRUST BY THE UNITED STATES FOR THE INDIANS (EXCLUSIVE OF ALASKA AND HAWAII)

State	Indian Population Compiled by The Bureau of the Census (1960)*	Indian Population Compiled by the B.I.A. Within Units and Adjacent to Units (Includes Indians Terminated Since 1960)†	Acres of Indian Land—Tribal and Allotted— Held Under Government Trust, 1960–61†
Alabama	1,276	—	—
Arizona	83,387	69,345	21,491,414
Arkansas	580	—	
California	39,014	8,861	557,942
Colorado	4,288	1,263	751,551
Connecticut	923	—	—
Delaware	597		
District of Columbia	587	—	—
Florida	2,504	683	78,974

* From *Advance Reports, General Population Characteristics, 1960 Census of Population* (Bureau of the Census, March 31, 1961), PC (A2) 1, page 2:

"*Race* used by the Bureau of the Census is derived from the concept usually accepted by the general public. It does not necessarily reflect clear-cut definitions of biological stock. Persons of mixed racial parentage are classified according to the race of the non-white parent. However, all Indians of one-fourth or more Indian blood are considered Indians. Those of less than one-fourth Indian blood are also classified as Indians if they are regarded as Indians in the community. Persons of mixed Indian and Negro blood are counted as Negro unless, (1) Indian characteristics predominate or (2) they are accepted as Indians in the community.

"Census forms for 1960 were mailed in advance, most people filled in their own entries for 'race'; but many people in typical Indian country are beyond mailing range, and enumerators may or may not ask respondents to what race they belong. This may account for the lower census figure obtained by the Bureau of the Census, in South Dakota, as compared to that obtained by the Bureau of Indian Affairs."

† *United States Indian Population and Land, 1960–61* (Bureau of Indian Affairs, 1961), pages 2–4:

"The Bureau obtains its population data from listings prepared from Agency

Georgia	749	—	—
Idaho	5,231	4,178	792,777
Illinois	4,704	—	—
Indiana	943	—	—
Iowa	1,708	485	4,105
Kansas	5,069	1,163	28,321
Kentucky	391	—	—
Louisiana	3,587	259	262
Maine	1,879	—	—
Maryland	1,538	—	—
Massachusetts	2,118	—	—
Michigan	9,701	1,119	16,659
Minnesota	15,496	11,470	726,257
Mississippi	3,119	3,410	16,479
Missouri	1,723	—	372
Montana	21,181	18,739	5,278,779
Nebraska	5,545	2,255	67,288
Nevada	6,681	3,694	1,142,586
New Hampshire	135	—	—
New Jersey	1,699	—	—
New Mexico	56,255	52,102	6,464,857
New York	16,491	—	—
North Carolina	38,129	5,246	56,414
North Dakota	11,736	10,693	870,082
Ohio	1,910	—	—
Oklahoma	64,689	57,763	1,760,408
Oregon	8,026	3,383	693,663
Pennsylvania	2,122	—	—

records, local enumerations, special surveys and from Superintendents' estimates.

"Indians defined by the Bureau of Indian Affairs as living 'within' and 'adjacent to' units are those for whom the Bureau may provide some *direct* service such as education, welfare, credit, etc. The Alabama and Coushatta Tribes of Texas were terminated August 23, 1954. They are not counted in this group in spite of the fact that they are eligible for admission to schools maintained by the Bureau of Indian Affairs on the same terms that apply to other Indians (Public Law 627, sec. 2).

"The Indian population 'within' and 'adjacent to' units (344,951) is not however, the total number for whom the Bureau does actually provide some sort of service. There are many off-reservation Indians who may get some *indirect* services, such as irrigation, forestry, mineral, leasing, range management, road construction, etc. It is reasonable to assume that 360,000 or more than half of the Indians in the United States, which includes Alaska and Hawaii, receive some service from the Bureau. The number of off-reservation Indians receiving some services cannot be estimated accurately, because the figure varies depending on claims awards, lease payments, private actions and land turnover."

State	Indian Population Compiled by The Bureau of the Census (1960)*	Indian Population Compiled by the B.I.A. Within Units and Adjacent to Units (Includes Indians Terminated Since 1960)†	Acres of Indian Land—Tribal and Allotted— Held Under Government Trust, 1960–61†
Rhode Island	932	—	—
South Carolina	1,098	353	3,389
South Dakota	25,794	25,990	4,878,073
Tennessee	638	—	—
Texas	5,750	—	11
Utah	6,961	4,454	2,115,950
Vermont	57	—	—
Virginia	2,155	—	—
Washington	21,076	10,928	2,566,601
West Virginia	181	—	—
Wisconsin	14,297	6,495	147,289
Wyoming	4,020	3,772	1,888,062
Totals	508,675	308,103	52,398,565
Alaska	14,444	36,848	96,788
Hawaii	472	—	—
Totals	523,591	344,951	52,495,353

Addenda

The highest figure for the Indian population in the United States (excluding Alaska and Hawaii) was estimated by Professor Sol Tax, of the University of Chicago, from figures available in 1950. He included communities, small reservations, *rancherias* or colonies, scattered individuals or families, and reservations as — 571,824‡

The difference between the enumeration of total Indians by the Bureau of the Census (508,675) and the population of Indians compiled by the Bureau of Indian Affairs for whom it provides direct services (308,103) is — 200,572

Included in the latter group (200,572) are

Indians who never came under B. I. A. control, mostly on the eastern seaboard — 96,603§

Indians who relinquish their rights in reservations or to government services, who are indistinguishable from the general population. No figures have been compiled or estimates made for this group. — ?

Indians from whom the government itself withdrew services under the "termination" laws, beginning in 1954 and extending to the time of the 1960 Census — 5,024

---

‡ Preliminary edition prepared for purposes of discussion at the American Anthropological Association, Annual Meeting, December, 1956, to accompany a paper by Sol Tax, University of Chicago. Data compiled by Samuel Stanley and Robert Thomas, 1950.

§ William Harlan Gilbert, Jr., "Surviving Indian Groups of the Eastern United States," Smithsonian Institution *Annual Report, 1948* (Washington, G. P. O., 1949), 407–38.

TABLE 2

COMPARATIVE POPULATION OF INDIANS IN THE UNITED STATES
(EXCLUSIVE OF ALASKA AND HAWAII)*

Year	Total Number of Indian in United States†	Total Number of Indians "on Reservation"‡	Per Cent of Total "on Reservation"
1938	348,000	213,611	61.4
1940	355,000	231,242	65.1
1945	379,000	243,652	64.3
1960	508,675	243,412	47.8

* Several population estimates have been made by the B. I. A. over the last twenty years. The above figures were chosen by Clement C. Jeck, reports officer, B. I. A., as being the most accurate for comparative purposes. Letter dated April 24, 1962 (Commission files).

† *Decennial Censuses 1930 and 1960, Bureau of the Census.* Figures for 1938, 1940, and 1945 were estimated by using the 1930 census count plus births, minus deaths, and minus allowance for under-reporting of deaths to the year shown.

‡ In order to make the data comparable, it was necessary to *exclude* Indians living within the boundaries of the Five Civilized Tribes in Oklahoma (38,503), counted in 1960, since they were not counted in the previous years.

"On-reservation" Indians for 1938, 1940, and 1945 were those reported as "current enrollees living on own reservation or on reservation other than their own." For 1960, "on-reservation" Indians were those reported as "residing on reservations, or living nearby who were intermittent residents or otherwise regarded as residents for service purposes." Although there might be some small differences, generally the number of Indians covered by these definitions would be about the same.

TABLE 3

INDIAN TRUST LAND BY AREA OFFICE
SHOWING SHRINKAGE IN LAND BASE*

Individual Land Removed from All Trust Status

Area Office	1948–52	1953–57	Total Land Lost 1948–57
Aberdeen	291,300.02	333,799.93	625,099.95
Anadarko	107,709.95	154,539.87	262,249.82
Billings	184,309.65	897,954.18	1,082,263.83
Gallup	5,500.00†	1,080.00‡	6,580.00
Minneapolis	2,155.00§	117,798.00	119,953.00
Muskogee	112,549.00	202,014.73	314,563.73
Phoenix	943.30¶	1,319.04	2,262.34
Portland	15,605.91	56,310.14	71,916.05
Sacramento	84,691.01	25,833.93	110,524.94
Washington	**	**	**
Totals	804,763.84	1,790,649.82	2,595,413.66

* *Indian Land Transactions,* 85 Cong., 2 sess., Committee Print, Committee on Interior and Insular Affairs, U.S. Senate, 45. The total Indian trust land removed from all trust status during the period under study includes "takings for public purposes," but excludes land in the category of "sold to tribe," since it is believed that this land remained in trust status.

† Three years only—1950, 1951, and 1952.

‡ Four years only—1953, 1954, 1956, and 1957.

§ Two years only—1951 and 1952.

¶ Four years only—1948, 1949, 1950, and 1951.

** No figures given.

TABLE 4

BRIEF ANALYSIS OF FINANCIAL ASSISTANCE STATUTES RELEVANT TO INDIANS*

Area Redevelopment Act, 75 Stat. 47 (42 USC 2501)

Loans		Grants	
Purposes	*Principal Conditions*	*Purposes*	*Principal Conditions*
Sec. 6—Purchase or development of lands & facilities (including machinery & equipment) for industrial or commercial use (including rehabilitation, construction, & enlargement of existing buildings).	No funds available from private sources or federal agencies on reasonable terms; assurance of repayment; not to be used for working capital or plant relocation; must aid permanent unemployment relief & be consistent with O.E.D.P. Maximum 25 yrs. & 65% of project cost. Tribe furnishes not less than 10% & non-governmental sources 5% of cost.	Sec. 8—Land acquisition or development for public facility usage & construction, rehabilitation, alteration, and expansion or improvement of public facilities.	Project must: (1) aid permanent unemployment relief; (2) fill pressing need to establish industrial & commercial plants; (3) be consistent with O.E.D.P.; (4) not compete with existing privately owned public utility; and (5) tribe pays according to its ability. Maximum grant is the difference between completion cost & funds available.
Sec. 7—Purchase or development of land for public facility usage & construction, rehabilitation, alteration, expansion, or improvement of public facilities.	Same as above but maximum term 40 yrs.; facility must not compete with privately owned public utility unless need exists for increased service, & must aid establishment of industrial or commercial plants.	Sec. 11 — Technical assistance study in evaluating needs & assessing economic potentialities of redevelopment or other needy areas.	
		Sec. 16—Studies of size, skills, characteristics, adaptability, & occupational potentialities of redevelopment area labor force; referral of unemployed—occupational training with not more than 16 weeks training payments (on or off the job).	Reasonable expectation of employment after training.

*From the Division of Economic Development, Bureau of Indian Affairs.

Self-Help Housing Act, 63 Stat. 429 as amended (42 USC 1401)

Purpose	Loans	Grants	Limitations
Provide ultimate ownership of decent, safe, & sanitary dwellings for individual Indians in urban & rural non-farm areas.	Loan to local housing agency not in excess of 90% of development cost. Tribe or individual supplies land, labor, & some materials & maintains home during term of loan.	Same as above, but annual contributions help pay off development cost within prescribed term.	Not in excess of 40 years & exemption from all real and personal property taxes.

Urban Renewal Act, 63 Stat. 413 (42 USC 1450)

Purpose	Loans	Grants	Limitations
Clear slums and blighted areas; aid community development; provide adequate housing for urban and rural non-farm, low-income families.	Not in excess of project cost to local public agency on proof of lack of resources and inability to secure credit on reasonable terms; tribal workable program for community improvement; loans bearing interest, not in excess of 40 yrs. (10 yrs. on open lands).	Same purpose as for loans, but no grants for improvements on open land.	Same conditions but in A.R.A. and for communities under 50,000; grants up to ¾, otherwise not in excess of ⅔ of project cost.

Rural Housing Act, 63 Stat. 432 (42 USC 1471)

Purpose	Loans	Grants	Limitations
Sec. 503—Aid farm owners (those holding patent in fee, restricted or trust lands, or 50-yr. leases of tribal lands) and non-farm residents to construct, repair, improve, or replace farm buildings and provide decent, safe, and sanitary living conditions and adequate farm buildings.	Proof of ownership and farm or building site in rural area without decent, safe, and sanitary dwellings or adequate farm buildings; lack of financial resources and inability to secure credit on reasonable terms; furnish security for not over 33-yr. loan repayable with 4% interest.	For farm owners in need of better buildings, up 5 yrs. annual contributions in form of credits for annual interest and 50% of principal payments due on loan.	Proof of good faith and inadequacy of income to repay loan, principal, and interest but reasonable expectation to do so after 5 yrs.
Sec. 504—Repair and improve farm dwellings and buildings by removing hazardous conditions.	Applicant ineligible under Sec. 503, but no loan (or loans and grants) in excess of $1,000.	Same purposes as for loans.	Applicant ineligible under Sec. 503, but no grant or grants in excess of $1,000.

Loans   Grants

Public Works Acceleration Act, 76 Stat. 541 (42 USC 2641)

Purposes	*Principal Conditions*
Provide aid for unemployed through improvement of federal, state, or local public works projects for which federal financial assistance is authorized, such as roads, soil, & moisture conservation, irrigation, reforestation, employee housing, office buildings, warehouses, recreational facilities.	(1) Initiation or acceleration in short time; (2) meets essential public need; (3) completion in 12 months; (4) consistent with O.E.D.P. No loan in excess of 75% of cost, or if project eligible under another federal grant program. Tribal fiscal year capital improvement monies must be increased by amounts equal to non-federal funds used in project.

Indian Sanitation Facilities Act, 73 Stat. 267 (42 USC 2001)

Joint participation of tribe & Public Health Service to construct essential sanitation facilities including domestic & community water supplies, drainage, sewage & waste disposal facilities (ultimately to be transferred to tribe), & to provide needed equipment for homes, communities, & lands.	Tribal contribution in proportion to its resources—at least tribal labor.

Planned Public Works Act, 68 Stat. 590 (40 USC 462)

Purposes	*Principal Conditions*
Encourage tribes to maintain adequate reserve & planned public works, which can be rapidly commenced when desirable.	Engineering & architectural surveys, designs, plans, working drawings, & specifications for construction within a reasonable period in conformity to over-all

area plan & agreement to repay without interest when construction started.

Community Facilities Act, 75 Stat. 175, 76 Stat. 920 (42 USC 1491)

Finance specific projects for public works (including water storage, treatment, purification, or distribution; sewage, sewage treatment, & sewage facilities; gas distribution systems; other utility systems; community halls, jails, recreational facilities, libraries); acquisition, construction, reconstruction, & improvement of facilities & equipment in mass transportation in urban areas & in co-ordinating transportation facilities

When no other funds available on reasonable terms & there is reasonable security; when there is a mass transportation development program & facilities proposed are needed therefor. Maximum term, 40 yrs.

Low-Rent Public Housing Act, 63 Stat. 429 as amended (42 USC 1401)

Provide and rent decent, safe, & sanitary dwellings to families of low income in urban & rural non-farm areas.

Not in excess of 40 yrs. and 90% of development cost with interest, guaranteed by Public Housing Administration; project to be built on tribal land and exempt from all taxes; unsafe and insanitary dwelling units to be eliminated.

Annual contributions by government to maintain low-rent character of project.

Not in excess of 40 yrs. & exemption from all real & personal taxes.

Housing for Elderly Act, 63 Stat. 429 as amended (42 USC 1401)

Same as above.

Same as above.

Same as above except annual contribution may be greater.

Same as above.

Loans | Grants

	Loans		Grants	
	Purposes	Principal Conditions	Purposes	Principal Conditions

Manpower Development & Training Act, 76 Stat. 23 (42 USC 2571)

Purposes	Principal Conditions	Purposes	Principal Conditions
		Appraise manpower requirements & develop training programs including on-job training to equip workers with new skills; pay weekly training allowances.	Reasonable expectation of employment after training of more than 2 weeks but of reasonable duration; 3 yrs. previous work experience required for allowances, except for youths over 19 but under 22 yrs. old.

Federal Housing Act, 71 Stat. 294 as amended (12 USC 1709)

Purposes	Principal Conditions	Purposes	Principal Conditions
Sec. 203—Encourage improvement in housing standards & home ownership by insurance against loss on specific types of loans made by private lending institutions.	Land held under fee patent or 50-yr. lease, or Secretary of Interior (under 25 USCA 483a) approves mortgage of trust land or land restricted against alienation, and B.I.A. gives assurance it will approve mortgage.		

Small Business Act, 72 Stat. 384 as amended (15 USC 631)

Purposes	Principal Conditions	Purposes	Principal Conditions
Finance business construction, conversion, or expansion (including land acquisition) & acquisition equipment, facilities, machinery, supplies, or materials; supply working capital; provide technical & managerial aids; help business displaced by urban renewal or federally aided projects.	Monies not otherwise available to Indians or tribes on reasonable terms (tribal non-profit enterprises may be ineligible); reasonable assurance of repayment; loans not in excess of $350,000 or 10 yrs. & until construction completed, under $12,000 for 5 yrs. Different conditions for pool & disaster loans.		

Farm Credit Act, 48 Stat. 257 (12 USC 1131)

Aid farmers to get short-term credit from local production credit associations for all types farm & ranch operations including purchase of land, livestock, & machinery, & payment of farm debts & expenses.	Loans only to local credit associations; ability to repay without impairment of farm operations; usually 1 year at interest but renewable if credit remains satisfactory; 5 yrs. for capital loans.
Aid farmers to get long-term credit from federal land bank associations for agricultural purposes.	Loans only to federal land bank associations; not in excess of 65% of appraised farm value on interest & secured by mortgage approved by Secretary of Interior.

Rural Electrification Act, 49 Stat. 1363, 63 Stat. 948 (7 USC 901); Ex. Ord. 7037 (5/1/35)

Finance construction & operation of generating plants, electric transmission & distribution lines or systems, wiring of premises, & installation of electrical & plumbing appliances & equipment in rural areas.	Loans only to corporations (tribes), not to individual consumers. Maximum term 35 yrs.; 2% interest; ability to repay from operating revenues.

Fisheries Loan Act (Fish & Wildlife Act of 1956, 16 USC 742c), 50 CFR, Part 250

Approve loans to owners of fishing vessels & fishing gear & to persons conducting research in basic fisheries problems.	To owners only (not tribes) if no other financing reasonably available, ability to operate vessel successfully, & repayment from earnings assured. Maximum term 10 yrs.; 5% interest; sound collateral insured. No financing shore oper-

	Loans		Grants	
	Purposes	*Principal Conditions*	*Purposes*	*Principal Conditions*
		ations or refinancing existing loans (not secured by vessel) or undesirable vessel mortgages, or vessel purchase or replacement if applicant has less than 20% interest.		
Fishing Vessel Mortgage & Loan Insurance Act, 52 Stat. 969 as amended (14 USC 1271), 70 Stat. 1119 (16 USC 742a)	Assist fishing industry to finance construction, reconstruction, or reconditioning of fishing vessels by insuring loans from non-governmental lenders.	Secretarial approval of borrower, lender, & work plans & specifications; not in excess of 75% of cost, 5% interest; secured by chattel & ship mortgages; insurance & performance bond.		
Economic Opportunity Act of 1964, 78 Stat. 508			To mobilize the human and financial resources of the nation to combat poverty in the United States.	

TABLE 5

Infant Death Rates
(Based on 1,000 Live Births)

Year	National Indian Rates*	Rates for Indian Groups Where Records Were Compiled or Collected by Research Workers	All Races— National Rates*
1960	—	88.2†	—
1959	—	—	—
1957–59	53.7	—	27.1 (1958)
1955–57	58.5	—	26.0 (1956)
1953–55	68.2	—	26.6 (1954)
1949–51	85.1	—	29.2 (1950)
1944	—	135.3‡	41.4 (1945)‡
1955–59 (average)	—	58.5§	—

* *Indian Health Highlights,* November, 1961, p. 8.

† "Health Needs of Ute Mountain Ute Tribe," Preliminary Survey of the Survey Team of the Ute Indian Project, University of Colorado, School of Medicine, November 19, 1962.

‡ "A Sampling of Statistical Material for Health Personnel," Bureau of Indian Affairs, undated, probably about 1933. This material was based on figures in states where the Indian population comprises approximately 95 per cent of the rural non-white population.

§ *The Navajo Year Book, 1951–1961: A Decade of Progress,* Report VIII, 116.

Index